Praise for *Running with the Champ*

"When I heard that Tim Shanahan was writing a book about Muhammad Ali, I was excited, because for the first time we'd get a chance to look at the Champ from the perspective of a real friend. In the years that I have spoken to Tim, it seems that we never run out of stories about the Great Ali. Tim has taken the term 'brother' to another level; no one has been as close to the Champ as Tim Shanahan. Read with me and celebrate true friendship."

—George Foreman

"Oh my! This is the reader's opportunity to get inside the ropes with the Greatest. Tim Shanahan's book is a knockout read, offering rare insight into the man regarded as the most powerful and prominent athlete of his time."

—Dick Enberg

"Of all of his great achievements in life, from champion prizefighter to goodwill ambassador to instrument of hope for the underprivileged, it is quite lovely to learn that Muhammad Ali was also a devoted friend. In his affectionate memoir of their long and durable bond, Tim Shanahan reminds us of a sometimes overlooked aspect of the Champ—that in stride with the wonderful talent and wild antics that kept us so entertained walked a man of profound decency."

—Mark Kram, Jr., author of the PEN Literary
Award–winning *Like Any Normal Day*

"Has its share of touching moments . . . give[s] glimpses of Ali's dignified, decades-long struggle with Parkinson's."

—Michiko Kakutani, *The New York Times*

"An affectionate portrait of boxing legend Muhammad Ali . . . Charming moments abound . . . If you're wondering why Ali is called 'the Greatest,' this . . . pleasant memoir makes for a good place to start."

—*Kirkus Reviews*

"An engrossing story . . . of an enviable friendship . . . Shanahan comes off as a likable guy . . . it's easy to understand why the fighter allowed him into his inner circle."

—*Publishers Weekly*

"Shanahan presents a complex but less bombastic person than is popularly associated with the name; generous to a fault, devoted to his religion and . . . family, and a champion of the less fortunate. This view of a fabled boxer from the unusual angle of friendship offers justification beyond the boxing ring for calling Ali 'the Greatest.' "

—*Library Journal*

"Poignant moments during morning workouts and rare glimpses into Muhammad Ali's personal life punctuate this tale of the unlikely relationship between the boxing champ and author Tim Shanahan."

—*American Way*

PHOTO BY TIM SHANAHAN

RUNNING

WITH THE

CHAMP

My Forty-Year Friendship with

MUHAMMAD ALI

TIM SHANAHAN

with Chuck Crisafulli

SIMON & SCHUSTER PAPERBACKS

New York   London   Toronto   Sydney   New Delhi

Simon & Schuster Paperbacks
An Imprint of Simon & Schuster, Inc.
1230 Avenue of the Americas
New York, NY 10020

First Simon & Schuster trade paperback edition May 2017

SIMON & SCHUSTER PAPERBACKS and colophon are
registered trademarks of Simon & Schuster, Inc.

For information about special discounts for bulk purchases,
please contact Simon & Schuster Special Sales at
1-866-506-1949 or business@simonandschuster.com.

The Simon & Schuster Speakers Bureau can bring authors to your live event.
For more information or to book an event, contact the
Simon & Schuster Speakers Bureau at 1-866-248-3049
or visit our website at www.simonspeakers.com.

Designed by Ruth Lee-Mui

Manufactured in the United States of America

1   3   5   7   9   10   8   6   4   2

The Library of Congress has cataloged the hardcover edition as follows:

Names: Shanahan, Tim. | Crisafulli, Chuck.
Title: Running with the champ : my heavyweight friendship with Muhammad Ali /
by Tim Shanahan with Chuck Crisafulli.
Description: First Simon & Schuster hardcover edition. | New York : Simon &
Schuster, [2016] | Includes index.
Identifiers: LCCN 2015034685| ISBN 9781501102301 (hardcover) | ISBN
1501102303 (hardcover) | ISBN 9781501102356 (ebook)
Subjects: LCSH: Ali, Muhammad, 1942– —Friends and associates. | Boxers
(Sports)—United States—Biography.
Classification: LCC GV1132.A44 S424 2015 | DDC 796.83092—dc23
LC record available at http://lccn.loc.gov/2015034685

ISBN 978-1-5011-0230-1
ISBN 978-1-5011-0234-9 (pbk)
ISBN 978-1-5011-0235-6 (ebook)

PHOTO CREDITS
Pages 107, 177, and 247: Photograph courtesy of Howard Bingham
All others: Photograph courtesy of the author

To my gorgeous and creative wife, Helga,
who has shared a beautiful life with me.

CONTENTS

RUNNING

WITH THE

CHAMP

ONE

BACK TO PARADISE

October 2013

AS I DROVE THROUGH THE security gates and into the community of luxury homes in Paradise Valley, Arizona, some very familiar feelings began to surge up once again. After all these years—nearly forty—those feelings hadn't ever really gone away. Steering the car toward a home back by the communal tennis courts, I thought about all that had been packed into those four decades: ups and downs, laughter and tears, one-of-a-kind moments and incredible adventures. The years could be measured in mansions and penthouse suites, Rolls-Royces and private jets, Hollywood encounters and Las Vegas events. But they could also be measured in quieter moments: morning runs, family dinners, late-night talks. Mostly it had been close to forty years of love, trust, and the deepest friendship I'd ever known.

I was here in Paradise Valley to visit my old friend Muhammad Ali. I pulled up in front of his home and couldn't help smiling. After all this time, the thought of spending a day with Muhammad still filled me with happiness and excitement. I felt the warmth and the joy that anyone might feel at the prospect of spending precious hours with a loved one. Even after all we'd been through, I still felt that our friendship was an incredible honor and privilege.

Back in 2005, Muhammad and his wife, Lonnie, purchased this second home in Paradise Valley and moved here from their longtime residence in Berrien Springs, Michigan. They hoped that the warmer, drier weather would help in Muhammad's ongoing battle with the symptoms of Parkinson's disease that had been slowly and steadily affecting him since his retirement from boxing in 1981 (he'd been officially diagnosed with Parkinson's in 1984, at the age of forty-two). In fact, the move had turned out to be extremely beneficial. The weather, intensive physical therapy, and a regimen of cutting-edge medications put Ali in the position he had been in many times in his career: the statistical underdog who astonishes everyone by battling back against a fierce opponent.

Of course, in the ring Ali was often able to finish off his opponents with a knockout. That wasn't the case now. The disease had weakened and stiffened his muscles, limiting his mobility and making speech difficult. The man who had once thrilled the press and the public with his loud, fast, funny rhymes and over-the-top braggadocio now spoke in a low, hoarse, barely intelligible growl, rarely getting out more than three or four words at a time. And on his bad days, the simplest of tasks was almost impossible without the assistance of Lonnie or her sister Marilyn, who worked as his live-in caregiver. But there were still plenty of good days, when despite his physical limitations, the twinkle in his eyes and the look of recognition and understanding told you he was still fully there: Muhammad Ali, three-time heavyweight champion of the world, and one of the brightest, wittiest, most beloved figures of our time.

Since his move to Paradise Valley, it had become much easier for me to see him. I was living in Southern California and working as regional sales manager for a medical products company. I oversaw eight distribution managers and more than three hundred sales reps across four western states, one of which was Arizona. It had been hard for me to get to Michigan, but now a couple of times a month I could find some reason to do business in Phoenix or Tucson, and whenever I set up those business trips I'd set aside a couple of days to spend time with

Muhammad. As a business traveler, I wasn't very fussy. All I needed was a decent bed in a first-floor room, access to a business center, and a location that was easy to get in and out of. The accommodations were never important to me. What really mattered was spending as much time as possible with Muhammad without becoming an inconvenience to Lonnie or Marilyn. My wife, Helga, and I have always gotten along well with both of them and really appreciated the trust they extended to us. We didn't ever want to take for granted the fact that we had been allowed to remain an active part of Muhammad's life.

This particular trip had been thrown together quickly, so my visit with the Champ was going to be a surprise for him. I'd called Lonnie to make sure it was OK to come by, and she told me that while she'd be away for the day, Marilyn would be there with him and I could come by early and spend the entire afternoon with him.

IT'S ABOUT TEN A.M. AS I ring the bell at the front door of Muhammad's beautiful home. Marilyn greets me, shows me in, and tells me that Muhammad is still in bed. He's on some new medications and has been sleeping much later into the day. Marilyn is always completely focused on Muhammad's needs, and does a great job of making sure that his days are balanced between what he wants to do and what he's required to do as part of his ongoing treatment.

"I don't know what time he's going to get up," she says, "but yesterday it was noon."

It is actually good to hear that he is getting a good rest every night. As long as I've known Ali, he has been a chronic insomniac, and it has always been hard for him to get as much sleep as his body needed. He used to tell me that whenever he closed his eyes, he would start thinking about all the world's troubles and would stay wide awake figuring out how and where he might use his fame to help solve problems.

Muhammad is currently recovering from a medical procedure. He has recently had surgery on his throat to loosen his rigid vocal cords. The surgeon in Boston gave Lonnie and Marilyn high hopes that the surgery would release the pressure on Muhammad's larynx and trachea and would make it easier for him to swallow and speak. Marilyn tells me that she's been doing voice exercises with the Champ and that he is responding with enthusiasm. But it's still not clear whether the results of the surgery will be a brief relief or an ongoing success.

Marilyn walks me into the home's sunny kitchen, where Muhammad spends a good portion of his day. In the breakfast area there's Ali's throne—a high-end easy chair (with built-in vibrator), placed in front of a TV and DVD player that run almost constantly for Muhammad's benefit. He has a large library of favorite films, and as soon as one ends, Marilyn asks him what he wants to watch next. I am not at all surprised to see that the DVD currently loaded is a Clint Eastwood feature, *The Good, the Bad and the Ugly*. Muhammad loves westerns, and he always enjoys watching Clint, whom he first met back in 1969 in the greenroom of *The David Frost Show*. As Marilyn goes about her daily routine, I sit down at the breakfast table, pick up the remote, and start watching the film from where Muhammad left off.

After a while, Marilyn heads into Muhammad's bedroom to check on him. She comes back to tell me that he's awake and wants to get up, so she's going to help him get dressed. A few minutes later, he shuffles slowly into the kitchen with Marilyn at his side. Even on his bad days, he always wants to be fully dressed when he leaves his bedroom, and today he's in tracksuit pants and a knit T-shirt. But it does indeed look like this is one of his bad days—he has his eyes closed tightly and is letting Marilyn guide him to the kitchen table. I'm about to get up and help her, but she motions for me to stay seated. She helps him sit down, and puts his breakfast in front of him. With his eyes still closed and his head hanging down, he picks up his spoon and begins to eat.

I'm not terribly shocked, because I have seen this before. Light can bother some Parkinson's patients, and Muhammad will often keep his eyes closed to relieve the irritation. And sometimes—whether the light is bothering him or not—if he isn't feeling fully himself, he'll keep his eyes closed until he really feels ready to let the world in.

"Muhammad," says Marilyn in a cheerful voice. "Open your eyes.

Somebody's here to see you, Muhammad. Open your eyes, Muhammad, you have a visitor."

I wait to see how long it takes for him to notice who's sitting at his table. I keep waiting for him to look at me but he doesn't look up. He just keeps his head down and continues to eat.

"Muhammad," I say softly. No response.

Marilyn speaks in an even quieter, gentler voice. "Muhammad, you have a surprise visitor. Open your eyes. Look who's here to see you."

Slowly, he lifts his head and focuses. His eyes light up and he makes a funny face at me—his "mocking" face. Then, he speaks.

"TIM SHANAHAN."

Now I am shocked. His voice is louder and clearer than it's been in years. It's loud enough that I'm actually knocked back in my chair. Marilyn is just as shocked, and almost instantly she has tears in her eyes.

"Muhammad Ali!" I shout back. "The heavyweight champion of the world! The Greatest of All Times! Muhammad Ali is saying my name. I haven't heard you say my name like that in twenty years. I don't even remember the last time I heard you say my name."

I'm smiling and laughing and looking at him across the table. He's looking straight back at me—his "mocking" face has shifted into a no-nonsense expression.

"Can you say that again, Muhammad?" I repeat my name for him.

"TIM SHANAHAN," he shouts back.

Now I'm a little choked up, too. In the earliest days of our friendship, this was his way of saying hello to me—booming out my name whenever he saw me, no matter where we were or who else was around. After a while, he stopped using the distinctive bellow and would just quietly say, "Shanahan," giving it a little emphasis as if it were a word from a magic spell. I knew from the start that he was certainly not the kind of friend from whom I was going to hear "Hi, Tim, how you doing?" or "Hey, Tim, what's going on?" and that was fine by me. I was very happy to get the occasional "Shanahan" mixed in with the more common "What's happenin'?" or "What it is?" But over the years, as it got harder and harder for him to speak, he just didn't say my name at all. He would simply find some other way to acknowledge me. I think it had been years since I had heard a "Shanahan" and probably decades since I had heard "Tim." Hearing my full name as loud and clear as he had shouted it was like taking a ride in a time machine.

Muhammad turns his attention back to his breakfast, and it doesn't look as though he's going to say anything more. That doesn't bother me at all.

"OK, Marilyn," I say. "If I die today, I'm a happy man."

I MET MUHAMMAD WHEN HE was the reigning heavyweight champ, and it hasn't been easy over the years to watch a man who had been such a perfect physical specimen become more and more dependent upon the care of others. He never surrendered his spirit to his physical problems, though, and anyone who knew Muhammad was not surprised that, through all his struggles, he maintained his dignity and his sense of humor. He made it clear to me that the last thing in the world he wanted was for people to pity him, and he had said to me many times, "Tell people I'm not suffering. I'm not in pain. I just get tired." He still appreciated what a unique, remarkable life he lived, and he didn't see any reason to view his circumstances in a negative way. I often thought of something he told me years ago when I asked him if he was satisfied with his life.

"I've lived the lives of a hundred men," he responded. "And I wouldn't do anything differently. My middle name is 'Controversy' and that's what made my life interesting."

As his illness progressed, Muhammad was always defying expectations. One day I would call him on the phone and could barely get a word out of him. Then just a few days later he'd be on the phone sounding sharp and responsive and would actually be initiating the conversation with prompts such as "Tell me about when we bought the Rolls in Chicago." I loved to retell our old stories to him, and on some of my visits we'd watch a DVD collection of his old interviews, some dating back to when he was just eighteen years old. I always got a kick out of hearing him hush the people around him because he wanted to hear once more how brilliantly "The Greatest" answered some decades-old question. In reliving those better days from the past, he could keep his mind alert and active.

Throughout his career, whenever he had obstacles to overcome or hard times to get through, his philosophy had been that the difficulties were challenges from God that he was expected to pass. To Ali, Parkinson's was simply one of the bigger tests he'd been faced with.

"God tests me every day that I wake up with my disease," he'd say, "and I pass the test every time."

With all that in mind, when I came to visit with him I made a point of treating him as I always had, never allowing his medical condition to come between us. I didn't put on an "act"—I just let the tone of our friendship be what it always had been—upbeat and full of humor. I'd talk the way I'd always talked to him, and I knew him well enough that I could speak his half of the conversation for him when I knew it would be too much trouble for him to respond. He'd told me that he actually preferred this form of communication, pointing out that it took him twice as much energy to respond as it did to listen. He'd rather listen intently than interrupt the flow of a story.

I know some people found it difficult or awkward to be around Ali now because they didn't know how to engage him. I never had a problem dealing with Muhammad's Parkinson's, maybe because I saw the disease develop from its onset over the years and knew what to expect each time I saw him. It helped that we had those decades of experiences to draw on, so when I launched into a story, I knew that he knew exactly what I was talking about.

Muhammad always loved getting gifts—any kind of gift—and ripped into a package like a kid at Christmas. I got into the habit of bringing a few special things along with me on my visits. I learned through Marilyn that Muhammad enjoyed playing any kind of board game that required mental agility and strategy. She was always buying new games to play with him, and I tried to find gifts that would give him pleasure but also challenge him. I sat with him for some very competitive hours of rolling dice and moving pieces, and was always happy to see that his will to win was not affected by his disease. He still loved showing off his ability to outthink an opponent, and when Marilyn or I lost a game to him, it was never on purpose. It was because he beat us.

I also always brought a big stack of eight-by-ten photos for us to look through. These would generally be all kinds of photos from our times together—shots from training camps, parties, family dinners, and get-togethers. I knew Muhammad still enjoyed the sight of a beautiful woman, so I'd make sure to include photos of him standing with such beauties as Sophia Loren, Lola Falana, Christie Brinkley, Bo Derek, and Diana Ross. When Helga and I first met Ali, he was with his third wife, Veronica Porche Ali, and within a couple of years they had two children, Hana and Laila. I had many pictures of Helga and me together with Muhammad, Veronica, Hana, and Laila, and Muhammad always seemed to enjoy these very much. Muhammad always wanted to hold all the pictures himself and go through them one at a time, deciding how long he wanted to look at each one (he tended to linger on pictures of the very beautiful Veronica). He would study them carefully and listen to me describe who was in the shot and where it was taken. I was always looking for signs of recognition, ready to give answers to whatever he might ask about. His most common questions were "How old is he?" "Where is he now?" "How many grandchildren?" "Is he still married?" "Is he still making money?" and "Is she still a fox?"

I might try to jog his memory once or twice, asking him if he remembered a particular day or place or person. If he didn't answer, I would move on.

"Sometimes I can remember thirty years ago but I can't remember three weeks ago," he would say—not as a complaint, just a statement of fact.

I would also bring Muhammad coffee-table books full of photos I knew he would like, though I had learned the hard way that these books often didn't last too long. Parkinson's patients can have a compulsion to engage in repetitive movements and one of the things that was very satisfying for Muhammad was tearing the pages out of books. He'd enjoy whatever the photos were, but with great concentration he'd rip them out, page by page, slowly and methodically. He was aware of what he was doing, and you could see that the tearing was soothing and relaxing for him. I never saw this ritual as the waste of a good book—I liked seeing Muhammad enjoy himself, and if tearing the books was what gave him pleasure, then so be it. I brought him some beautiful photo books of his favorite celebrities—Marilyn Monroe, Elvis, Sophia Loren, Cher, Clint Eastwood, the Beatles—and would actually look on with joy as he tore up each of them.

AFTER ALI FINISHES HIS BREAKFAST, we stay at the kitchen table and watch the rest of *The Good, the Bad and the Ugly* together. He grew up watching TV westerns such as *Gunsmoke, Rawhide, Have Gun—Will Travel,* and *Wyatt Earp,* and still loves anything that involves a showdown between the good guys and the bad guys. In addition to westerns, he is particularly fond of horror films—especially anything with Christopher Lee's Dracula—as well as films with great dance scenes (as an athlete who moved so well on his feet, he has a great appreciation for the grace of Fred Astaire and the athleticism of Gene Kelly, and he often said about them what people said about him: they made amazing moves look easy).

On this visit I've brought Muhammad two picture books—one on Marilyn Monroe and one on the Beatles. Not surprisingly, he asks to see the Marilyn Monroe book first. And by the time Clint Eastwood is staring down his opponents in the film's climactic "Mexican standoff," Muhammad has carefully torn half the Marilyn photos out of the book. I produce my usual stack of personal photos for him, and we start to go through them together. This time I've brought fifty or so pictures of Muhammad with some of his better-known celebrity friends.

"Do you remember him?" I ask.

"Travolta."

"Do you know who that is, Muhammad?"

"Kris." It's Kris Kristofferson, with whom Muhammad has had one of his longest-running Hollywood friendships. "Where is he now?"

"I think he's in his home on Maui, but he wants to come visit you again soon."

I show Muhammad a photo of him standing between Sir Paul McCartney and his then-wife, Heather Mills.

"Are they still married?" Muhammad asks.

"No, they got divorced."

"Was it bad?" he asks.

"Well, it was bad for Paul," I say. "It cost him a lot. But the good news is that it's a wonderful picture of you two. We can crop out the ex-wife and you and Paul will look terrific together."

Muhammad laughs his low, guttural laugh. Boy, do I love that laugh.

We work our way through the rest of the photos like that, and then he pulls out some of the shots of Veronica, Hana, and Laila and sets them aside—a sign that he wants me to leave these with him (I always leave all the photos with Marilyn anyway).

When we've made it through the pictures, Muhammad starts to get out of his chair. Part of maintaining his dignity comes in doing as much as he can for himself, no matter how long it takes. Marilyn is always there to help him, as am I, but we let him do whatever he can for himself. Now he stands, without my help, and begins to walk back toward the refrigerator. This is part of the routine of his day. He's gotten up and gotten dressed. He's taken his medicine and entertained his guest. Now he's earned a reward: ice cream.

He gets to the refrigerator, opens the freezer, selects a half-gallon container of vanilla, and sets it on the counter. Marilyn takes over and begins to scoop up a couple of bowls of ice cream. "Muhammad, you are one spoiled child. You get your way too much," she says, scolding him and granting his request at the same time. She has told me that the ice cream is not just a treat—it soothes his throat and makes it easier for him to swallow solid foods, and it is also an excellent medium for masking the taste of his medications.

Muhammad seems to be moving very well on his feet today, so I decide to ask if he can pull off one of his old magic tricks.

"Hey, Muhammad, can you still levitate?"

"Yeah."

For as long as I've known him, Muhammad has had a fascination with magic, and over the years he has actually become fairly proficient at sleight-of-hand tricks. Muhammad once hired Terry Lasorda—a very talented magician and the nephew of the former Dodgers manager Tommy Lasorda—to move into his training camp so that he could learn new tricks as he prepared for a fight. Mostly Muhammad stuck with card tricks, but he had one larger classic illusion he loved to show people. He would angle himself with his back to a group of observers, and then, while holding his heels tightly together, would lean all of his weight on the toes of his right foot. He could then bring both heels up while balancing his body so that he appeared to be floating. I'd seen him mystify groups of fans with the trick many times, though just as often people seemed to assume he was showing off another of his natural abilities: He's Muhammad Ali—of course he can levitate.

This illusion is a hard move to pull off for a fit athlete, let alone a seventy-year-old man with Parkinson's. But, with some encouragement from Marilyn, Muhammad goes for it. He places one hand on the kitchen counter, one hand on my shoulder, and somehow manages to get all his weight on the toes of one foot so that he is up in the air for several seconds. I love it—in some ways the fact that he can still pull off a levitation is as wonderful as hearing him say my name so clearly and loudly. I make a fuss over the fact that he can still float like a butterfly, and ask if he can still "sting like a bee." He flicks a couple of quick, accurate jabs just shy of my face, then digs into his ice cream.

I have never had much of a sweet tooth, but for as long as I've known Muhammad, ice cream has been his main vice and a constant source of pleasure. And when Muhammad eats ice cream, he likes to see that you are sharing that pleasure with him. I couldn't possibly count the number of scoops of chocolate and vanilla I have eaten alongside

Muhammad through the years. Today, I have another bowl of ice cream with the Champ.

I stay awhile longer, just joking around with Muhammad and going over some of our favorite stories. I don't ever really feel ready to leave Muhammad, but there always comes a time when it is clear that he's had enough activity for the day. There's never any big deal about my leaving—no "Thanks for coming" or special goodbyes. I don't need that. I always want to be confident that this will not be the last time I see my friend, and I want our goodbye to be as happy and easy as our goodbyes always have been.

I tell him it's time for me to leave and, as always, he puts both of his hands on the arms of the chair—he wants to get up and see me to the door. I go to his chair and kneel down next to him before he makes the effort to get up. I put my arm over his shoulders behind his neck and give him a kiss on the left cheek. Then I say what I always say at the end of our visits: "I love you, Champ."

And he says what he always says in these situations: "Maaaan . . ."

THERE HAVE BEEN TIMES WHEN I drive away from a visit with Muhammad feeling sad, mostly because my time with him has come to an end and I don't know when I will see him again. Even though I know he is being well cared for by Lonnie and Marilyn, I often can't help but worry about what his days are like when he doesn't have a visitor to break up the routine. He is the man responsible for the most exciting times in my life, and though his body has slowed, I know his amazing mind is still active. I hate the idea of him being alone, far from so many of the family members and friends who love him. After many of my visits, I find myself hoping that Muhammad still wants to be here. I hope that his moments of joy can still balance out the moments of pain.

Leaving his home this day, though, I do not feel sad. On the way from Muhammad's house to the airport, I am focused on all the amazing moments of our thirty-eight years of friendship, and I am grateful that I have just been able to spend a few more cherished moments with my friend. As I think about our friendship, I am aware that my own name is ringing in my ears. It's ringing that way because Muhammad Ali has shouted it out, loud and clear, and that has me beaming with happiness, hope, and love. I concentrate on that wonderful sound and as I do, it feels as if thirty-eight years have just melted away.

TWO

MAIN MAN

ALL I HAD TO DO was ring a doorbell. And I had never been so nervous in my life.

I had been in nerve-rattling situations before. Like in June 1970 when, with the war in Vietnam raging, I received my draft notice just two weeks after graduating college. In the army, I dealt with the surges of adrenaline and anxiety that came with the live-ammo training that was part of officer candidate school. When I got out of the service, I played semipro basketball in Germany, and had experienced the unsettling feeling of being on the foul line in front of a hostile crowd with the game on the line. And since returning to the States and beginning a career as a surgical technician, I'd been in operating rooms where the decisions being made were literally a matter of life or death.

I had handled nerves before, but this time they took me by surprise. I felt perfectly confident walking up to the main door of this massive home in the Hyde Park neighborhood of Chicago. It was only as I prepared to ring the doorbell that I actually got weak in the knees. I was an expected visitor here and all I needed to do was put my finger to the bell. Simple enough. But when I rang the bell, it was going to be answered by the heavyweight champion of the world: Muhammad Ali.

I was living in Chicago with my wife, Helga, a native of Wiesbaden, Germany, who had come to live with me in the States the year before. We had an apartment in a little complex near O'Hare Airport. The place was definitely modest, but Helga loved the fact that it had a balcony overlooking courtyard gardens and a pool, which we used as much as the Chicago weather would allow. In my spare time, I got involved with a charity called Athletes for a Better Education. The group lined up adult mentors for high school athletes from Chicago's poorest and most crime-ridden neighborhoods, and once a month a player from one of Chicago's pro teams would deliver a motivational speech to the students at a special dinner. Already, I had worked with such stars as Bob Love and Chet Walker of the Bulls, Bobby Hull and Stan Mikita of the Blackhawks, and Ernie Banks and Ferguson Jenkins of the Cubs. Through the charity, I became especially close to a dynamic young running back who'd just come to town from Jackson State in Mississippi to play for the Bears, Walter Payton.

It was a chance connection at the University of Chicago Medical Center that led me to this Hyde Park doorbell. A nurse had heard I was looking for pro athletes who could address a banquet hall full of kids, and she suggested I speak with Dr. Charles Williams. Dr. Williams, it turned out, was a personal physician to Muhammad Ali.

At first, it seemed crazy that I might actually be able to get Ali to come speak to our kids. This was the fall of 1975, and Muhammad Ali wasn't just heavyweight champion of the world—he was the world's most popular celebrity. In the past year alone, he had won a thrilling victory against George Foreman in the ferocious "Rumble in the Jungle" match in Zaire, during which he'd pioneered the "rope-a-dope" tactic. Then he had gone on to defeat his archrival Joe Frazier in their third fight, the "Thrilla in Manila." Sports fans acknowledged him to be one of the greatest athletes who had ever lived, and his humor, good looks, intelligence, and compassion made him a hero to millions of people all over the world.

I had always been a huge fan of Ali's. In 1964, when I was attending Marquette University High School in Milwaukee and he was still

Cassius Clay, I was captivated listening to the radio broadcast of his epic fight with Sonny Liston, in which Ali became the youngest heavyweight champion in history. Even though I served in the military, I respected the courage it took for Ali to stand up for his principles as a conscientious objector in 1966—a stand that cost him his title and got him banned from boxing for three and a half years. When Ali fought Foreman, my brothers and I rented a room at the O'Hare Sheraton because the hotel was one of the few local places showing the closed-circuit satellite broadcast of the fight. Foreman, a young, strong, menacing champion, had quickly demolished two of Ali's greatest foes, Joe Frazier and Ken Norton, winning both fights with technical knockouts in the second round. Most sportswriters expected that Ali—still working his way back after the hiatus—would suffer a similar defeat. My brothers and I were Ali fans, but we worried, too, that he was going to get hurt.

Foreman was indeed a formidable adversary for Ali and landed a lot of powerful blows. But Ali took his skills to a new level, proving to the world that he was able to absorb a lot more punishment than anyone had suspected before dropping Foreman in the eighth round with a massive left hook to the jaw and a hard right to the face. The fight—from its weeks-long buildup to Ali's final knockout punch—was the most dramatic sporting event I had ever seen. As a fan, I went from actually fearing for Ali's life to feeling joy at his triumph, and I wholeheartedly agreed with Ali when he proclaimed from the locker room in his postfight interview, "Don't ever doubt me again—I'm still the Greatest."

I had the chance to approach Dr. Williams in mid-October, and he thought it was a fine idea to have Ali as a speaker for the kids. He told me that my timing was perfect—the following month Ali would be moving from Cherry Hill, New Jersey, to Chicago. Ali had strong ties to the city: he'd fought to become a national Golden Gloves champion here, had announced his conversion to Islam in the Chicago Coliseum, had lived in the city with his first wife, Sonji Roi, and had met his current wife, Khalilah (Belinda Boyd), here. Chicago had also been home to Elijah Muhammad, leader of the Nation of Islam. After becoming a

Muslim, Ali developed a personal relationship with Elijah Muhammad, whom he considered to be a messenger of Allah. Elijah Muhammad had just passed away in February, but his home remained the central headquarters of the Nation of Islam, and apparently Ali wanted to return to Chicago so he could live closer to those premises.

Without much fanfare Dr. Williams picked up the phone, called Ali, gave him a brief pitch about the speaking engagement—and handed the phone to me.

"Hello?" I said.

"Yeah," a voice responded.

"Hello, Mr. Ali. My name is Tim Shanahan and I, and I—"

"Yeah, I know. Dr. Williams told me," said Ali. His voice was low and surprisingly soft for such a big, powerful guy. "I know you're trying to help these kids who need your help to get into college. That's good."

I hadn't expected to find myself on the phone with the heavyweight champion of the world, and I think I started to thank him for agreeing to appear at the dinner before he had even said that he would do it.

There was a pause. Then he said, "You're like me. You want to help people. Get me the date and the time for your dinner. I'll be there."

"Thank you again. We'll schedule the dinner for when we know you're going to be in town."

"Good. Get my number from Dr. Charles," he said without much emotion.

After the call, I learned from Dr. Williams that Ali had been planning his move to Chicago for some time, but hadn't yet found a house he wanted to buy. I knew that Elijah Muhammad had lived in the Hyde Park neighborhood, and I asked some of the nurses I was friendly with at the University of Chicago Medical Center if they knew of any homes in the area that might be right for Ali. One of them told me that the president of the university, Edward Levi, was retiring and moving back east. He had a mansion on South Woodlawn, just a few blocks from Elijah Muhammad's house. I passed this information back to Dr. Williams, who scouted the place and then got the OK from Muhammad to close the deal through his business manager, Gene Dibble. A few weeks later, Muhammad Ali was a resident of Chicago, living at 4944 South Woodlawn.

True to his word, Muhammad agreed to speak at an upcoming Athletes for a Better Education dinner on the Friday after Thanksgiving week. I spoke to him briefly on the phone one more time on Wednesday of that week to confirm the final details. He surprised me when he said he wanted me to come to his house the next night to talk about the organization and what it did for kids.

SO HERE I WAS IN front of a South Woodlawn mansion, trying to muster the courage to ring the doorbell. I rang the bell and suddenly I was all nerves. All sorts of panicky questions started zooming through my mind: What am I supposed to say? How am I supposed to act? What do I even call him? Champ? Muhammad? Mr. Ali? Mr. Champ?

There were panes of stained glass on each side of the door, and I looked through the clear glass border of one of them. I saw a beautiful wood table that held a flower arrangement at the base of a curving stairway. Suddenly there was a hand on the rail of the staircase and then

South Woodlawn Avenue, Chicago—where I first met Muhammad Ali.

a large figure descending the stairs. I darted back up from the window so that I wouldn't get caught peeking in. In the few seconds it took for that figure to get to the door, I managed to become even more nervous.

Oh, boy. Here we go.

The door opened and there he stood, looking every bit the majestic heavyweight champ in a beautiful gray-and-maroon boxer's robe with a great big hood. I was suddenly shaking the biggest, meatiest hand I had ever encountered, though his handshake was very gentle. He seemed to be taking great care not to hurt a hand that he could easily crush (I'd learn later that he shook hands this way partly because his own hands were perpetually sore).

"Hi, Mr. Ali, I'm Tim Shanahan." I was extremely self-conscious about getting my words out, and there was a chance I had just introduced myself as "Tim Shahanahan."

"I know who you are, man. Come on in," he said.

I couldn't quite get my legs to move. "I just wanted to come by and—"

"Yeah, I know. Come in."

I forced my uncooperative legs to step through the doorway and into Muhammad Ali's home. "I don't know how much Dr. Williams told you about this event but I just want to thank you again . . ."

"He told me all about it," Ali said. I'd heard his voice on the phone but I was still surprised in person to hear how soft-spoken he was. "Look, I like people that want to help other people and that's what you're doing. Anybody that comes to me for help with things like you're doing for the kids, I'll do it every time. Don't be afraid to call."

We walked across the entranceway to the staircase. He sat down on the steps and motioned for me to sit beside him. I clicked into business mode and started to give him a rundown on what Athletes for a Better Education had done so far, which pro athletes were involved, and what he could expect at the event the next night.

He nodded politely as I delivered my spiel, then said, "Man—you've really got a handle on this. I wish I would have known about it earlier. I would have come out here sooner."

He had some more questions about the event and we talked for another couple of minutes. Once business was out of the way, I figured he would show me right back out the door. But he didn't seem in any hurry to get our meeting over with. It occurred to me that because he was being so warm and relaxed, I had calmed down—my knees weren't knocking anymore and I didn't feel any of the jitters I'd felt at the front door.

"Boy, Mr. Ali," I said. "I've been a fan since you beat Sonny Liston for the championship and I've seen all your fights. It is so great to finally meet you, but I have to say I was a little nervous about coming here."

"Why were you nervous?" he asked.

The question was so direct it caught me off guard. "Uh, well—for one thing, you're Muhammad Ali, the most famous athlete on the planet."

"Maaan—I'm not *that* big," he said. He reached across the staircase to a little table that sat in the entryway. On top of it were a phone and a small but thick black book. He picked up the book and flipped it open. I was looking at Muhammad Ali's personal contact book, full of names and numbers.

"There's a lot of people bigger than me," he shrugged. "You know him?" He was pointing to a name: Leonard Bernstein.

"Sure."

"He's more famous than me. How about this one?" He was pointing at another name: Johnny Carson.

"Uh, yeah."

"See—more famous."

He slowly paged through the book, pointing out other entries, sometimes mentioning how and where he had met each famous figure, or suggesting that a certain name might be a good speaker for the Athletes program. I concentrated hard enough to etch the passing names in my memory: Arthur Ashe, Milton Berle, James Brown, Chubby Checker, Bill Cosby, Bob Dylan, Elvis (in the "E"s rather than the "P"s), Lola Falana, Eddie Kendricks (of the Temptations), Norman Mailer, Dean Martin, Tony Orlando, Lloyd Price. Things began to get a little blurry toward the end of the alphabet, though I do remember that Frank Sinatra was in there.

There was no reason in the world for Muhammad Ali to humble himself before Tim Shanahan, yet here he was, pointing at names and shaking his head and telling me how much more famous his friends were. Of course, at the same time, he was showing off exactly who his friends were and casually underscoring the point that, in fact, nobody was as famous as he was. If he wanted to impress me, it was working.

"Let's call her," he said. He was pointing to Diana Ross's name.

"OK."

He dialed a Manhattan number, spoke with someone for a moment, then said, "All right—tell her Ali called." To me he said, "That was the maid. Diana's not home. Who else should we call. Hmmm—how about him?" He was pointing to Tony Orlando's name.

Tony was enjoying the peak of success that fall, riding a string of hits such as "Tie a Yellow Ribbon" and starring in the top-rated *Tony Orlando and Dawn* variety show on TV. Muhammad dialed his number, and it seemed that Tony himself answered, because Muhammad began talking in a very relaxed, familiar way. Then he said, "Tony—I've got a friend here who wants to say hello. His name is Tim Shanahan."

He handed me the phone.

"Uh—hi, Tony, how are you doing?"

"Pretty good, Tim. So you're friends with the Champ?" Orlando asked.

"Well, I guess I'm a very recent friend—I just met him tonight."

"Oh." Orlando laughed. "So you're one of Muhammad's million closest friends, too?"

"Yeah, that's about right," I said.

"Well, so am I," said Tony.

Muhammad took the phone back and said a couple more things to Tony, then ended the conversation with a quick goodbye. He closed the phone book, put it back on the table, and got up from the stairs.

"Follow me," he said. "I want to show you something."

We took a few steps around the corner of the staircase and there

I saw a feature I had never seen in a private home before: an elevator. Ali pointed at it like a kid showing off a new Christmas present, and seemed to take pleasure in my stunned expression.

"The heavyweight champion of the world needs to have an elevator in his home," he said. He pulled the elevator gate open and gestured for me to step in. "Let's go upstairs. I'll show you my forty-six-inch TV."

He pressed a button that would take us up to the third floor. As the elevator slowly shuddered its way upward, he turned toward me and asked another direct question: "What nationality are you?"

I explained that the Shanahans were Black Irish. According to some historical theories, somewhere in our family tree there had been a mixture of genes from invading Spanish Moors, dark-skinned Basques, and native Irish. I happened to know that Ali had a similarly mixed heritage: I was such a fan that I had asked a Mormon doctor I worked with if he could use the Mormon genealogical archives to do some research into Ali's lineage. I learned that Ali's mother Odessa's grandfather was an Irishman named Grady. Grady's son, Odessa's father, had married a black woman. I mentioned this to Ali, and said that, since my great-grandparents and his great-grandfather were both born in Ireland, we could be considered Black Irish cousins.

"We're both Black Irish?" he asked, incredulously. "You mean, you're a nigga like me?"

"Well—I guess so. But I've been passing for years."

He clapped his hands and let out a big laugh: "Maaaaan." I was relieved to see he got my sense of humor.

We stepped off the elevator and into Ali's third-floor rec room, which contained the biggest TV I had ever seen. It looked more like a film theater system than a television, with a huge screen angled to catch the light from three large red, blue, and yellow projectors. The TV was hooked up to what looked like an industrial-sized videotape player. This was before the era of the VCR, so the very idea of being able to watch your own tapes was amazing. There were some shelves on which Ali had created a library of tapes (the tapes themselves were the size of dictionaries). I looked closely enough to see that these were tapes of his fights, and the two that were out by the TV were tapes of the Foreman fight and the Thrilla in Manila.

Ali noted my interest in the tapes, and told me that he kept them organized in the order of their importance to him. It looked to me like that meant he considered his most important fight to have been his first battle with Sonny Liston back in 1964. Ali told me the first Liston fight remained his most memorable one, because he considered Liston to be his most frightening opponent.

"I was twenty-two years old and everyone expected me to be annihilated by this ex-con," he said. "He was scary. But I beat him. And that made me champion for the first time. I dreamt of it, and then it happened."

He popped the tape of the Foreman fight back into its big case and put it on the shelf. "Going to Africa to fight Foreman—knowing that he had destroyed Norton and Frazier—that was scary, too," he said. "Whenever I fought Frazier, there were lots of people who thought I could beat him, but nobody thought I could beat Foreman."

"Who would you say was your toughest fight?" I asked.

"My first wife," he said. "Then Liston, Frazier, and Foreman."

He showed me around the house a little more, which he still hadn't fully moved into. Then he asked if I was hungry. It was about nine p.m. and I had eaten dinner earlier, but I wasn't going to do anything to cut this night short. I told him I would eat something if he was going to. We went back down the elevator and walked to the kitchen. The only cooking-related item out on the kitchen counter was a toaster, and as Ali opened up cupboards I noticed there wasn't much in them. He managed to scrounge up enough supplies to make us each a toasted American cheese sandwich with mayo and mustard, served along with two large glasses of orange juice.

We settled in at the small kitchen table to eat, and I asked him if it was OK to ask a question about the Thrilla in Manila. He nodded.

"That was a fourteen-round fight, and you were up against one of the hardest punchers out there. After being hit so much and after throwing so many punches, how did you even get your hands up for round fourteen? I don't know how you could take that much punishment and last that long in the ring."

He nodded, and I could tell he appreciated a question that indicated some understanding of his sport.

"You don't know, and neither do I. I knew God was with me, but I died in the ring that night. I died in the ring with Frazier. I left something of me in that ring. I was determined to beat him, and I beat him, but I don't know how I did it except that it was with Allah's help."

After we ate our sandwiches, Ali produced a couple of bowls and served up sizable helpings of ice cream. Sitting close to him, under the kitchen lights, it struck me that, for a guy who'd spent the last fifteen years punching and being punched, his skin was absolutely perfect—tight and fine and without a blemish. At one point, though, he leaned over a bit and, from the way the light hit him, I noticed that there was a little scar above his left eye, just under the eyebrow.

"Muhammad, is that a scar from one of your earlier fights? I don't remember you ever getting cut."

"No. I did that myself. That's from when I was eleven years old. I rode my bike into a brick wall, fell off, and got cut." He looked hard at me and gestured toward my eyes. "You've got the same scar. Did you box?"

I'd forgotten about my own scar. I told him that I hadn't been a boxer but, like him, had an accident as a kid. I was five or six and was running down a steep hillside with my older brothers. They dug in their heels and stayed in control but I just ran straight down the hill and flew into a pile of rocks.

"Hmm. So we were both crazy kids," said Ali.

We finished our ice cream, and it seemed to me that it was finally time for the night to end. I thanked him for such a great evening, and told him I would be on my way.

"How far do you have to drive home?" he asked.

I told him I lived in Arlington Heights, by the airport. It was maybe forty minutes away.

"Call me when you want to watch a fight."

I had just enough control not to shout out, "Wow!" Muhammad Ali had welcomed me into his home. He had even fed me. And now he was asking if I wanted to come back some time to watch a fight with him. He seemed so warm and sincere, I was convinced that he was treating me the way he would treat any other guest he might have had in his home that night. I was just shocked that I happened to be that guest, and I felt honored that he thought I was worthy of the kind of courtesy he was showing me.

"Thanks, Muhammad, I would love that."

Then he surprised me again, asking if I would come by the next night to give him a ride to the dinner event. Of course I would. I remember thinking how casual that exchange sounded: a new acquaintance was asking for a ride, and I was saying yes. But at the same time, there was a little voice that kept screaming in the back of my head, as it had been doing all night long, *You're talking to Muhammad Ali!*

He was still in his robe, and the November night had grown quite cold, but he walked me out to my car. I had a '75 Buick Regal, with a black-and-white exterior and an all-white interior. The car caught Ali's eye.

"You like that car?"

"Yeah, I love it. It's got power and it handles beautifully."

He pulled the door open and got his big frame halfway into the driver's seat, one foot still planted on the street. "Feels good," he said. "I've got to drive this sometime."

"Anytime, Muhammad," I said. "Maybe tomorrow when I pick you up."

"Black and white," he said as he climbed back out. "Your car's Black Irish, too."

I laughed, and I noticed he was pulling his robe closed tight against the cold. "You better get back inside, Muhammad."

"What time are you coming tomorrow?" he asked.

"Well, the event is at seven—I could come get you at six."

"Be here at five thirty. We'll talk some more."

We shook hands again. "It was a pleasure meeting you, Muhammad."
"OK" was all he said.

I waited and watched him walk into the house and close the door.
Then I saw him peeking through the window, waiting to see me drive off.

I did get home safely. Helga was already asleep, so I didn't have
anyone to share my excitement with. I'm pretty sure I just stared at the
ceiling all night, as the events of the evening played over and over again
in my head. My life had taken a few interesting twists and turns before,
but did I really just spend an evening with Muhammad Ali?

AS I DROVE BACK TO Ali's the next night, I wondered if our first meeting had
been a fluke. Maybe I had just caught him in a friendlier-than-usual
mood, and from now on our relationship would be more businesslike.
Would he even remember that he had invited me to watch a fight with
him, or that he wanted to drive my car? I also thought about the fact
that he'd been home by himself the night before. Here was the biggest
superstar in the world, and there wasn't any security at all around him.
I knew he was married and had four children, but what I didn't know at
the time was that he and his wife, Khalilah, were having marital troubles that would soon lead to a separation. She was staying with the kids
at an apartment close to both her parents' home and Muhammad's new
place. I supposed that even a superstar could get lonely, and maybe Muhammad had just wanted some company the night before. The more I
thought about how Ali might receive me now, the more nervous I got.
By the time I was standing in front of that Hyde Park doorbell for a
second time, my knees were just as wobbly, and I got panicky enough
that I began to doubt that the night before had even happened. It took
even more effort this time to put my finger to the bell.

"My main man, Tim Shanahan," Ali practically shouted as he pulled
open the door. With that he turned around and walked into the house.
OK. Apparently, last night had actually happened, and I didn't have to
worry about him being any less friendly tonight. Again, I forced my feet
to step over that threshold and into Muhammad Ali's home.

He looked extremely sharp in a suit custom-tailored to fit his big frame—a dark blue pinstripe wool suit over a bright white shirt and a flashy red tie. He strode into his living room to pick up a briefcase on the floor.

"Everybody is so excited to see you tonight, Muhammad," I said. "Do you know what you're going to talk about?"

He sat down, set the briefcase on his lap, and popped it open. Inside were thick stacks of five-by-seven index cards wrapped with rubber bands. In 1967, in the wake of his refusal to be inducted into the military, Ali had been banned from boxing. Denied the chance to earn a living in the ring, Ali supported his family by developing a series of talks he could give in front of a variety of audiences, and became an in-demand lecturer on college campuses. Even after his return to boxing, he maintained a busy speaking schedule, and was still using the same cards.

He had about a dozen different speeches that he had written himself. He handed me one of the wrapped stacks of index cards. It was for a speech titled "The Heart." He handed me another stack for a speech titled "Greatness," and then one for a speech titled "Friendship." The cards weren't just notes—they had every word of the speeches written out. But he had delivered each of them enough times to have them all completely memorized, and he started reciting some of the lines from each of them. He looked through the case a little more, then decided that his speech on friendship was best for the audience of high school kids that night.

We talked a little while longer about the kids that the organization was helping, and about how one of its main goals was to stress to these kids the importance of a college education. Ali was a big advocate of higher education, no matter what kind of athletic skills a kid might have. Muhammad said that he had been moved along from grade to grade and ended up with a diploma, but was frustrated at leaving school without being able to read or write at a high school level. He clearly had an athletic career ahead of him, but still he took it on himself to improve his reading and writing. It seemed to me that the effort had paid off greatly—he had taught himself well enough to become one of the world's great public speakers.

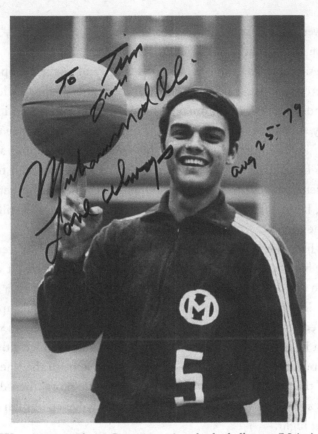

Warming up with my German semipro basketball team (Mainz).
Muhammad liked this shot so much that he wanted to sign it.

We got in my Black Irish Buick and headed for the Chicago Conrad Hilton Hotel. On the way over, he asked me if working for Athletes for a Better Education meant that I was an athlete. I filled him in on my athletic background—that I had played college basketball at Creighton, that I'd been part of the USA handball squad at the 1972 Olympics, and that I'd played a couple of seasons of semipro basketball in a German league after I got out of the army. After that, I told him, I was ready to leave my athletic days behind and begin a career as a surgical products sales rep, specializing in open-heart surgery.

"Are you a surgeon?" he asked.

"Not even close," I said. I explained that I was more a salesman than a physician technician, and I was in operating rooms to observe how the products I sold were being used by the cardiologists actually doing the surgery. With that, I expected that we might talk a little more about my athletic background—I was certainly ready to go over my career highlights with him. But Ali didn't seem all that impressed and didn't ask any follow-up questions.

We got to the Hilton and headed in. The place was packed with a couple hundred attendees, and they all went nuts as soon as he stepped into the banquet hall. The kids broke into ecstatic applause, and even the other pro sports guys sat there with big grins on their faces, clapping just as loudly as the kids. Muhammad and I were seated together on the dais, and I had the chance to introduce him to some of the other attendees who'd been involved with the charity: Ray Burris, José Cardenal, and Ernie Banks from the Cubs; Chet Walker of the Bulls; and my buddy Walter Payton from the Bears.

I think everyone gobbled down dinner as fast as they could, because everyone wanted to get to Muhammad's speech. There were some announcements and some presentations of awards to kids who had made great improvements in their grades. Then it was time for the main event. The kids went crazy all over again when Ali stood up to speak and he was fantastic with them—patient and good-natured and very funny. Once he got them quieted down and launched into his talk on friendship, the crowd hung on every word. I don't remember a lot of the speech, but I do remember it ended with some powerful lines of poetry: "I looked for my God, but my God I could not see. I looked for my soul, but my soul eluded me. I looked for a friend, and then I found all three."

Then, for dramatic effect, he said, "Heavy."

He got a standing ovation that seemed like it would have lasted all weekend if we hadn't finally moved to close things down.

When I dropped him off back at his place that night he said, "I'm going to be working out at the Southside Gym. Do you know where that is?"

I told him I did.

"Do you want to watch me work out?"

Of course I did.

"Well, pick me up at five thirty Monday morning and get me over there. We'll talk some more."

For the first time in our brief friendship, I was going to have to say no to Muhammad Ali. "I'm supposed to be with a doctor in surgery on Monday morning, Muhammad. There's just no way I can get out of that."

"See—you're trying to help people. That's all right. I'll get there myself. You get over there when you can."

THE MONDAY MORNING SURGERY WAS a routine pacemaker implant—no complications—and by 8:30 I was in my Buick, racing from the University of Chicago Medical Center to the Southside Gym to see if I could catch Ali before he finished working out. I didn't have to race far—the gym was on Fifty-fifth Street, very close to the university, in a large second-floor space above a block of storefronts. As I headed up the rickety wooden steps to where the action was, I got nervous all over again. I had seen Ali twice and I still couldn't believe I'd spent even that much time with him. It had felt so natural and enjoyable, but I wondered how long the connection might last. The nights I had spent with him had both been related to the Athletes for a Better Education event. I had met with him in private, and I had been with him at a public event. But now, I was stepping into his life as world heavyweight champion. At this gym, he was in his element, doing a part of what it was that had made him so famous to begin with. Maybe now that he was turning his attention back to boxing, our brief connection wouldn't seem so important to him. Maybe now I'd really just be one of a million, as Tony Orlando had put it.

I assumed a superstar like Ali could train anyplace he wanted. If so, he sure hadn't picked the Southside Gym for the decor. It was a beat-up, seen-better-days kind of place that looked exactly what you would expect an old-time boxing gym to look like—cracked windows, yellowed posters unsuccessfully trying to cover up the holes in the walls, the stink of sweat and cheap cigar smoke hanging in the air. There was a well-worn boxing ring in the center of the big, dimly lit room, and a whole bunch of tough-looking black guys were milling around watching Ali shadow box. I stood at the edge of the crowd. Nobody acknowledged me with so much as a nod. Ali bobbed and danced in the ring, throwing occasional lightning-fast combinations.

After a few minutes he stopped boxing and laid his gloves on the top rope as he caught his breath. He looked down at some of the people standing closest to the ring and said something that got them laughing. Then he looked up and surveyed the rest of the crowd. Suddenly his face lit up.

"Look who it is!" he said loudly. He pointed a glove in my direction, and I turned to look over my shoulder at who he was so excited to see. "My main man, Tim Shanahan!"

Even though he said my name out loud, for a split second I was so shocked I didn't recognize it. My mind raced with the same question that I'm sure was puzzling everybody else around the gym—"Who's Tim Shanahan?"

Oh, yeah—it was me.

The tough guys around the ring were checking me out now. From the dirty looks coming my way, I could only guess that these guys did not feel very welcoming toward the only white guy in the room, who also happened to be the only guy in a business suit. Ali went back to work in the ring, and once his focus shifted away from the crowd, the looks coming my way only got dirtier and even less welcoming. I didn't care. They could stare at me as coldly as they wanted, and they could try as hard as they wanted to make me feel out of place. Muhammad Ali had just called me his "main man." He had welcomed me into his home, and now he had welcomed me into his gym. As far as I was concerned, I was exactly where I was supposed to be—though I still couldn't believe I was lucky enough to be here.

I walked away from the group gathered around the ring and sat on a bench by the windows, where I still had a good view of Ali. He moved around the ring and threw punches for a few more minutes, and as people sensed that he was close to the end of his workout, those in training went back to their own workouts, while the staff returned to their tasks around the gym. People weren't standing around staring at Ali anymore, but you knew they all had one eye on whatever he was doing.

He finished in the ring and somebody from the gym helped him get his gloves off. When he came down the steps he was just a few feet away from me. As he passed he waved me toward him.

"C'mon."

I sprang to my feet and started following him. He headed across the gym and went through a door into a smaller room, and I stayed close behind him. On the wall across from us Ali's street clothes hung on some hooks. In the middle of the room was a rubdown table. I was alone in a locker room with Muhammad Ali. There were some showers off to the side of the room, and I assumed he was going to head in there and that I was supposed to wait for him by the table. But without a second's hesitation, Ali simply dropped his boxing trunks and underwear (he hadn't been sparring so hadn't needed the protection of a jock). He sat down on the massage table and crossed one leg and then the other as he took off his boxing shoes and socks. Then he stood up again. I was alone in a locker room with a completely naked Muhammad Ali.

I'd had years of experience being in locker rooms with naked teammates, but I think my Catholic upbringing left me with such conflicted feelings about casual nudity that I was never entirely comfortable in those situations. Muhammad was obviously as comfortable as could be, and because he was so at ease, I guess, I was able to overcome my usual shyness enough to notice that he had the most impressive physique I'd ever encountered. People use Michelangelo's *David* as the standard for an ideal male body, but looking at a naked Ali, I couldn't imagine a more perfect form. In fact, Ali was definitely more impressive than David when it came to the size of his most masculine body part.

Ali walked away to take a quick shower, then came back to the massage table, smoothed out a big towel very neatly on it, and lay down on his stomach.

Hmm. What now? He had invited me in here but I really wasn't sure what I was supposed to do. He'd spoken at my event—was I supposed to return the favor by giving him his rubdown? I started to feel a little flustered, but before I had a chance to ask what would have turned out to be a very stupid question, a masseur stepped into the room and quickly got to work giving Ali a hard, deep tissue massage. Ali had some personal masseurs he worked with, but this was a local guy who ran a nearby judo school and worked for the gym when somebody put in a special request. As he leaned hard into Ali's muscles, the Champ didn't grunt or groan—he just started talking to me in a soft, relaxed voice, mainly asking me more questions about how Athlete's for a Better Education was run, and indicating that someday he wanted to set up a similar sort of organization that could help as many people as possible.

When the rubdown was finally finished Muhammad jumped off the table and headed for the showers. Once he was dressed we headed out together. He shouted a few goodbyes to people in the gym, and then we went down the stairs and were back out on the street.

"Thank you, Muhammad, for letting me watch you work out. That was really great."

"Where's your car?"

Was he worried about how far I had to walk to my Buick? Of course not.

"Ohhh—Muhammad—am I driving you home?"

"Yeah."

And so my brand-new friendship with the heavyweight champion of the world was cemented a little further. The Hyde Park home wasn't far from the gym, and on the way there we talked a little bit about his training, especially his preference for 5:30 a.m. runs. When we got to his house I pulled into his driveway and this time I didn't wait for a

"C'mon." I simply got out of the car and followed him into the house. I was done with work for the day, and whatever else I had thought I was going to do had just been canceled by the chance to spend more time with the Champ.

Elijah Muhammad's son Herbert had arranged for Muhammad to have a housekeeper, and she greeted us as we walked into the kitchen. Well, she greeted Muhammad. She was in her mid-sixties, quite large, and had the darkest skin I'd ever seen. She wore a scowl that warned me of a deeply ornery nature. She seemed almost stricken that a white guy was on the premises, and when Ali asked if she could put out some lunch for us I could tell she was not happy at all about serving me. But there wasn't much serving to do—the kitchen still hadn't been stocked with much of anything, so she simply put out some cold fast-food chicken and paper plates on the dining room table.

Muhammad and I talked a little more while we ate, but mostly he focused on going through a big pile of personal mail. When the food and the mail were dealt with, he got up and headed toward the main staircase. Again, I didn't wait for an invitation to join him—I just followed. I was starting to learn that this was the way Muhammad liked things—he had let me into his home but he certainly wasn't going to be the doting host. He wasn't going to ask me what I wanted to do or take time to explain what he wanted to do. He seemed to want his guest to be in sync with him. If I could figure out how to do that without asking a lot of questions or acting awkward or formal, then apparently I could stick around.

We skipped the elevator this time and walked up to the third-floor TV room, where he went over to his shelf of fight tapes. If he had asked me which fight I wanted to watch, I would have chosen the Foreman fight or one of the Frazier fights. But he wasn't asking me. There was a fight he wanted to watch—his eleven-round knockout of Ron Lyle, which had happened several months before the Thrilla in Manila. We settled into the couch across from the big TV screen and Ali started the tape. Nobody had given Lyle much of a chance against Ali, and while the fight wasn't a great one, it was a good one. It was also one of the few Ali fights that had been broadcast on network television. Ali said he liked Lyle both personally and as a fighter. He said it felt like he'd been up against a mirror image of himself—Lyle was a good-looking, well-muscled six-foot-three black guy, who moved more quickly in the ring than you'd expect of a big man.

"See—he's fast. He's a good athlete," Ali said whenever Lyle made a strong move on the TV screen.

He was watching the fight intently, and I couldn't help darting my eyes over to watch him watching himself. I heard what he was saying, but I also felt like I was having the closest thing to an out-of-body experience I had ever had. I flashed back to a year earlier, when I sat with my brothers Pat and Michael in the O'Hare Sheraton, watching Muhammad Ali battle George Foreman. Now I was in Muhammad Ali's house, sitting on Muhammad Ali's couch, sitting next to Muhammad Ali, watching a Muhammad Ali fight. It was as if I were living inside a dream, and I couldn't imagine anything else in my life that would match this feeling.

After the fight was over, Muhammad said he was going to take a nap, which I took as a pretty clear signal that it was time to go. Just a few days before, I had stood outside this house, so nervous I could barely ring the doorbell. Now I felt comfortable enough inside that it was going to be hard to say goodbye.

But saying goodbye wasn't Muhammad Ali's style. Instead, he asked, "Do you run?"

"I try to run three miles a day. I've been doing that since college."

"Where?"

"Well, Washington Park is close to the hospital—and not too far from here. I like to run there in the mornings, before I have my appointments in the downtown hospitals."

"Are we going to run tomorrow?"

"Uhh . . . sure, Muhammad."

"What time?"

I remembered what he'd told me about his training regimen. "How about five thirty?"

"Mm." He picked up a scrap of paper and a pencil and wrote something down, then handed it to me. When I had contacted him for the Athletes event, I had called his business line. Now he was giving me his personal number. The same number that he had given to Tony Orlando and Diana Ross and Elvis and the rest of the million best friends in his little black book.

"Call me when you're coming over."

The Champ wanted me to call him on his private line. If I was living in a dream, the dream wasn't over quite yet.

THREE

COUSIN TIM

THE NEXT MORNING, AT 5:30 sharp, I was back at the house on South Woodlawn ready to head off for a training run with the heavyweight champion of the world. This time, it was a little easier to walk up to his door. Muhammad greeted me and let me in. He was barefoot, in a gray Russell sweatsuit. He headed into the kitchen and I sat down at the dining room table. A moment later he reappeared with a pair of socks and a large pair of combat boots. He sat down and began to put them on.

"What are you doing today?" he asked.

"Well, I have to go to Loyola University Medical Center for a surgery."

"You're going to be in surgery?"

"Yeah. But not until ten. I have plenty of time." I watched him lace up a combat boot. "Muhammad—what size shoe do you wear? Those look awfully big."

"Size thirteen. Not that big."

I asked him why he wanted to run in such heavy boots. He explained the weight of the boots helped strengthen his legs, and that the boots' sturdy construction made it less likely that he'd turn an ankle while training. He told me he kept the boots on all day before a fight, because then when he stepped into the ring, his feet would feel lighter and he could move more quickly. His father had told him that's how Joe Louis trained, so Muhammad started doing the same.

A few minutes later we were in Muhammad's most luxurious car—a gleaming gold '74 Stutz Blackhawk—driving over to the edge of Washington Park at Sixtieth Street and Cottage Grove. The park was surrounded by quiet residential neighborhoods on three sides and a sleepy business district on the other. Muhammad preferred to run in the streets around the park rather than on the trails in the park (his boots would be too slippery on moist morning grass). At that hour of the morning we had the streets to ourselves. Muhammad did a quick set of exercises before the run—twenty-five each of jumping jacks, push-ups, and toe touches. I copied what he was doing. It seemed to me that he was more focused now than he had been when I saw him work out in the ring. There, he'd been quick to kid around and entertain the bystanders. Now it was as if he were going into a state of deep meditation. His runs were a crucial part of his staying in shape, both mentally and physically, and it looked like he took them very seriously.

We began to run alongside the park, and when I saw the pace he set for himself, I knew right away that I could probably hold a faster pace— I was an avid tennis player and had been running five days a week for more than ten years. I prided myself on staying fit. I also knew that getting out ahead of him would be exactly the wrong move. I hadn't come out with him to try to show off. I understood that he had not invited me along to try to race him, and I wouldn't even think of doing anything that might seem competitive. He set the pace, and I kept up with him.

I guess he was comfortable with me as a running partner, because over the next couple of weeks those 5:30 runs became our daily ritual. We would run for an hour, sit in the park awhile to cool down and talk, and head back to his house for breakfast (he could make pancakes; my specialty was scrambled eggs with tomatoes and toast). Then I could head straight over to my appointments at the hospital.

It seemed to puzzle Muhammad that I could go from a casual cup of coffee straight to an operating room. One morning as we sat at his table after a run, he asked, "Do you see a lot of blood when they cut somebody open?"

I explained to him that the surgeons I worked with were skilled enough that they avoided cutting any major arteries—there was less blood than he might think.

"Maaan." I think he still had a hard time imagining that I started my workday looking into open chest cavities.

Muhammad was driven to remain champion, but he was open about the fact that he really hated training, and especially hated getting up early to run. He told me that when he was young, he had loved being in training—he would run all day—and if he had never stopped his early routine, he might still approach it with the same desire. But his involuntary three-and-a-half-year hiatus from boxing had thrown off his body's rhythms, and now he approached training as something that was necessary but very unpleasant.

He told me that for most of his career, his morning runs had been solo efforts. He might run with Jimmy Ellis, a boxer and training partner he had known since he was fourteen—but most of the time he preferred to have training staff shadow him in a car. He didn't make a big deal about having invited me to run with him, but I understood I was being given a rare privilege. Muhammad hadn't seemed to take much notice when I had told him about my past athletic experiences, but he did seem impressed that I could not only keep up with him but would be willing to keep running hard after he got tired. He didn't seem to mind when I started running the final hundred yards of our three-mile runs as fast as I could. He would be shaking his head as we found a place to sit down in the park.

"What are *you* in training for, Shanahan?"

"Nothing, Muhammad. I just like to stay in shape."

"You're crazy, white boy."

It was a privilege enough to be running with Ali, but my favorite moments of our mornings together came during the drives to and from the park, and after the runs when we would lie on our backs on an embankment of park grass and stare up at the morning sky. It was then that we started to really talk to each other, as any two guys getting to know each other might. We started to talk a lot about our childhoods, his in Louisville, Kentucky, and mine in West Allis, Wisconsin, just outside of Milwaukee. Growing up in Louisville he'd worked odd jobs at the local library and at Churchill Downs, home of the Kentucky Derby. He was fifteen years old when he worked at the track and, having won the Louisville Golden Gloves the year before, was in training for the national Golden Gloves competition. One day, as part of his training, he decided to see if he could outrun a thoroughbred. He thought maybe he could beat the horse in a hundred-yard dash if he could hit his top speed while the horse was still accelerating. For a while he was able to get out on the track while a complicit jockey would ride alongside him, but eventually some other jockeys complained that the big kid running on the turf was spooking the horses, and that particular training regimen came to an end.

"Did you ever outrace a horse?" I asked.

"It was close for fifty yards."

One of the first very personal things Muhammad shared with me was that he'd been deathly afraid of the dark as a child. He wanted to know if I had felt the same way. I had, but I told him it was not just the dark but the sounds of the dark that terrified me, especially the barking dogs and yowling stray cats. He laughed and agreed that the sound of a screaming cat at night could be scary, but the thing that terrified him most as a kid was crashing thunder and wild lightning. I grew up in a devout Catholic household and had attended church almost every day. I said that when I had to make the dark walks home from the movie theater six blocks away, it was the dogs and cats that had me on edge (especially after something like *Brides of Dracula*). Once I was home in bed, though, nothing put the jolt of fear in me like the sounds of a storm. Even with all that churchgoing, prayer never did much to ease my fears on those stormy nights. I asked Muhammad if he ever prayed when he was little.

"My mama took us to church every Sunday," he said. "I prayed a little. My aunt Coretta had this prayer hanging in a frame over her bed, though: 'Only one life, it will soon pass, only what you do for God will last.' I liked that."

The prayer reminded me of the final lines of his "Friendship" speech at the Athletes for a Better Education event.

"Yeah, that's a good one," said Ali. "Aunt Coretta told me that, too."

He had grown up with a mother and father who encouraged his athletic career early but it was through his relationship with Aunt Coretta—his father's sister—that he gained a true sense of purpose. He told me that she had converted the back half of her house into a home-cooking restaurant, House of Goodies, and that he and his younger brother, Rudy, spent many dinner hours there waiting for their mother to come home from work. Muhammad told me that while he always knew that his parents loved him, Aunt Coretta was the one who told him to expect extraordinary things in his life.

"She used to say, 'God has a plan for you. You have the finger of God touching your forehead and you will be special.' So I used to lie on our front lawn at night and look up at the stars and wonder if God really was up there above it all, and I would ask God, 'What do you want me to do? Do you have a plan for me? Tell me what I should do.'"

"What happened?" I asked.

"He never answered. But I still believed Aunt Coretta."

On days when I didn't have to head straight from breakfast with Muhammad to surgery, I'd spend more time at his home. He set the pace for our runs and for just about everything else we did, but one morning I decided to see if I might be able to steer things a bit. After he finished his bowl of corn flakes, I said, "Boy, I sure would like to see that Foreman fight again sometime."

"Let's go," he said. He got up from the dining room table and headed for the stairs. I followed. Up in the TV room, he loaded the tape of the fight and we sat down on his couch just as we had to watch the Lyle fight. Soon I was experiencing that same out-of-body feeling, as I sat next to Muhammad Ali while watching Muhammad Ali on screen. But this time something else fell into place for me. In my first meetings with him, I saw him as the same larger-than-life figure that the world knew through the TV screen. The more I spent time with him, though, the more I got used to the fact that he was not actually "larger than life." Muhammad Ali was an exceptional, extraordinary icon and one of the most recognized faces in the world, but he was not just a hero. He was, of course, a real person. And I was sitting next to this real person, in his rec room, as a new friend.

Muhammad was sitting back on the couch, perfectly relaxed. But to me the Foreman fight was too epic to be watched simply as entertainment, and I started asking questions about what we were watching. The more I asked, the more Muhammad became engaged. He told me that the ring itself had been a ramshackle affair, not built to the usual professional specifications. The posts holding up the ring weren't steady, and the canvas was very soft, with a lot of give. That made it slow, which favored Foreman. Ali had quickly realized that he would not be able to bounce around and move away from Foreman the way he had planned to. He told me that by the end of the first round, he was already tired. Foreman was quicker than Muhammad had expected, and was very effective at cutting off the ring and limiting Ali's movement. When Ali got back to his corner he told them, "I can't keep this up for fifteen rounds."

At the start of the second round, forced to rethink his strategy, Muhammad came up with the now famous "rope-a-dope" tactic, in which he lay back against the ropes and let Foreman punch himself out while he saved his energy. The strategy was a surprise to his trainer, Angelo Dundee, who was furious at the sight of Muhammad absorbing punishment and initially urged him to fight back more. But Muhammad told me that the rope-a-dope was a test to see if Foreman could hurt him when given the opportunity. He said that if he felt he was getting hurt, he wouldn't have stayed on the ropes. But the rope-a-dope worked. By the middle rounds of the fight, Ali could see the exhaustion and frustration on Foreman's face, and knew that everyone watching was starting to think that maybe he—an eight-to-one Vegas underdog—could win this fight after all.

"See, I keep talking to him," Muhammad said, pointing at the screen. "Right here I was saying, 'George, that didn't hurt. You hit like a sissy. Swing harder—I'll tell you when it hurts. Try it again, chump. Is that all you got?'"

At the end of the seventh round I could see that Foreman finally responded to Ali, and I asked Muhammad what he said.

"He said, 'Yup—that's about it.'"

Muhammad knocked him out in the eighth round with a flurry of five or six punches ending with a heavy straight right. Once again, Muhammad Ali was the heavyweight champion of the world.

SOME MORNINGS AS WE DROVE over to the park in the Stutz Blackhawk, Muhammad would blast the radio and sing along with his favorite songs: "Just My Imagination" and "Ball of Confusion" by the Temptations, anything by Aretha Franklin, James Brown, the Isley Brothers, and the Chi-Lites. This was the music I had grown up loving, too, along with the Miracles, the Four-Tops, the Marvelettes, the Dells, and Marvin Gaye (my taste in music was always considered highly unusual by my white schoolmates back in West Allis).

I was a little surprised the first time Muhammad sang along with a Beach Boys tune, but he told me that not only did he like Brian Wilson's music, but he had read somewhere that Brian used to lie on the grass and stare up at the stars for inspiration just like he did as a kid. He'd goad me into singing along with Brian's soaring falsetto, sometimes suddenly cutting the radio volume to see how well I was sticking to the part.

I was a little less surprised to learn that Muhammad loved the music of Elvis Presley. I knew he had met Elvis years earlier in Las Vegas, and that Elvis had even presented Muhammad with a custom-designed robe to wear into the ring for Muhammad's match against Joe Bugner. (That moment was captured in some amazing photos taken in Elvis's suite at the Las Vegas Hilton by Muhammad's good friend and personal photographer Howard Bingham.) Elvis wanted the bejeweled robe to say "People's Champion" across the back but a miscommunication rendered it "People's Choice." Muhammad didn't wear the robe for the

Bugner fight, but did have it on for his first fight against Ken Norton in 1973.

One morning, one of Elvis's lesser-known singles, "Someone You Can Never Forget," began to play over the car radio.

"Do you like Elvis?" Muhammad asked.

"Do I like Elvis? I'm a huge fan. I saw him on *The Ed Sullivan Show* when I was nine years old, and 'Don't Be Cruel' was the first song I ever knew all the words to."

"Do you remember that Elvis said when he became famous the one thing he wanted to do was buy his mother a car? He bought her a pink Cadillac. Then he bought his mother a house."

"Yeah, Muhammad. I did know that."

"I was fourteen years old when I heard Elvis say that, and that made me want to do the same thing. I said, 'When I get rich and famous I'm going to buy my mother a car and then a house.' After my first pro fight, I bought my mother a pink Cadillac. An Eldorado. It had to be a used one, but I got it. I did something different than Elvis, though. I bought my mother a convertible. I bought her a convertible because I wanted everyone in Louisville to see her riding with the top down and say, 'There goes Muhammad Ali's mother! He bought her that car. He's the greatest boxer in the world and he's the greatest son in the world, too!' And after my second fight I bought my folks a house. Just like Elvis."

Muhammad grew up in a lower-middle-class black area of Louisville, and his parents both had to work very hard just to get by. Muhammad's father, Cassius Clay Sr. ("Cash"), made a living working steadily as a sign painter, and his mother, Odessa—nicknamed "Bird"—was a domestic worker who would often catch a bus to the wealthier parts of town before Muhammad and his brother, Rudy (who later took the name Rahaman), were awake, and would not see the boys until she picked them up at Aunt Coretta's in the evening. The family was intact, but the home could be volatile, as well. Cash was a drinker and a womanizer who had a hard time controlling his temper. Money was always tight, and sometimes Cash and Odessa shared a meal so that there would be enough food for the boys. Muhammad told me that when he and Rudy didn't have the twenty cents they needed for two bus tickets, Rudy would board the bus and Muhammad would run alongside it. He could maintain his pride by telling anyone that asked that he was running because he was in training for the Golden Gloves—not because he didn't have a dime.

I knew there hadn't been any luxuries in Muhammad's childhood, but one time when he said that he "grew up poor," I gave him a little pushback.

"Muhammad, you weren't any poorer than me."

"What do you mean?"

"Look, I grew up in a very small house with fourteen kids and four adults. My family had one tiny bathroom that didn't even have a full-sized bathtub—it was a half-tub. I slept in the 'dining room' on a fold-out couch with one of my brothers, and I didn't get a bed to myself until I went off to college."

He looked at me hard, then arched an eyebrow. "So you really are 'BLACK' Irish?"

"I told you so."

"See, you're like me," he said. "You're serious when you have to be, but then you can be funny and loose at other times. And, besides that, you can sing like Eddie Kendricks."

AS WE SPENT MORE TIME together, the little voice that had shouted, "You're with Muhammad Ali!" quieted down. It didn't seem as much of a shock to be in his presence—if I hadn't gotten over the shock, I don't think we would have been able to get any closer. Muhammad got comfortable with people when they understood what he wanted without him having to explain himself. He didn't like small talk—unless he was doing the talking. I seemed to know what he was saying or what he wanted without asking a lot of questions, so we got along well right away. The key was probably that, despite how I felt about him at first, I didn't let my awe show. That's not to say I forgot who I was with: the nervousness faded away, but the excitement of being with Muhammad Ali was always there.

I would often call that private number he had given me, and once in a while when I would answer the phone I would hear his voice. Usually the conversations were short—just to confirm our next run or to make sure I'd seen the latest episode of one his favorite TV shows (*The Six Million Dollar Man*, *Kojak*, and *Police Woman*). I had also given him my beeper number—back in pre–cell phone days doctors and hospital staff carried beepers so that they could be reachable in emergencies. The first time he beeped me, I called him back as quickly as I could.

"What time are you coming over?" he asked, sounding very serious.

"I can get there in an hour and a half, Muhammad."

"Good." *Click*.

I finished up at work and hurried over as soon as I could. When I showed up, he told me what his emergency was: he wanted to watch a tape he had of a 1964 Mike Wallace interview with Malcolm X. I knew very little about Malcolm X at the time, except that he had been shot dead in 1965. I found him to be a very persuasive speaker, and Muhammad told me he never got tired of hearing Malcolm's "words of wisdom"—he loved the deep, confident tone of Malcolm's voice. When the interview was over, Muhammad wanted to go out for a drive.

It was about 8:30 at night, and when we got to the local 31 Flavors there were maybe ten people at the counter. To put it mildly, they were surprised to see Muhammad Ali walk into the place and stand in line behind them. The people who put in orders ahead of us stuck around, and when it was our turn, I ordered a chocolate cone, Muhammad got a banana split, and we took a table by the door. Everyone in the place was just standing there staring at him, and Muhammad did something that really surprised me. He waved everyone in the place over, making it clear that they could feel free to approach him. The first person to come up to him was a teenage girl.

"Hello, pretty lady. How old are you?" When the girl told him that she was fifteen, Muhammad said, "I won the Olympic gold medal when you were just a little baby." He took a napkin and signed it for her. He motioned for a younger girl—maybe eight—to come sit next to him, while he continued to sign napkins for the rest of the patrons, taking bites of his banana split in between autographs. When he had signed something for everybody, he set the little girl on his lap and asked, "Do you know who I am?"

The little girl shook her head no.

"I am Muhammad Ali, the heavyweight champion of the world, and now you can tell your children and your grandchildren that you and your daddy had ice cream with me at a 31 Flavors. Now, give me some jaws." With that, he gave the girl a nuzzling kiss that made her burst into giggles.

That was the first of many times I got to see just how much Muhammad Ali loved his public. No matter how many people swarmed around him, no matter how many autographs he was asked to sign, no matter how much a crowd interfered with him getting a banana split, he stayed "on"—absolutely generous of spirit and happy to spend a special moment with everybody who wanted to shake his hand. It was amazing to be a witness to such moments, and the fact that he had me with him to share those experiences was one of the early signs to me that maybe a real friendship was developing between us.

Relaxing in Washington Park, site of our morning runs,
Muhammad is watching me sing "Just My Imagination
(Running Away with Me)" by the Temptations.

One morning when we were sitting on the grass of Washington Park after running, I said, "Muhammad, it's wonderful the way you treat people when you're out in public. But people would understand if you said you couldn't stay long enough to talk to every single person. People know you're busy—they wouldn't hold it against you."

He looked at me with a serious expression—one I would come to know as his "listen carefully to what I have to say" expression. "Remember. I am Muhammad Ali. When these people meet me, it's going to be a special moment that they will never forget. I know that, and I want them to remember meeting me as one of the best experiences of their life. If I can give a lot of people a great memory, then that's what I am going to do."

He didn't say this as if he were bragging about his own importance—more that he recognized that there was a service he could do for others ("I never forget that God is watching," he told me later).

We were quiet for a moment, then Muhammad said, "I wish Elvis would go out and meet the people like me instead of being holed up in his hotel rooms not wanting to go out. Doesn't he know that the people love him and just want to get a look at him in person? That it would mean everything to them if they could see him in person, just a glimpse, just to see him? Most people never get a chance to see a famous person like us in their lifetime. If you're famous, you can make people happy with a handshake, a kiss, a hug, an autograph. So why not do it? It doesn't cost you anything but a little time."

"Well, I've never had to worry about being famous," I said, "but it seems to me that people have different ideas about how to handle fame. For some people it's a burden. For you it's uplifting. You seem to be inspired by the fact that other people are inspired by you. You have the power to affect people just by looking at them. You have the power to affect people's lives just by shaking their hands, and because you enjoy having this power, you want to share it with everyone that you can."

He said, "Heavy."

• • •

I KNEW MUHAMMAD HAD OTHER friends and other people in his life—people that had been around a lot longer than I had. Howard Bingham was the friend he had known the longest, and was someone Muhammad trusted completely. But Howard's home was in Los Angeles. I got the feeling that, at least in Chicago, I was the only person getting the kind of calls (and beeps) I was receiving from him. There were people who were part of his "fight life," people he dealt with for business, and his Muslim brothers, but after the move to Chicago I seemed to be his one-man short list when he wanted someone to run with him, to watch TV, to eat ice cream, or just to kill time.

It didn't occur to me then, but looking back it is strange that this black superstar—one who had come to Chicago to get closer to the leadership of the Nation of Islam—was spending so much time with a Catholic white guy. I would hear Muhammad quote the Quran, and he would talk with others about how the Nation of Islam could help blacks around the world, but he and I spoke very little of his faith and he never gave any hint of racial bitterness or any indication that my skin color made any difference to him. Muhammad Ali knew what it was like to be denounced and demeaned, and he had been at the center of a racial firestorm through most of his career. But he was still absolutely willing to judge people on the basis of their character, and I guess he judged me to be a guy who was trustworthy.

Eventually, I met some of the other people in his circle. Herbert Muhammad, the son of Elijah Muhammad, a key figure in the Nation of Islam, had been involved in Muhammad Ali's business affairs since 1966. Herbert was important in Ali's turn to the Muslim faith, and, from what I could tell, had been a strong advocate for welcoming Ali into the Nation of Islam when Elijah Muhammad had doubts about whether a professional fighter could be a proper representative of Islamic principles. With the passing of Elijah Muhammad, the Nation of Islam was now overseen by Herbert's younger brother, Wallace D. Muhammad. Ali told me that Wallace was promoting a new, less racially charged message for the organization. While his father had referred to "white devils," Wallace believed that blacks could not simply turn their backs on that much of the world and would not get anywhere if they didn't know how to negotiate business with the whites. Ali supported this shift, though I don't think it had anything to do with his deciding to hang out with a guy named Shanahan.

With the Nation of Islam in transition and Ali riding high in the wake of the Thrilla in Manila and the Rumble in the Jungle, Herbert Muhammad became an increasingly dominating force in all of Ali's career decisions, and he had clearly earned Ali's trust. Usually Muhammad would meet Herbert at the Nation of Islam headquarters up the street, but sometimes Herbert would come by Ali's house, and we crossed paths occasionally after runs. Despite the softening of the Nation of Islam's antiwhite rhetoric, the very first time I met Herbert he didn't seem very happy to find a white guy in Muhammad's house. But when Muhammad eventually explained who I was and how we had met through Athletes for a Better Education, Herbert seemed impressed and became much friendlier. He knew the organization, liked that it was aiming to help inner-city kids, and was working with some of the same black athletes I was working with.

Still, while Herbert was always very polite and would answer me cordially if I spoke to him, he would never speak to me directly. As far as I was concerned, we didn't have much to talk about anyway. Herbert was handling the larger issues around Muhammad's private business affairs, and I certainly didn't feel I had any voice in those matters. Whenever it looked like Herbert and Ali needed to really get into deeper discussions, I left them alone. Sometimes, if I saw Herbert's car parked at Muhammad's house, I didn't go in. Herbert and I recognized that we were both a part of Muhammad's life, but we kept our distance from each other.

I had a better connection with Gene Dibble, an investment banker who had been one of the first black stockbrokers working in Chicago in the late '50s. For the last few years, he had been working as Ali's financial adviser. While Herbert Muhammad was a bit defensive about a new face showing up in Muhammad's life, Dibble went in the other direction. As soon as he heard Muhammad say a couple of complimentary things about me and could sense that Muhammad liked me, then Dibble decided he was going to like me, too. He was a smart guy with a lot of charm and I didn't mind if he wanted to charm me into thinking of him as a friendly acquaintance. I think Dibble also realized I might be a useful acquaintance—I ended up introducing him as an investment counselor to Walter Payton, Ernie Banks, and Bob Love.

The one friend of Muhammad's I clicked with right away was his other running partner, Jimmy Ellis. Jimmy was also a boxer from Louisville who had briefly reigned as heavyweight champion when he successfully fought his way through the tournament that was organized to find a replacement champ when Ali's titles were vacated. Ellis had one successful title defense against Floyd Patterson, then lost his title to Joe Frazier in 1970. At the beginning of 1975, Ellis lost a brutal rematch with Frazier and then, after one more loss, retired from the ring. Now he was interested in working as a training partner with Ali (whom he'd fought and lost to in 1971 when Ali was beginning his comeback). Jimmy was a sweet, quiet guy who was very easy to be around, and from the first moments of meeting him when he came to visit Muhammad in Chicago, we got along extremely well.

Muhammad loved to make a fuss over Jimmy and play up the fact that they had titles and a hometown in common. "The only time in history," he'd proclaim in a loud, ring announcer voice, "two heavyweight champions have come out of one small town. Ladies and gentlemen, right here, from the little town of Louisville—not one, but two heavyweight champions of the world. Jimmy Ellis! Muhammad Ali! From Louisville, Kentucky!"

Not long after Jimmy came to visit, Dibble showed up at the house with an important announcement. Muhammad had been looking to buy some property outside of Chicago to use as a training camp when he didn't want to travel back to his established camp in Deer Lake, Pennsylvania. Dibble had found an 80-acre former chicken farm in Berrien Springs, Michigan, about a two-hour drive from Chicago around the south end of Lake Michigan. Chicken farming didn't mean anything to Ali, but he got very excited when Dibble shared another aspect of the property's heritage: it had once been a hideaway for Al Capone, with the unprofitable chicken business serving as a means of mob money laundering. The front gate to the place was visible from almost anywhere on the property—the better to cut the chances of being surprised by an FBI raid. Local legend held that if you poked around enough you'd find a maze of secret tunnels for fast getaways. Muhammad couldn't wait to see the place.

So, one Friday five of us piled into Muhammad's Cadillac and headed for Berrien Springs. Muhammad was driving, with Dibble riding shotgun. Dibble had invited me to come along, and Jimmy Ellis was with us to give his opinion on how the property might be used as a training camp. Jimmy and I shared the backseat with Pat Patterson, a black Chicago policeman. Mayor Richard Daley had decided it was in Chicago's interest to assign an officer to serve as Muhammad Ali's personal bodyguard, and Patterson got the job. It was a little tight with three big guys in the backseat, but we weren't cramped for long—with Muhammad at the wheel, we covered the two-hour drive in about ninety minutes. The ride did last long enough for Dibble to lay out a game plan, though.

"Look, Muhammad," he said. "I talked to some friends in real estate and they connected me to the guy who owns this farm. He's going to ask for four hundred thousand but my friends think it's only worth about two fifty. Don't let him screw you—don't go for the first offer. You just tell him you're going to think about it and then leave. I'll take over with the lawyers."

The place lived up to the billing Dibble had given it. It was a beautiful expanse of wooded land right on the St. Joseph River, with horse trails running along the water. There was one main farmhouse, an Olympic-size pool, and several other smaller structures, one of which looked perfect for converting into a gym. A real estate agent gave us a tour of the property, and we even found the remnants of a tunnel under a chicken coop near one of the guesthouses. After a while Ali headed back into the main house with the agent, but not before Dibble reminded him not to bite at any offers before Dibble negotiated the price down. Jimmy and Patterson and I walked around looking for more tunnels, and Dibble got on a phone to check once more with his real estate buddies.

About twenty minutes later we all headed into the kitchen of the main house, where we found Muhammad signing the offer sheet—at the asking price.

"What are you doing, Muhammad?" asked Dibble.

"I just made a deal with this guy," he said. "This place is perfect. I love it."

Muhammad had agreed to pay the $400,000 asking price without one bit of negotiation. Dibble was obviously upset, but to his credit he held his tongue until we were all back in the car on the way home.

"Muhammad, I told you the plan. You just paid a hundred and fifty thousand more than that place is worth."

"That real estate guy's got to make a living, too, doesn't he?" answered Muhammad. "He's got a family to feed. He showed us the right place—he deserves the money."

"Oh my God," sighed Dibble, sinking down in his seat. "I've never met anyone who loves money so much and has so little regard for it."

"Come on, man," said Ali. "You know how much they're paying me to fight? I can afford to spread it around a little."

NOT TOO LONG AFTER THAT trip, I got to introduce Muhammad to the most important person in my life, my beautiful wife, Helga. After being drafted into the army, I served the last two years of my three-year commitment stationed in Germany. In my last year of service, I began moonlighting as the only American member of a German semipro basketball team. Through those teammates, I met a beautiful German schoolteacher. In addition to being completely smitten with her, I also felt that I'd never been so comfortable around another person, let alone a beautiful woman. When my army time was up, I stayed in Germany another year playing with the team and getting closer to Helga Feldmann. Eventually, we were spending every possible moment together.

We faced a major obstacle together when I realized I couldn't really make a living out of semipro ball and had to come back to the States to start a career. Helga had a great teaching position with a guaranteed pension that she wasn't eager to give up. The most difficult day of my life was when we had to part ways at the Frankfort airport, where Helga told me, "I don't know if we'll ever see each other again but remember—once you love someone, you never forget."

We didn't forget. I wrote to her twice a week for a year, and when I was firmly established in my medical sales job, I begged Helga to give America a chance. I knew it was a lot to ask someone to leave their country behind, but she surprised me with a call after Thanksgiving 1974 to tell me that she'd sold her car and all her possessions and had purchased a one-way ticket to John F. Kennedy Airport in New York. We spent that Christmas together, and have been happily building our life together ever since.

Helga got a job helping to restore paintings at the Art Institute of Chicago and stayed busy creating her own art projects. She was a very independent spirit and didn't mind at all when I began to spend time with Muhammad. In fact, at first she didn't seem all that impressed that I'd met him, and was in no rush to try to meet him herself. She had no interest in celebrities, and didn't see how a professional fighter could be any more or less interesting than the sports figures I'd already met through the charity work.

I had a feeling that the two of them would see something special in each other, though, so one morning after a run I asked Muhammad if he would like to meet my "beautiful German wife."

That definitely got his attention. "Yeah. Bring her over tonight. We'll have some Chinese food."

That evening, Helga and I showed up at the South Woodlawn house with Chinese food and some mocha ice cream, and had a wonderful meal with Muhammad. Just as I suspected, Helga was completely disarmed by Muhammad's warmth and his sense of humor, and Muhammad was fascinated by Helga's direct manner and her passionate nature. After dinner, we decided to go out to the movies—*Jaws*, which had terrified swimmers everywhere that summer, was still playing in a few Chicago theaters, and Muhammad hadn't seen it yet. By the time we got to the movie theater, the lines were too long to get into *Jaws*, so we saw *Three Days of the Condor* with Robert Redford and Faye Dunaway instead. As I drove Helga home that night, I asked her what she thought of Muhammad. She put into words what I had been feeling but had not been able to articulate: "He's so full of love."

In early 1976, I met the new woman in Muhammad's life, Veronica Porche. Veronica's goal in life was to become a doctor, and she had been in her second year of premed studies at USC when she heard a radio ad seeking "good-looking girls to travel to Africa with Muhammad Ali." The ad was the work of the promoter Don King, who wanted to put together a team of beauties to serve as promotions girls for the Foreman-Ali Rumble in the Jungle. Scores of women responded to the ad, and Veronica was one of only four to make the cut. Muhammad first saw Veronica in Salt Lake City at a promotional event leading up to the fight. He was married to Khalilah at the time, but that didn't stop him from pursuing a romance with Veronica. Soon she was a constant companion.

When I first met Muhammad, he was living alone, separated from Khalilah, but by January 1976, Veronica was at South Woodlawn more frequently. The first time I met her I was in the entranceway of the house waiting for Muhammad to come downstairs. As he did, she came out of the kitchen, and Muhammad introduced us. She was strikingly beautiful—and we barely spoke to each other. I'd learn soon enough that Veronica was not very fond of the boxing people Muhammad surrounded himself with and, assuming I was one of those guys, was in no hurry to get to know me.

Veronica's position in the house became a little clearer the next time I met her. I was sitting in Muhammad's kitchen, sipping coffee after a morning run, when she appeared wearing a bathrobe. This time we said hello to each other a little more warmly, and that little voice in my head said, "Oh—I think I get it now." Veronica had been living in an apartment a few blocks away from Muhammad, but in the early months of '76 she moved to his house and they began living openly as a couple.

I quickly learned that when you were part of Muhammad's world, you had to be ready for surprises. One Friday, Muhammad asked me to come by the house as soon as I was out of that morning's surgery. As I walked into his dining room I could hear that Muhammad was not alone, but I nearly stopped in my tracks when I saw who he was talking to: at the end of the dining room table, right next to Muhammad, sat Warren Beatty.

I walked forward and extended a hand. "Hi, Mr. Beatty—it's great to meet you."

He shook my hand, looking a little puzzled over who was interrupting his meeting with Ali.

So Ali introduced me this way: "This is my cousin Tim Shanahan. He looks white, doesn't he?"

Warren looked stunned.

"He's a brotha like me," continued Muhammad, without any hint of a smile. "He's been passing all these years."

Warren didn't say a word. Muhammad had asked me to be there, and for the first time I had the feeling that being his friend made it almost impossible to be starstruck by anyone else, even a star as big as Warren Beatty. I felt perfectly comfortable pulling up a chair and sitting across from the actor. What looked to me like a couple of movie scripts lay on the table.

"What's going on?" I asked Muhammad.

"Warren wants me to do a movie."

"Oh." I looked to Beatty. "Is it something that you're producing or directing?"

"I'm doing both," he said. "It's called *Heaven Can Wait*. A remake of an old film called *Here Comes Mr. Jordan*, about a boxer who dies too soon because of an angel's mistake, and then gets a second chance on earth in a different body."

He explained the story a little more, and I'm not sure I understood it too well. But it was clear that Warren was very excited about having Muhammad star in the movie.

"Muhammad is going to be great in this," Beatty said. "It'll be a breakout performance for him, and after boxing he's going to be a very popular actor."

"Yeah—I'm going to grow a mustache and be the black Gable," said Muhammad. "I'll be Dark Gable."

Muhammad did have some concerns about the actual work of acting. He'd done some commercials in which he'd become extremely frustrated with the time it took to set up cameras and lights, and he hated the process of doing dozens of takes to get one shot. He wasn't sure he had the patience to make it through a whole movie. Warren assured him that there were ways to keep himself from being bored and talked awhile about some of the ways he passed time on sets to keep his mind active. His tips made sense to Muhammad, and by the time Warren was getting ready to leave to catch his flight to Los Angeles, he and Muhammad were telling each other how excited they were to be working together.

"Where's Veronica?" I asked. "Does she know Warren's here?"

"No—she's sleeping in," said Muhammad. Suddenly he had an odd expression, like a lightbulb had just gone off above his head.

"Warren, do me a favor," he said. "Come with me."

They headed upstairs and I followed behind. Muhammad quietly pushed open the door to the master bedroom and indicated that Warren should go in and sit on the bed. Warren didn't want to, but Ali grabbed him by the arm and pushed him in. "Go on!"

"Muhammad?" asked Veronica, still half-asleep.

"Veronica, wake up. I've got a surprise for you," he answered.

Veronica turned over, saw Warren Beatty sitting on her bed, and promptly yanked the covers up over her head.

"MUHAMMAD!" she screamed.

Warren looked incredibly embarrassed, and Muhammad got him out of there fast, looking as though he realized his big idea hadn't gone quite the way he wanted it to.

Whatever the repercussions, Muhammad and Veronica's relationship survived the Beatty-in-bed prank. However, the plans for Muhammad to star in *Heaven Can Wait* did not last long. He never lost his enthusiasm for the project, but after he sent the script and contract to Herbert Muhammad, Herbert passed them along to Wallace Muhammad, and Wallace strongly discouraged Ali from pursuing the project. Wallace felt that a movie based on the concept of reincarnation was inconsistent with Muslim principles, and he found a number of scenes in the film that he felt violated the teachings of the Nation of Islam. Ali put up some resistance at first, arguing that the public would not confuse a movie role with his religious beliefs. But Wallace objected so strongly that Muhammad eventually gave up on it. Instead of becoming the next Gable, he'd keep fighting.

I felt sad for Muhammad because I could see how disappointed he was over the lost opportunity. But I kept thinking about the way he had introduced me to Warren Beatty: "Cousin Tim." It was a shame that Muhammad wasn't going to get the chance to showcase his talents as an actor. But I couldn't help feeling happy that I'd gone from being "White Boy" to being a part of the family.

FOUR

WAITING FOR BARDOT

I THINK MOST CHILDREN GROW up believing that the way their homes are run is the normal way for families to live. "Normal" was pretty chaotic for me. As I told Muhammad, by the time I was thirteen years old I was one of eighteen people living in a small duplex row house in the less-desirable part of a working-class neighborhood in West Allis, Wisconsin. My mother, father, and four brothers and I lived upstairs, and my mother's sister, her husband, and their nine kids lived downstairs. With four tiny bedrooms, and two tiny bathrooms, the home would have felt crowded under any conditions, but my uncle's alcoholism and the cloud of my mother's emotional problems made things a lot worse. It's hard for me to remember any moments of quiet in that house. When it was time for me to head off to Nebraska to attend Creighton University, I bought a one-way bus ticket for sixteen dollars and never looked back.

That's not to say I had a terrible childhood. My father and mother would take us out for lakeside picnics once in a while, and my dad—a good athlete himself—enjoyed giving me baseball and basketball tips. But Dad worked long hours trying to keep his auto repair parts store running and was hardly ever around, and Mom was often over-whelmed by the challenge of managing the home. When I was about four years old, I started seeking out peace and comfort on my own at McKinley Park just two blocks away. One of the recreation directors there was a woman named Stell Keinrath, a former underhand fast-pitch softball champ who became like a second mother to me. She must have thought I had athletic potential, because as soon as I turned six she signed me up for a youth baseball league. Oddly enough, of the fourteen kids in my house, I was the only one who had a keen interest in sports, so playing ball was not only a respite from the craziness of home, it was also an experience that I could feel was uniquely mine. Coming from a house in which hand-me-downs were the rule and dinner servings had to be battled over ("Hey! Mikey got two pork chops!"), that meant a lot.

Athletics felt easy and natural to me, and from an early age I began to excel at baseball and basketball. Maybe it was through sports—where your value was clearly established through plays made and points scored—that I learned not to care too much about skin color. I was just barely aware that racial conflicts were a part of the news stories in late-'50s America. But, to me, whether a guy made a good teammate or not was a matter of character, not race. The neighborhood I lived in was mostly white—a mix of working-class families of German, Irish, Italian, and Polish descent. The black parts of town were only a few blocks away. To my young eyes, it looked like everybody was working just as hard to get by and there didn't seem to be any good reason to look down on each other. I was equally comfortable hanging out with the white friends at my all-white school and with the black friends I played basketball with at the city parks in the summer league.

Muhammad Ali was not the first world-famous figure I'd had the chance to meet. Fifteen years before I showed up at Muhammad's door, I shook hands with a president-to-be. In the fall of 1960, John F. Kennedy was campaigning heavily throughout the Midwest for the November election, and on October 23 he delivered an address at the Milwaukee Arena. One of my father's best friends was friends with Kennedy's Wisconsin campaign manager and scored three tickets to the event, with an invitation to meet John and Jackie Kennedy afterward at a private party in a suite at Milwaukee's renowned Pfister Hotel. My dad's friend thought it might impress the Kennedys to meet a young ballplayer who had just played in the VFW's World Series, which I had just done, so I was tapped to accompany my parents.

I don't remember much about JFK's speech except that I was awfully uncomfortable in loose shoes and a too-large sport coat that, as usual, had been handed down to me from my brothers Pat and Mike. I was greatly impressed by the hotel, though, which was by far the fanciest building I had ever been inside. The spectacular lobby was full of marble columns and gilded woodwork, and you looked upward to a two-story vaulted ceiling painted with clouds. JFK's suite felt a little less glamorous, mainly because it was packed with people and the air-conditioning was having a hard time keeping up with a surprise Indian summer. I seemed to be the only young person in the room. My dad's friend found us and ushered us through the line to meet the candidate.

JFK comes to Milwaukee. He shakes hands with young Tim Shanahan and then wins the 1960 presidential election. Coincidence?

Suddenly, there I was, shaking the hand of JFK as he gave me a smile and a wink, as if he were truly happy to see me. I think I had built up an image of him so much in my head that it was a little strange to discover that he was just a regular guy in a suit. He was handsome, but he had such a down-to-earth manner that he could easily have been one of my dad's friends, not a man running for president. At the same time, I could feel that this man had power. He was the star at the center of all this activity around him, and the fact that he seemed like the friendliest, most relaxed guy in the room made him even more powerful.

I moved along almost as soon as our handshake was done, and a few steps away I found myself standing at the edge of the throng around the candidate.

"Sit down," a voice behind me said.

I turned and saw that Jackie Kennedy, very pregnant with John Jr., was sitting on a couch and was beckoning me to take a seat next to her. I did.

"What's your name?" she asked. You could see that she was feeling the heat in the room—there was a fine sheen of perspiration on her brow and her thick black hair looked a little damp. She was an attractive woman, and her voice was gentle and friendly, but I wasn't sure why she wanted to talk to me.

"Timmy Shanahan," I answered.

"Oh, you're Irish, I knew it," she said with a smile. "Where do you go to school?"

"Holy Assumption in West Allis."

"What kind of nuns teach there?"

"The Notre Dame nuns."

"Do you like the nuns?"

"Yes." I thought Mrs. Kennedy seemed like a very nice person, and I could tell she was trying to be nice to me, but—like most thirteen-year-old boys—I just wasn't very interested in having a conversation with an adult, especially while wearing an uncomfortable jacket and tie. Mrs. Kennedy went on to tell me that she was Catholic like me, but that she had gone to a private grade school. Right about then my mother came over for her chance to say hello to Jackie, and I felt relieved to have a reason to get up and go stand by my dad and his friend. I'm not sure how much the Shanahans' support had to do with it, but JFK was elected president two weeks later.

MUHAMMAD ALI WAS NOT EVEN the first record-setting sports celebrity I'd met. One morning in the summer of 1961, as my VFW baseball teammates began showing up for practice, I saw something astounding: right there on our playground, watching a Pee Wee league game of six- and seven-year-olds, was my greatest sports hero, the Milwaukee Braves slugger Henry Aaron. I was a huge Braves fan, and had been thrilled when the team beat Mickey Mantle and the New York Yankees to win the 1957 World Series (the Yankees won a rematch the next year). Aaron was now in his eighth season with the Braves and had already clobbered more than two hundred home runs on his way to besting Babe Ruth's record. And here he was, standing on West Allis grass.

Nobody seemed to be paying him much attention. Nobody crowded around him for autographs. I guess everybody—kids and the few adults around alike—was so surprised and intimidated by his presence that we didn't know what to do, so we didn't do anything. My teammates and I finally figured out an explanation for Hank's visit. We knew that one of those little Pee Wee players was Felix Mantilla Jr., son of a Braves infielder. Apparently Hank and Felix Sr. were close enough that the slugger had come to watch his friend's son play. I didn't feel any impulse to approach Aaron, but I did make a point of checking out the car he'd driven to our field: a brand-new powder-blue Corvair, with a white plastic St. Christopher statue prominently displayed on the dashboard.

A couple of weeks later, I attended a Braves game at Milwaukee County Stadium with my friend Bruce Triplett, whose mother was willing to stake us three dollars for bus fare and a pair of fifty-cent bleachers tickets (for years I was under the impression that any friend who had a couple of quarters in his pocket for candy bars and Cokes must come from a very wealthy family). One of the benefits of coming from a house of fourteen kids was that nobody noticed much when you weren't around, so I met Bruce at the bus stop and headed off to the stadium. It was a great game, with the Braves' ace Lew Burdette taking on the Philadelphia Phillies. I had never been to a night game before, and it was thrilling to be next to the left-field foul pole in the upper deck, looking down upon the brightly lit field. We got even more of a thrill when Aaron hit a monster shot that came right toward us. We were instantly on our feet, ready to cheer the home run, but at the last moment the ball hooked foul (the vision of that ball arcing high under the night lights remains a favorite childhood memory). Hank got a couple of hits anyway, and Burdette pitched a complete game. When Burdette got the Phillies out in order in the top of the ninth, the Braves had a 4–1 win. It was a Friday-night game and it was 10:15 as we headed out of the park, but I decided my night wasn't over. I told Bruce I was going to go to the players' parking lot to wait for Aaron and get his autograph. Bruce told me he wouldn't come with me—he had to be home by eleven. My curfew was ten—I was already in trouble, so why not make the most of it? Bruce walked off to catch his bus, and I walked around to the back of the stadium.

There wasn't as much worry about security back then, and there wasn't even a fence separating the players' lot from the general parking area. I strolled into the lot, took a look around, and then I spotted it—the powder-blue Corvair with the St. Christopher statue on the dashboard. I knew it might take awhile for the players to shower and change, so I sat on the ground with my back against the driver's door of Hammerin' Hank's Corvair and closed my eyes for just a moment.

I woke up to the sound of approaching voices. I jumped to my feet and found myself staring up into the face of Hank Aaron.

"Hey, buddy. What are you doing here?" he asked, more puzzled than angry. "What's your name?"

"I'm Tim Shanahan. I knew this was your car and I just wanted to get your autograph." I could feel my face turning ten shades of red.

"How did you know this was my car?"

"I saw you at our Little League game in Hoyt Park."

"OK, sure. Where's your mother and father?" asked Hank.

"I'm here by myself."

"You're alone? Where do you live?"

"West Allis."

"How are you getting home?"

"I'm going to take the bus down Wisconsin Avenue."

He stared at me for a moment, then spoke to someone on the other side of the car.

"It's too late for this kid to take the bus. Should we give him a ride home?"

I turned toward the car to see who Hank Aaron was talking to. Lew Burdette was smoking a cigarette and drinking from a can of Schlitz beer. Four remaining cans of a six-pack were nestled in the crook of his pitching arm.

"West Allis? That's a two-beer drive." Burdette shrugged. "Sure, give the kid a ride."

Aaron let me into the backseat. I was so excited I had to stop myself from giggling.

"What's your address, son?" he asked.

I told him I lived on South Seventy-second Street, right off Greenfield Avenue. Burdette said he was familiar with the neighborhood. He got his suits made at a tailor shop called Johnnie Walker's, which was just around the corner from my house. We pulled out of the stadium lot, and as Henry Aaron drove his car down Wisconsin Avenue toward my house, the two ballplayers seemed to forget that I was there, talking about the game they had just played. The year before, Burdette had pitched a no-hitter against the Phillies. This night, the Phillies' only run came from a home run by the first baseman, Don Demeter.

"Demeter, can you believe that?" asked Burdette. "I know his weakness. I know what he can and can't hit and I give him that pitch?"

"It was a good pitch, Lew," said Aaron. "It wasn't over the plate. He had to reach out to get that one, and he did."

They started talking about their families. I noticed a bag of batting-practice balls on the floor in the backseat, and I took out one that didn't look too scuffed up. When there was a lull in the players' conversation, I asked, "Mr. Aaron, could I have your autograph on this baseball?"

I handed it to Burdette, and at the next stoplight, Aaron signed it and put it down on the seat next to him as the light changed. Just a few lights later we pulled up in front of Johnnie Walker's. Burdette insisted that Aaron get out of the car and take a look in Johnnie's show window, and I got out with them. When they turned to go back to the car, I told Hank that I could walk the rest of the way.

"All right, son, but you go straight home now, right?"

"Yes, sir. And thank you very much. It was great meeting you."

"OK, son, but no more sleeping in the parking lot."

They drove off and I started running home—so happy it felt like I was flying. I was halfway home when that happiness crumbled: I'd forgotten to get the autographed ball off the front seat. I turned around and ran as fast as I could back to Greenfield Avenue, hoping the blue Corvair might still be in sight. It was, but was already far off down the street. Too late. I cried for the next ten minutes straight. And I cried through the night, wondering what was wrong with me that I could lose an autographed ball from Hank Aaron before I'd even held it. I felt like a world-champion idiot.

I CONTINUED TO LIVE A split social life, hanging out with white kids at school and black kids in my neighborhood. Occasionally, I was made aware that my crossing of color lines was unacceptable. My family knew that I played basketball with black players in the summer leagues, but I knew better than to ever describe those teammates as "friends" when talking to my mother or my brothers. In their eyes, I was a proper white boy going to a proper white school, soon to be applying for scholarships to a proper white college. To my family, black kids were a bad influence by definition, and hanging out with them would only jeopardize my future. I remember when a couple of very tall, black teammates came to pick me up at my house, my mother actually gasped in horror. As I headed out to their car, she said with disgust, "Now who are you running with?"

My white Marquette University High School teammates began to call me "Spook" or "Nigger." In 1962 the latter word still had all the power and weight of a taboo and, in my experience, was a word used only by whites—at that time my black friends never used it to refer to each other. (When Muhammad Ali refused to serve in the army, he said, "No Vietcong ever called me nigger." The usage had changed by 1975, when Muhammad could casually refer to me as a "nigga.") Still, my impression was that my teammates were not intending the harsh word to sound hateful when they applied to me. It was more a way of saying, "You definitely have some black blood in those Irish genes." It seemed a natural part of the juvenile teasing and trash-talking that happens in groups of athletes. Of course, others didn't hear it that way. Once, when we played an all-black team from Milwaukee's North Side, one of my teammates called me by my nickname and ended up in a fistfight with an opposing player that almost turned into a bench-clearing brawl.

My black neighborhood friends called me "Shan" or "Shanny." I was especially proud of myself for being able to keep up with those friends athletically, because the level of play in the local city park league was extremely competitive. (A couple of those friends, Johnny Johnson and Freddy "Downtown" Brown, were stars in the summer league, and they amazed all of us local boys by going on to play together and win a Big 10 basketball championship for Iowa State and an NBA championship for the 1978–79 Seattle Supersonics.) My black friends got so comfortable having me around that they sometimes didn't seem to notice the difference in skin tone between us. I remember one of my more irascible black buddies complaining about how much he hated white people. When I reminded him that I was white, he responded, "No, you ain't white. You're Shanny."

I WAS HOPING MY BASEBALL and basketball skills might win me a scholarship to an athletically competitive university such as Arizona State or, closer to home, the University of Wisconsin. Didn't happen. A couple of my uncles were Jesuit priests teaching at Creighton University in Omaha,

Nebraska, so, with my mother's encouragement I applied and was accepted there. At Creighton my circle of friends was white, mostly because there were only a handful of black students on the campus. These new friends did notice there was something a little different about my moves and my tastes: they were amazed by the fact that I danced like James Brown, played basketball like Earl Monroe, and sang falsetto like Eddie Kendricks of the Temptations. I focused hard on both athletics and academics, played on the basketball practice squad and the baseball team, and ended up putting together a strong-enough transcript to get into the University of Wisconsin's law school. I graduated from Creighton on June 1, 1969. I was well aware of the war in Vietnam, and I knew that as soon as I started law school in the fall my student deferment would be extended. But on June 14, I received my draft notice for induction into the army.

I did eight weeks of basic training at Fort Leonard Wood, Missouri, and hated every minute of it. I was angry that my plans for the future had been snatched away by forces beyond my control and felt like I'd gone from being my own person to being just another number in the army. My only salvation was basketball. No matter how hard the day of training, I was in the base gym every evening looking for guys to play pick-up games with. After basic training I moved on to Artillery Officer Candidate School, at Fort Sill, Oklahoma, which was even more grueling, and which still stands out as the worst six months of my life. Toward the end of those six months, not only was I miserable, I was also a nervous wreck. Two weeks after the OCS graduation ceremony, the newly trained officers would receive their orders to ship out, and most of them went straight into combat. One of our OCS trainers was a master sergeant who had already done three tours in Vietnam, and he told us that the life expectancy of a forward observer—which is what he was training us to be—was two months. He told us that it was folly to send green recruits into the madness of war and expect them to be leaders of seasoned veterans. If the enemy didn't kill them, their own soldiers would.

But basketball came to the rescue. I graduated from OCS, but during the two-week waiting period before my orders came through I managed to break my ankle on the basketball court, and couldn't ship out with the rest of the OCS graduates. While I healed in the base hospital, I received an offer from General Buford Moss, the base commander: if I was willing to waive my OCS commission as a second lieutenant and allow my military occupation specialty to be shifted from Artillery to Special Services, he would allow me to try out for the post basketball team. If I made that team, I would go to Fort Ord to try out for the all-army basketball team. The general was a diehard basketball fan who wanted his post represented on the all-army team, but he wasn't sure if I would accept his offer. He thought I might have my heart set on being an officer or might feel committed to the brotherhood of the OCS. Uh—no. If I could serve my country by playing basketball instead of getting shot at, that was fine by me. I was so excited about the opportunity that I started working out on the basketball court before I even had my cast off, passing and shooting just to try and stay in shape.

When it came time to join the post team and switch to Special Services, I realized that the general had a point: it was very hard to say goodbye to the band of brothers I'd trained with, especially knowing that so many of them were off to war, while I was off to make foul shots. For months I felt guilty about it, and I've never stopped feeling lucky: of the twenty-eight graduates from my OCS class who shipped out to Vietnam, nine were killed in combat.

To cap it off, the basketball competition was tough enough that I did not make the all-army team. The Special Services unit was divided into four specialties, "Craft," "Recreation," "Physical Activity," and "Entertainer" (folks like Sammy Davis Jr. and Burt Lancaster served in the military as Special Services entertainers). I was now a Physical Activity specialist, at a pay grade higher than a second lieutenant, and though I was still required to serve one year overseas, there wasn't much calling for my specialty on the front lines. I received orders for a posting in Germany. Instead of having to worry about artillery, I was going to oversee the gymnasium at the army base in a town called Bad Kreuznach. That base had the best basketball court in the area, and members of some of the German semipro teams worked out there. Through one of those German players I learned that each of their teams was allowed to carry one foreign player. I tried out for the local Mainz team and made the squad. Every weekend our basketball team's sponsor, Siemens, provided each player with a cut of the live gate, usually around 300 marks apiece—a nice addition to my army paycheck. Each player also received a case of Mainzer beer, a local specialty. I wasn't much of a beer drinker at the time, but the more beer I gave away, the more popular I became with my teammates and my fellow soldiers.

Germany was getting ready to host the 1972 Olympics in Munich, and one of the exhibition sports to be showcased was team handball—a sport played with a ball smaller than a soccer ball, on a court bigger than a basketball court, with the aim of getting the ball into the other team's soccer-style net. An army friend of mine had been charged with putting together an American handball team, and that team ended up surprising everyone by beating enough international teams to qualify for Olympic competition. When the American team came to Germany before the Olympics, I helped organize some exhibition matches for them, and in return I was chosen as one of two alternate players for the twelve-man squad. I didn't play and wasn't even allowed to suit up, but when the games began in Munich, there I was in the Olympic Village. As a guy who'd always had sports at the center of his life, being in that Olympic Village, surrounded by amazing athletes from around the world, was an unbelievable experience. I remember the color-coded water pipes above the walkways between buildings—each color representing an area where a different nation resided. I remember the sight of the tiny gold medal gymnast Olga Korbut sitting on the shoulder of the 380-pound gold medal weight lifter Vasily Alekseyev, the better to get around in a crowded cafeteria. I recall the excitement as the seemingly unbeatable Mark Spitz swam his way toward winning seven gold medals and setting seven world records. I remember feeling the heartache when two top American runners, Eddie Hart and Rey Robinson, missed their own quarter-final track heats because of a coach's miscalculation of the event's start time. I was enthralled by the connections taking place around the large tables in the Village game room, where athletes sat down in front of their country's flag and exchanged Olympic pins with each other.

There was so much of the Olympics that was wonderful, humbling, and inspiring. But of course what I remember most is the tragedy that unfolded there. I was in one of those crowded cafeterias getting breakfast when a corps of machine-gun toting German officers in tracksuits appeared and had us march single-file back to our dorms. My handball teammates and I tried to figure out what was going on by watching our TV, until we realized that from our eighth-floor balcony in Building 12, we could see that what was being broadcast was happening in the two-story dormitory right across from ours: a Palestinian terrorist group called Black September had taken eleven Israeli athletes hostage.

We weren't supposed to leave our rooms, but as the negotiations proceeded into the afternoon, a few of us decided we might get a better handle on what was happening if we made our way down to the ABC TV command center, housed in a large trailer just behind our dorm. I'd previously met the sportscaster Curt Gowdy, and he welcomed us into the trailer, where he was working with his colleagues Howard Cosell, Chris Schenkel, and Keith Jackson. One of the trailer's most prominent features was a large portable bar stocked with every imaginable liquor, and people were hitting the bar now in search of some kind of solace. It wasn't working. The sportscasters and their tech crew were all absolutely distraught, some almost in tears, and they kept asking one another the same questions: Who could do this? Who could take this moment away from athletes who had trained so hard all their lives? How could the Olympics recover from something that was so tragic on every level? Gowdy offered us drinks, too, but we knew that wasn't going to help us feel any better about what was happening around us. The trailer had a separate editing room, and we watched as an editor cut together scenes from fresh footage of the Olympic Village in crisis mode.

Early the next morning we heard our worst fears confirmed: two athletes had been killed during the initial hostage-taking. The terrorists had gotten a group of nine hostages as far as a NATO airbase, but in an ensuing firefight all nine of those athletes were slaughtered by their captors. Five of the eight terrorists were killed, as well. For the first time in its history the Olympic Games were suspended for a day, while organizers decided what to do. After a huge memorial service attended by almost every athlete present, the president of the International Olympic Committee, Avery Brundage, announced that canceling the Olympiad would serve only to hand the terrorists a victory. The games did go on, but something begun with such joy and hope now had an aura of sadness and loss.

I HAD MET HELGA THROUGH my basketball teammates before the Olympics, and I saw her a couple of times in the Olympic Village, as one of her high school students was part of the German gymnastics team. After the games, I called her to ask her out on a date and in her perfect English she said "yes." Then she called back a couple of days later to cancel, telling me quite straightforwardly, "I got a better offer." I didn't like getting the brush-off, but I couldn't stop thinking about this German blonde. A month later, I tried her again, and this time she invited me to come over for dinner at her apartment in the village of Wöllstein. Before I could stop myself, I made the bonehead move of asking if I should also bring along the basketball teammate who had introduced us—a guy who I knew also had romantic designs on Helga. She seemed a little surprised, but said that would be OK. She prepared a magnificent five-course dinner for the three of us, and at the end of the evening, when my training-conscious teammate was ready to leave and get to bed early, Helga whispered to me that I should stay. The teammate got the message and went out the door in a huff. I stayed—and never left. We didn't begin our relationship with a night of wild sex, though. The culture of the time may have encouraged flings and one-night stands, but we both wanted to feel emotionally close to each other before we became physically intimate. That first night, we simply talked and laughed and shared secrets and felt as connected as two people could be.

I was back at Helga's for dinner the next night, and the night after that, and in a matter of weeks, everything I owned was over at her place. My army tour came to an end, and it was not hard to decide that I would stay in Germany—living with my new love, playing for my German basketball team, and working as a bartender at the army base officers' club. As a high school teacher, Helga had six weeks of vacation over the summer that coincided with my basketball off-season. We decided we wanted to travel together, so the day after her last class, we piled into Helga's Karmann Ghia and headed for the sunshine of St. Tropez. Helga said she wanted to show me a place so beautiful that it spoke to the artistic soul—a place that had inspired artists as diverse as Picasso, Matisse, Colette, and Helmut Newton. And the French Riviera did seem like a vision of paradise to me—the kind of place I had imagined but never really knew existed. I still remember the moment we crested a hill and suddenly saw stretching before us the sight of a perfect blue sky meeting the deep blue ocean. We both actually gasped at the beauty. I had been away from home and overseas for some time now, but this moment crystallized something for me. I was in a speeding sports car, sitting next to a beautiful woman I was completely in love with, looking at a view more spectacular than anything I had ever seen. I felt as though I were suddenly seeing the world through brand-new eyes, and it looked amazing.

The house Helga and I were staying in wasn't quite overlooking the beach, but it was just a short walk away. Helga had been to St. Tropez the previous summer, and our first morning there she couldn't wait to get me down to her favorite secluded beach, Escalet. We went, and that's when I realized that—in this particular paradise—people enjoyed the sun and the surf by taking off all their clothes. I guess that whenever I'd previously heard about the existence of "nude beaches," I'd pictured a bevy of *Playboy* centerfolds sunning themselves. There were definitely some attractive women on the beach in St. Tropez, but there were a lot more ordinary folks. Completely naked ordinary folks—kids, grandparents, families, bodies of all shapes and sizes. Part of me appreciated how natural this was, and how comfortable everyone seemed to be. But all the years I had spent being schooled by nuns and priests had instilled in me a fine sense of shame when it came to the human body. I wasn't going to take my clothes off in public, no way, no how. Helga was amused by my modesty, but she assured me that nudity was not mandatory. I left my trunks on, lay on my towel, and was very careful not to stare too hard at my fellow beachgoers. When, after a few more trips to the beach, I finally relaxed enough to attempt some nude sunbathing, my poor, pale Irish buttocks, having never been subjected to a single ray of sunlight, ended up so sunburned that for the following week it hurt just to put on pants.

Helga and I fell into a wonderfully lazy routine in St. Tropez. Every morning, she would sleep in and I would take my morning three-mile run on the beach and then stop off at the local pastry shop to get coffees and a couple of *Blätterteig*—puff pastries that had become our favorite breakfast (I loved the cherry, Helga wanted strawberry). One day when I got to the shop I noticed a young, good-looking guy in jeans and a black T-shirt seated on a Harley-Davidson Sportster right in front of the place. Harleys always caught my attention—the company was based in Milwaukee and one of my high school friends was Bob Harley, grandson of the founder, William Harley. Through Bob I got a summer job at the Harley plant and had mastered all fourteen positions of the Sportster assembly line, from mounting the engine to keying the ignition of the brand-new baby Harley and driving it off the factory floor for a test ride. I took a long, admiring look at the bike before entering the pastry shop, then went and stood in line behind a rather short, good-looking blonde in white shorts, pink blouse, and sunglasses. She got her order and stepped over to the side to put cream in her coffee.

I stepped up to the counter and asked for my usual from the proprietor, a very friendly woman named Analise. "Ahh, the strawberry, the cherry, and two coffees," Analis responded.

"*Oui.*"

"That's my usual, too, for me and my boyfriend," said the petite blonde.

I turned to look at the woman, who now had her sunglasses off. She was not just beautiful—she was Brigitte Bardot.

"Uh—hello," I sputtered. "I've really enjoyed your movies and—and—you are just so gorgeous in person. Absolutely beautiful."

"Thank you so much. That's sweet," she said.

"Is that your boyfriend on the Harley outside? That's a great bike."

"Oh, yes—so much fun to ride."

My order was ready, so I took it and left. Brigitte stayed in the shop, talking with Analise. I stepped outside in a bit of a daze. I thought back to 1957, when I was ten years old and happened to stroll past the local art house cinema. I had never thought much about the movies that played there before, but this time the theater had just put up a poster for *And God Created Woman*. The image of Brigitte Bardot in nothing but a bikini bottom had a powerful effect on me—it was in that very moment that I suddenly understood the allure of the opposite sex (ohh—so this is what the fuss is all about!). Now I was exchanging pleasantries with Bardot over *Blätterteig*. Incredible.

I realized that if I started up a conversation with the guy on the Harley, I could get some more face time with Brigitte, too. I introduced myself to him and told him that I might have helped assemble his bike. When he asked how that was possible, I told about my factory job. He told me he had loved Harleys since watching Marlon Brando in *The Wild One* (he was aware that Brando rode a Triumph in that film—he wanted the Brando look but a Harley for a ride). The guy told me his name was André. He was trying to make it as an actor and had met Brigitte on the set of one of her films. She was now divorced from her second husband, the German businessman Gunther Sachs, and she and André were spending a lot of time together.

While we were talking, Brigitte stepped out of the pastry shop and, without saying a word, sat side saddle on the back of the bike and began to eat her pastry and drink her coffee. She listened to us talk for a couple of minutes, then said, "Why don't you come meet us at the Café de Paris tonight? We're having dinner there with some friends."

"I'm here with my girlfriend," I told her, holding up the pair of *Blätterteig*.

"Well, she will come along with you, then," said Brigitte.

We quickly worked out details of time and place and then she and André roared off down the street on the Harley. I headed back to our place to deliver the pastry to Helga, in even more of a daze. But I had enough focus to know that it was probably not a great idea to let the woman I love see how excited I was about meeting an international sex symbol. I tried to play it cool. When we were halfway through our pastries, I said, "Hey, you'll never believe this, but I just met Brigitte Bardot at the pastry shop."

Helga wasn't surprised. She knew Brigitte had a home in St. Tropez and had seen her around town the year before. Celebrity sightings were not unusual here. St. Tropez attracted artists, but it also attracted an increasing number of jet-setters. (Mick and Bianca Jagger had been married there the year before.) That part of the St. Tropez scene didn't interest Helga much. She painted, sculpted, and designed her own clothes—she had the passions of a true artist and was not concerned with the comings and goings of "beautiful people" who treated St. Tropez as a moneyed playground. However, when I told her that Brigitte had actually invited us to dinner, she agreed that was something worth getting excited about.

That afternoon we worked together to figure out how to look our best for an evening with Bardot. In the early evening we hopped in the Karmann Ghia and drove to the address André had given me. The restaurant was a bustling bistro type of place right on the harbor, with an up-close view of some of the most luxurious yachts. The place was already quite crowded, and Brigitte and André were at a banquette across from the bar, with six or seven friends crowded around a few small tables. We waved to them, and they waved back, but there was no clear place for us to sit and join them, and suddenly Helga and I both felt a little awkward. We took a window table for two instead, enjoying our own meal and occasionally exchanging smiles across the room with Brigitte. We were done eating before Brigitte's group, so we simply waved adieu to her and left.

If we had never seen Brigitte again, perhaps we would regret not having joined her for dinner. But there turned out to be no need for

Helga and me in St. Tropez—Brigitte Bardot invited us to this restaurant, but there wasn't room to sit at her table of friends.

Beautiful Brigitte. This is the photo she carried around with her for fans. Helga's is signed—I wanted to keep mine pristine. I always thought that she was one of the most beautiful women in the world.

regrets. We saw Brigitte a few more times during our stay, and each time she treated us as if we were old friends (the fact that Helga spoke perfect French must have helped). She invited us to a beach party at her house—a fine affair at which we joined in with the artistic types and beautiful people, sipping cocktails while lounging about the surf and the sand on colorful inflatable rafts.

One night Helga and I were walking through town, and as we passed a side street, we heard the sound of a voice and a guitar. I looked down that small, winding street and caught a glimpse of who was making that music: it was Brigitte, sitting by herself on some stone steps. Helga and I approached her, and I took a picture of her as she sang. She looked up from her guitar and greeted us with a simple, smiling, "Oh, hello."

When she finished the song she was playing, we talked a bit. She told us that she had just made a recording of the Peruvian folk song "El Condor Pasa," and was surprised when I told her that it was one of my favorite melodies (I knew the version that Simon and Garfunkel recorded on their *Bridge Over Troubled Water* album.) Brigitte began strumming the chords to the song and started singing the melody. After a line or two, I very quietly joined in and sang along with her. She encouraged the accompaniment with another smile. The more Brigitte and I sang together, the louder we got, and by the song's final chorus our voices were echoing off the stone walls around us and filling this little street with music. There was beauty to be seen all around St. Tropez, but the vision of Brigitte Bardot sitting on those old stone steps, singing and smiling, sums up the magic of the place pretty well.

SOMETIMES I WONDER IF MY early brushes with famous people helped prepare me for my relationship with Muhammad. Shaking hands with JFK, meeting with Hank Aaron, and singing with Bardot had very different effects on me, of course, but all those experiences offered a chance to see that, at some basic level, people are people no matter how famous they might be. In any event, within a year of our beautiful time in St. Tropez, Helga and I went through our teary separation at the Frankfurt airport, unsure if we were going to see each other again. And just a year or so after that, the two of us were eating Chinese takeout with Muhammad Ali, happy that this worldwide celebrity did not seem to be a brief, random acquaintance but a new, true friend.

FIVE

LACE 'EM UP

THERE ARE NO SHORTCUTS TO being the Greatest."

Muhammad and I were standing on the grass of Washington Park, catching our breath after a morning run. I had gotten the chance to know him during a professional lull after his Thrilla in Manila fight with Joe Frazier. Now it was time for Muhammad to get back to work. His next fight was set for February, 20, 1976, when he would defend his heavyweight title against a largely unknown Belgian boxer named Jean-Pierre Coopman. I didn't think that Coopman would be much of a contender against the Champ, but Muhammad was telling me that he always needed to think about his own preparation rather than the skills of his opponent.

"You don't become the Greatest under the lights the night you win the championship," he said. "That's when they tell you you're the Greatest. But you *become* the Greatest in the early morning runs and in all those hours of work at the gym. When you're up before the world wakes up and you're running in the darkness and you are dead tired, then you have a choice: Do I quit or do I run another mile? That's when you become great—running the extra mile."

The fight was held in San Juan, Puerto Rico. Muhammad asked if

Helga and I wanted to come down to see it, and a Puerto Rican doctor I knew through Dr. Williams invited us to stay at his home. But as much as I wanted to see Muhammad in action in the ring, I couldn't get enough time off from work to make the trip, so Helga went without me. I did see the fight when it was broadcast in prime time on CBS. Athletically, Muhammad was always at his best when he was up against a skilled, dangerous foe like Foreman or Frazier. But as an entertainer, sometimes he put on his best shows when the fight was a mismatch. The Coopman fight was one of those. Coopman was billed as "The Lion of Flanders" but he turned out to be more of a house cat—he was all smiles during prefight press conferences and was clearly more of a fan of Ali's than a threat to him in the ring. The only real challenge that the Belgian presented to Muhammad was that Ali couldn't do anything to psych him out in the days before the fight because Coopman didn't speak a word of English—at the start of the fight the boxers' instructions had to be translated into Flemish for Coopman's benefit.

Muhammad might have used the mismatch as a chance to humiliate his less capable opponent, but he liked Coopman enough as a person to treat him with respect. Instead of simply pummeling "The Lion," Ali put on a show—dancing around the ring, talking to the crowd, and showing just enough of his lightning-fast left jab to remind everybody why he was the champion. Muhammad was recovering from a bad chest cold, and he had had one crucial night's sleep interrupted by a fire in his hotel, but he was in charge of the fight every second of every round, and knocked out Coopman decisively in the fifth.

Back home, he tried to stick to his training regimen as he prepared for his next match—an April fight against a journeyman heavyweight named Jimmy Young. (When people asked about the apparent dip in the quality of fighters he was taking on, Muhammad pointed out that he had done battle with Frazier just months before and was looking to set up a rematch with Ken Norton—he felt he'd earned the right to some easier matchups in between.)

On one of our morning runs, a question occurred to me: people always talked about how a fighter might change his strategy depending on who he was fighting, but I wondered how much effect the style of a referee had on a fight. Muhammad told me that you knew a referee was doing a good job when you didn't notice him in the ring.

"Some referees want to *be* the fight," he said. "They showboat in the ring like they're the center of attention. The boxers don't want that and the crowd doesn't want that. We all want a referee that will let us fight."

He started to tell me about referees that he liked and didn't like, and he mentioned that one of his favorites was Teddy Waltham, an older British ex-boxer who had worked as a judge or official for several of Muhammad's early fights in Europe and who was in the ring as referee for Muhammad's 1966 title defense against Karl Mildenberger (Muhammad told me he considered Mildenberger to be a tougher opponent than Sonny Liston).

"Waltham was an older guy. Didn't look like he could keep up with us in the ring," said Muhammad. "But he handled that fight well. I liked Mildenberger and I didn't want to hurt or embarrass him. Waltham was very professional and stopped the fight at just the right time, in the twelfth round. He was a good referee."

The Mildenberger fight was the first-ever heavyweight title bout held in Germany, and after the fight Muhammad and his cornermen, Waltham, and some American journalists were all on the same plane back to London. Muhammad told me that he was walking down the aisle and saw Waltham in tears, talking to some writers. The referee had been given a thousand pounds in cash—one of the biggest paydays he had ever received—but had been pickpocketed somewhere after the fight and had lost all the money. Muhammad said he wanted to cry too when he heard what had happened. He went back to his seat, asked somebody how much a thousand pounds would be in American money, wrote a personal check, went back down the aisle, and handed it to Waltham.

"Muhammad," I said. "That is so touching."

"I know it is," he said. "That's why I told you."

• • •

MUHAMMAD SCORED A UNANIMOUS DECISION against Jimmy Young, but didn't look good doing it. He had trained hard enough to have the stamina to go a full fifteen rounds, but he had also let his weight get up to 230, 14 pounds heavier than he had been for the Foreman fight a year and a half before. His famously fast hands and feet weren't quite so dazzling this time, and knowledgeable fight fans were beginning to worry about his well-being in the ring.

I had a firsthand view of just how much Muhammad had come to hate training and how hard it was for him to keep the fire in his belly that he'd had as a young fighter. I ran every morning with or without Muhammad, but of course I preferred running with him. I would call Muhammad—he never called me—to see if he wanted to run, and more and more often he would tell me he wasn't going to train that day. He was still an incredible athlete, and he certainly loved being Muhammad Ali, but it was getting harder for him to approach his sport with the same heart and energy that had made him the Greatest.

He did seem to make a commitment to get into better shape for his next fight, though, a May 24 bout in Munich against the British heavyweight Richard Dunn. His serious training would take place over four weeks at his camp in Deer Lake, Pennsylvania. Muhammad never actually invited me to come to the camp, but a couple of times he said things that sounded like he assumed I would be there. That was all I needed to hear. I rescheduled some work commitments and headed off for my first trip to Deer Lake.

The camp was set on a beautiful, wooded five-acre site about an hour northwest of Philadelphia that Muhammad had purchased in 1972 as he was fighting his way toward regaining the heavyweight championship. A treacherously steep road led up to a main parking area, from which one could easily stroll to a custom-built gym, basketball courts, a dining hall, a four-bedroom main cabin, and a cabin that was just for Muhammad (he wanted a cabin to himself, believing that conjugal relations should be put on hold while he was in training). Stretching up the hillside from the main buildings were log cabins that would become home to his trainers, sparring partners, and guests. There were stables, a barn, and a small white structure that Muhammad had built to use as a mosque. All around the site were giant boulders that Muhammad's father—the veteran sign painter—had painted with the names of great fighters of the past: Jack Johnson, Floyd Patterson, Jack Dempsey, Rocky Marciano, Sonny Liston, Sugar Ray Robinson, Joe Louis.

Muhammad and I had begun to forge a friendship through our morning runs and one-to-one conversations. In joining him at training camp, I found that I had to make the adjustment of trying to find my place among his inner circle of boxing people. Jimmy Ellis was working steadily as Muhammad's sparring partner, and since he and I already got along well, it was easy to decide that I would share a cabin with him while at the camp. His cabin was way up at the top of the hill, with a spectacular view of the countryside.

The rest of the team around Ali were new faces to me. My reactions to these people ranged from respect and admiration to anger and disappointment. On the respectful end, it was a real privilege to get to know Muhammad's legendary trainer, Angelo Dundee. Angelo first met Muhammad when Ali was still a Golden Gloves champion in Louisville, and had been in Muhammad's corner since his second professional fight, in 1961. (The one exception was when Ali fought Jimmy Ellis in 1971: Angelo was training Ellis at the time, and, with Ali's consent, he was in Ellis's corner for that fight.) After fighting as an amateur, Angelo never turned pro, but he had an incredible mind when it came to all the subtleties underlying the brute force of a boxing match. Angelo was based in Miami, where he and his brother Chris ran the Fifth Street Gym—the gym Muhammad trained in as a young fighter. Angelo would arrive in Deer Lake several weeks before a fight and serve as the calm center of authority during training.

Watching Angelo and Muhammad work together, I could see how much affection they had for each other. They seemed to have a perfect trust-based relationship between trainer and athletic superstar. Angelo was a big-picture guy—not worried about the timing of Muhammad's jabs and uppercuts but instead thinking of strategies he might use against particular fighters. Angelo believed "different styles make fights," and he and Muhammad would watch fight films to go over an opponent's weaknesses. Angelo would come up with what might work as a general plan of attack for a fight, and would counsel Ali on how to pace himself. But I never heard Angelo say anything to Muhammad about basic boxing mechanics—Angelo knew that Ali was so naturally gifted that anything a trainer tried to change would mess up more than it would help (Angelo once said to me, "If you're working with a Michelangelo, why would you want to change his style?").

Occasionally, if Angelo really wanted Muhammad to try something specific, he would use a little reverse psychology, knowing that if Muhammad thought something was his own idea, there was a better chance he'd embrace it. ("Muhammad, that was a great left hook you threw. I noticed how balanced you were before you threw it in order to get the leverage you needed. Beautiful!") Of course, Muhammad was smart enough to see through that ploy, but if the end result was helpful in the ring, fighter and trainer were both happy.

My first night at Deer Lake, when I told Muhammad how well I thought he and Angelo worked together, he said, "Angelo is the perfect trainer. No one knows me better psychologically than Angelo. And the reason I trust him is because he loves me."

I didn't ever hear Muhammad refer to Angelo as a "second father," but he was definitely like a favorite uncle or a great guidance counselor—the grown-up whose support can make all the difference in your life.

Ferdie Pacheco was a "fight doctor"—a physician who worked with many of the boxers Angelo trained, and who had been in Ali's corner since 1962. He and Angelo were close friends, and they both wanted only to help and support Muhammad. Ferdie believed that Angelo was the best thing that ever happened to Muhammad, and everything the doctor and the trainer did together for Ali seemed rooted in love and respect for Muhammad as both an athlete and a person.

Lana Shabazz was a wonderful, vibrant, earthy woman who served as the camp's cook. I knew from the moment I met her that she loved Muhammad dearly, and I could see she was committed to nurturing him with both her food and her motherly advice. I fell in love with her and her cooking right away.

Howard Bingham was a very talented photographer who first met Muhammad when he was assigned to take photos of him for a local Los Angeles newspaper. He and Muhammad had become extremely close over the years, and Bingham was someone whom Muhammad trusted very much. I had heard a lot about Bingham and had met him once in Chicago. At Deer Lake I had no trouble at all getting along with him. Howard was on the lookout for anyone getting close to Muhammad who might be a problem, but when Howard saw how Muhammad trusted me, he accepted me, too.

I was not as trusting of some of the other people around Muhammad, who, it seemed to me, were looking to take from him rather than give anything useful to him. It didn't really surprise me that a superstar like Muhammad would attract some questionable hangers-on, but I couldn't figure out how someone like him—so smart and with such a positive spirit—could let himself be surrounded by people who seemed to be taking advantage of him. Then again, I was new to Muhammad's camp and he was in his second reign as heavyweight champion—I had to believe that Muhammad felt that the people around him did serve a purpose.

Drew "Bundini" Brown was a familiar face to anyone who had spotted his distinctive hairdo in Ali's corner during televised fights. He had been a cornerman for Ali since 1963 and considered himself an "assistant trainer" although he had very little to do with Ali's actual training. Mostly he was around for emotional support—he was always the one shouting, "You're the Greatest," and he had a certain flair in the way he would put on or take off Ali's robe in the ring. Bundini was also pretty good with words himself and had come up with one of Ali's most famous rhymes, "Float like a butterfly, sting like a bee, your hands can't hit what your eyes can't see." One of Bundini's peculiar habits was that when he wanted something from Muhammad—usually money—he'd present a sob story and get himself worked up to the point of bursting into tears, right in front of everybody. And, every time, Muhammad—whether he felt pity or just wanted to make the crying stop—would give Bundini what he asked for.

Lloyd Wells and Walter "Blood" Youngblood were a couple of others who were always around at training camp. Wells had been a scout for the Kansas City Chiefs football team, and Blood had worked for Sugar Ray Robinson and as an aide to Malcolm X. They were tough guys, real street characters, who wanted nothing to do with me. The feeling was mutual.

There were a few other characters around, too, and as camp progressed, I became more convinced that I didn't want anything to do with many of the guys in Muhammad's inner circle, but I started to see why they were there. Muhammad was in camp with a singular goal—to train for a fight—and everything he did was leading toward the moment he would step into the ring. For everybody else in training camp, the days could be awfully long and uneventful. Muhammad's guys were with him for weeks at a time, cheering him on every day as he hit the heavy bag or sparred in the ring, and taking care of the trivial chores that kept the camp running. The experience of being in the heavyweight champion's training camp could be a lot more drudgery than good times, and Muhammad had surrounded himself with people—whatever their shortcomings—whom he could depend on to be with him consistently and to keep him in the right frame of mind. (Of course, Ali was paying them well to be with him consistently.)

Mostly, I was ignored by the boxing guys around Ali. The one guy who went out of his way to actually make me feel unwelcome was Gene Kilroy, a white guy who called himself Ali's "business manager." Kilroy was an ex-GI who had traveled with the army boxing team, met Ali when Muhammad boxed in the 1960 Rome Olympics, and began working for him when Ali returned to the ring in 1970 after his exile. Unlike some of the other guys, Kilroy really did seem to be working hard at the camp—he had a hand in managing everything that went on at Deer Lake. But while Angelo Dundee exuded quiet authority, it seemed to me that Kilroy was constantly asserting his top-dog position like a schoolyard bully.

In fact, most everybody in camp seemed to be worried about their position. They seemed jealous and sour toward me and my status as Muhammad's newest friend, but many of them were also jealous of one another. I didn't have to be in camp long to see the games many of them played, each trying to get closest to Muhammad. I didn't want any part of it. All I wanted to do was maintain an honest, straightforward connection with him. And, as an invited guest at his training camp, I was happy to stay in the background and do whatever I could to be of some assistance to him. I thought one of the ways I could help was in my usual role as running partner.

My first night at Deer Lake, in the main cabin after dinner, I asked Muhammad if he wanted me to run with him the next morning. Before he could answer, Kilroy practically snarled at me and said that Muhammad ran alone and wouldn't want to run with me. Muhammad just ignored him and said, "Yeah, meet me here at five thirty."

I could tell that Muhammad's response didn't make Kilroy feel any friendlier toward me, and he still seemed to be seething when I turned up in the gym the next morning in my tracksuit and running shoes. Muhammad was still getting dressed in his cabin, and Kilroy and Youngblood were waiting for him. Kilroy looked at me with disgust and told me again that Muhammad would not run with me. In so many words, he let me know that I was an unwelcome distraction. He spoke to me as if he owned the place—as if I were a complete stranger to Muhammad who shouldn't even be there. I had not come to the camp to make friends with somebody like Kilroy, but I hadn't come to make waves, either. If Kilroy was in charge, I would honor that. I sat down across the room. I figured I would at least say "Good morning" to Muhammad before he went on his run without me. After a while, Muhammad strode into the room in his gray Russell running suit and his combat boots. He surveyed the room and shot a look in my direction.

"Let's go," he said.

I got up and walked out the door with Muhammad, not even

glancing at the others. Then, without any distraction at all, Muhammad and I were off on our first Deer Lake run together.

MUHAMMAD'S DEMEANOR AT CAMP WASN'T too different from the one I had gotten to know in Chicago. He was serious and focused about training, but he still had the same sense of humor that was so much a part of him. Out of the ring, he would be mostly quiet and serious. When he did get into the ring to spar, he talked all the time, entertaining whatever visitors had shown up to watch him work out that day. He didn't run the camp as a dictator, but he knew exactly how he wanted the camp to run and expected everyone around him to follow through on that. He didn't pay close attention to any of those around him individually, he just expected us all to know what to do and how to handle ourselves. It did seem like there were times when he was entertained by the petty squabbles among his training crew—he would sometimes make an offhand comment that he knew would instigate some flare-up among Kilroy and the others, then sit back and watch as they got upset with one another.

Muhammad never made a big deal out of my being in Deer Lake, but I enjoyed the time I got to spend with him on our runs and in his private cabin. One night we were watching television and I told him how much I always liked his "mean face"—the distinctive, scowling overbite he employed when he wanted to play to the camera and look his craziest (he directed it memorably at Joe Frazier on the cover of *Sports Illustrated* before the Thrilla in Manila). He showed me the face now, and I made it right back at him. My variation was that I stuck my tongue out, too.

"Maaaan," he said. "You're the only person who looks uglier than me doing that."

"Well, I had some practice," I said. "My grandfather Albert used to make that same face when we watched pro wrestling together."

Muhammad looked at me with a curious expression.

"Mine did, too," he said.

"Really?"

"My grandfather Herman and I used to watch wrestling together," Muhammad explained. "Angelo Poffo, Cowboy Bob Ellis, Dick the Bruiser, and best of all, Gorgeous George—that's who we got the mean face from."

"My grandfather would make the Gorgeous George mean face, grab me, pull up my shirt, and rub his whiskers on my back until I couldn't take it anymore," I told Muhammad. "I started making the face back at him, but it didn't stop me from getting a whisker burn."

Muhammad laughed at that, and then we started talking more about the old wrestlers. Gorgeous George had been a favorite of his, and he told me that even as a kid he was fascinated by the fact that anytime George was interviewed, he would boast and brag about how great he was, and about how he was going to demolish his opponent. He was the most popular wrestler of his day not just because he was beloved, but because he also made people hate him enough that they'd watch his fights in hopes of seeing him get beaten. Ali told me he met George in 1961 when they were both interviewed on a Las Vegas radio station. Ali was still a young up-and-comer at the time, but after hearing the over-the-top way the wrestler promoted himself, Muhammad said he was inspired to take his own boasting to a new level.

"Cash—my father—used to tell me to believe I was the greatest and that I couldn't be beat. He told me that I was going to be bigger than Joe Louis before I ever won a fight. Gorgeous George told everybody he was the greatest, and people would show up at his wrestling match to see if he would kill or be killed. I realized that if I listened to my father and talked like Gorgeous George, I would always be fighting in front of a full house. I knew that if I was cocky and confident half the people there would be cheering for me, and the other half would want to see me get beat. But love me or hate me, they would all buy tickets to see me. It worked."

Muhammad borrowed the self-promotion from Gorgeous George, but as to his manner of speaking, he credited a different influence. When we watched TV together, instead of watching the late movie, Muhammad always wanted to flip around between a couple of channels that were running programs from preachers such as Billy Graham, Jimmy Swaggart, and Jim and Tammy Faye Bakker. I didn't really get why a devout Muslim would want to listen to these people, until he told me he was more interested in the style than the content. He loved the way they seemed to speak from the heart, modulating their tone, changing their rhythm, getting louder or softer as they spoke, and sometimes getting teary-eyed.

"It's amazing," he said. "All they've got to work with is their personal beliefs and their voice, and they captivate a TV audience. They have a story to tell and they know how to tell it. When you hear me talking before a fight, I'm doing the same thing as those preachers."

MUHAMMAD HAD INVITED HELGA AND me to come to Germany to see the Dunn fight, but, again, work got in the way and we had to settle for being two of the sixty million who watched the fight on TV (to air live in the States, the fight started at 3:30 in the morning in Munich). It was another uninspiring bout, which Ali won easily with a fifth-round knockout. He seemed to have some of his old speed back in his punches and footwork, but I couldn't tell if that was because he'd put in the extra effort to train hard, or if Dunn was just that much slower. What we didn't know at the time was that although Ali had many more rounds of fighting ahead of him, this would be the last knockout win of his career.

Back home in Chicago, we resumed our routine of (occasional) morning runs. I would bring cassette tapes of music I thought he might like to play in his Stutz Blackhawk on the rides to and from the park, and if I didn't have to work I would stay at his house while he went through his mail and returned phone calls. He seemed to enjoy having business-related conversations with the assorted promoters, lawyers, investors, and media people who were always trying to get in touch with him. I think he liked the opportunity to use his mind rather than his fists to solve the challenges of the day. He would say that he intended to be a successful businessman after he retired from boxing, and he liked being on the phone learning how to conduct business from "the smart people."

There were a few times when Muhammad added a stop on the way home—at the University of Chicago Medical Center's Children's Hospital. These visits were never set up by any public relations people, and usually the hospital had no idea he was coming. Muhammad would just decide he was in the mood to brighten the day for some sick kids.

I knew some of the nurses at the hospital because I sold equipment to the Pediatric Intensive Care Unit. But the first time Muhammad and I walked up to the nurses' station there, they sure didn't notice me. There was absolute silence and stares of disbelief as everyone tried to process the fact that Muhammad Ali was a visitor on their floor. The nurses scurried around with excitement and then took Muhammad around to meet some of the children. The hardest part of these nurses' job was trying to bring hope and happiness to the kids under their care, and having Muhammad as a visitor instantly made everyone's day sunnier.

Many of the kids knew exactly who Muhammad was and were thrilled to see him stroll up to their bedside, but if a kid didn't recognize the Champ he would say, "Do you know who I am? I am Muhammad Ali—the heavyweight champion of the world. Haven't you seen me on TV?" Whether the small patients recognized him or not, Muhammad's goal was to make their day a little better and to give them whatever encouragement he could. The smiles he could get out of those kids were incredible. And Muhammad always made sure to tell the staff how much he appreciated their work, which left them smiling just as brightly.

Because Muhammad seemed so comfortable on the visits to the Children's Hospital, I began to think he might like to meet the doctors that I worked with. He had let me watch him at work—I thought maybe I could return the favor. I got into the field of medical technology when I returned to the States after my time in Germany. I had never gotten any "A"s in science courses, but I found that I had a great facility for understanding the intersection of engineering and medicine in medical devices. Breakthroughs were happening every day in cardiology and that was fascinating to me, so before long I was training at the Texas Heart Institute and learning the nuances of cardiovascular surgery from Dr. Denton Cooley—a pioneer of the artificial heart. I became a surgical technician specializing in open heart surgery, and when a position opened with a medical products firm in Chicago I took it. Now I was assisting with open heart surgeries at Chicago's major heart institutions: Northwestern University Medical Center, Loyola University Medical Center, Michael Reese Medical Center, and more. One morning after a park run, I offered an invitation to Muhammad.

"Muhammad, open heart surgery really is an amazing thing to witness. Why don't you come in with me one morning and see how surgery in a big operating room functions?"

He looked at me like I was crazy. "Nooooo, maaaan," was his response.

"It's something that really only a handful of people ever get to see, Muhammad. We can go into an operating room supervisor's office and look through a window into the surgical suites and see everything that is going on, or if you want to we can actually 'gown up' like the doctors and walk into a suite and watch a procedure."

"No, man—I can't handle that."

Muhammad told me that he didn't even like seeing needles when he was getting his own shots, and had no interest in looking at a surgical procedure. He was a guy who loved monster movies and the shoot-'em-up scenes in westerns, and he didn't seem to have too much trouble bloodying an opponent when he boxed, but the thought of seeing a body opened up made him extremely squeamish. That was certainly understandable, and I knew better than to push the point, but I told him that if he just came to the surgical suite, he didn't have to go into an operating room—he could just meet the doctors and nurses. I told him that if we went to the University of Chicago Medical Center I would get Dr. Williams—Muhammad's doctor—to give us a tour. I asked Muhammad to think about how much it would mean to Dr. Williams and his colleagues to know that Muhammad Ali appreciated the lifesaving work they were doing so much that he wanted to see if for himself. That clinched it. Muhammad said he would come visit the hospital with me.

The surgical suite at the University of Chicago Medical Center consisted of twelve operating rooms along a lengthy corridor, and usually eight rooms at a time were scheduled for procedures. I got the OK from the hospital to bring Muhammad in on a day when I didn't have any surgeries to assist. The doctors welcomed him enthusiastically, and the nurses couldn't take their eyes off him. We joined Dr. Williams in the supervisor's office, which overlooked all the operating rooms. Dr. Williams explained a bit about what kind of things might take place in those rooms, and Muhammad's gaze was intense as he concentrated on everything he was hearing. He had never really reacted much when I told him about my work in operating rooms, but now that he was seeing what I was a part of at the hospital, he really got it. "You do this every day?" he asked at one point, actually sounding a little impressed.

"Yes, Muhammad. This is one of the places I come to work to after our runs."

"Heavy."

I GAVE MUHAMMAD A CLOSE-UP look at my place of work, and a couple of weeks later he gave me the closest possible look at his. We were at the Southside Gym, and he suggested I put on gloves and get in the ring with him. I'd been at the gym several times now and the guys there more or less accepted me—I'd actually started to get friendly with a few of them. So I felt comfortable accepting Muhammad's offer (I would never have gotten in the ring in front of the guys at Deer Lake). Muhammad didn't give me much more instruction than that we would spar for a three-minute round and that I should keep my gloves up.

As we were having our gloves put on, I decided to give Muhammad some Gorgeous George/Ali-style trash-talking.

"You've ducked me all these months, but today you have met your match, Mr. Big Stuff! You know what kind of shape I'm in. Think about all those mornings I run without you. I'm going to float like a hummingbird and sting like a wasp. The wasp's sting is mightier than the bee—after being in the ring with Shanny, the Champ will see!"

He did not take the bait, just emitting a low muffled laugh as I talked. Moments later we were in our corners, waiting for our round to start. As thrilling as it always was to walk into a room at Muhammad's side, it was a whole different feeling standing across from him in a boxing ring.

"Show me what you got, white boy," he said.

The canvas was slapped to signal the start of the round. Muhammad grimaced through his mouthpiece and then came rushing toward me like he was going to throw a big punch. My battle plan had been to simply try to stay away from him for the whole three minutes. I was confident that I could move around the ring without him cornering me—all I had to do was run away. I knew I was in good-enough shape to do that for three quick minutes. It sounded like a workable plan. I just had to control my breathing, as on a run. But with him coming at me so quickly, the ring suddenly seemed a lot smaller and I felt ridiculously vulnerable. And three minutes suddenly seemed like a very long time.

I tried to backpedal away from him and let loose a couple of "woo-woo" screams just like Curly from the Three Stooges (at least that got Muhammad to laugh). I was fast enough that he didn't corner me, but I hadn't counted on the fact that he didn't need to corner me to hit me. He started landing some jabs and straight rights on my arms and shoulders and a few to the face. I knew he wasn't hitting me with full force, but even his pulled punches had tremendous power in them—they definitely hurt—and it was scary to think about what it must have felt like to take the tremendous punches that landed on George Foreman or Joe Frazier, let alone what it felt like for him to take their punches.

I stopped a few times to throw some punches at him, but he wasn't very impressed. Now it was his turn to trash-talk.

"Come on, wasp—where's that sting?" he shouted. "You might float like a hummingbird, but you sting like a mosquito. You trying to hurt me, chump? I didn't feel a thing. Aunt Coretta has a harder punch than that. Come on, hummingbird—show me somethin'! Show me any-thing. Come on, is that all you've got?"

Suddenly I knew exactly how George Foreman must have felt at the end of round seven in their Rumble in the Jungle. "Yup—that's about it!"

Afterward, outside the ring, Muhammad told me that he wanted me to understand how much more athleticism there was to boxing than just throwing and taking punches.

"People don't understand how much stamina you have to have to be a boxer," he said. "Ask a normal person what it would feel like if they got up in the morning—they're tired, they just want to go back to bed—and right then they have to wrestle with their brother for forty-five straight minutes. That's a fifteen-round boxing match. You don't realize how much energy you have to burn up until you do it. There are times in the ring when it feels like all the energy has been drained out

A rare shot of Muhammad and Veronica dancing. We were
at a cancer benefit at the Playboy building in Chicago. This
is the second time that I saw Muhammad dancing.

of you, and it's a struggle just to keep your hands up. You have to pull from deep within, and that's when champions are made. You just went three minutes with me—imagine going the full fifteen rounds. I think you get the picture."

He'd made his point. I was happy to get the gloves and headgear off, and I imagined the "hummingbird" would get awfully tired trying to run away from the Champ for a whole fight and would end up taking a terrible beating.

THE BIGGEST NEWS IN MUHAMMAD'S home life was that Veronica was pregnant. They hadn't gotten married yet—he was still married to Khalilah. But Muhammad and Veronica were obviously very much in love and excited about starting a family together. The new baby would be Muhammad's seventh child. After a childless marriage to his first wife, he had four children with Khalilah: Maryum, the twins Jamillah and Rasheda, and Muhammad Jr. He also had two daughters, Miya and Khaliah, born from affairs with two other women.

Muhammad didn't talk to me much about his ex-wives or the women he had been with, but he was a proud father of all his children and was always concerned about whether he was doing enough to support them. That support extended unconditionally to the two girls born out of wedlock—he didn't consider them to be any less his children than the others.

It seemed to me that Muhammad now really wanted to be a settled family man, and that he wanted to build a home life with Veronica that he hadn't succeeded in maintaining with the others. Still, all those past relationships could create some craziness in the present, and I remember the first time I was pulled into that craziness. Muhammad beeped me, and when I called him back he said, "Do me a favor. I have a friend coming into town and I need you to pick her up at the airport at seven p.m. I'm going to be out with Veronica."

The "friend" coming into town was Wanda Bolton, Khaliah's mother. Muhammad had started an affair with Wanda while married to Khalilah, and their baby was now two years old. Wanda was attractive and was friendly toward me—at least after I explained who I was and why I was picking her up rather than Muhammad. Per Muhammad's instructions, I drove Wanda to a motel on Michigan Avenue in downtown Chicago, got her checked in, and then left. I didn't like being part of something that was being kept secret from Veronica, but I wasn't quite sure if Wanda's trip was part of Muhammad's old shenanigans or whether he was simply keeping in touch with the mother of one of his children. I didn't find out, because Muhammad never talked about it.

WHAT WE DID TALK ABOUT anytime we were together were movies, music, and food. One day I asked him to list his favorite foods.

Without much hesitation he said, "Fried chicken and macaroni and cheese."

"Who makes your favorite fried chicken?" I asked.

"Harold's," he said. I thought he might mention his mother or Aunt Coretta. But Harold's was short for Harold's Chicken Shack, a popular Chicago takeout chain that had a location on Cottage Grove close to Muhammad's place. The Chicken Shack was what came to mind for him because that was where a lot of his dinners had been coming from while Veronica had their kitchen remodeled.

"What else do you like?" I asked.

"Green peas. Spinach. Oh—and ice cream." He looked like he was imagining his next sundae for a moment, then he asked me, "Does Helga cook? Does she cook German food for you?"

"Helga is a fantastic cook—really more of a chef than a cook. You'd love her authentic German schnitzels, but she has learned to make all kinds of international specialties. She uses all fresh ingredients—never canned or frozen foods. She's even teaching me how to cook."

"Can she come over and cook one of her meals for us?" Muhammad asked excitedly. "We'll have a real family dinner in the dining room."

When I presented the proposition to Helga, she was thrilled at the chance to cook for Muhammad and set to work preparing a fitting menu. The one catch in the dinner plans was that not only was Helga doing all the cooking, but she and I had to supply all the cookware, all the plates and silver, and all the glassware. Veronica was still in the process of decorating their home, and the kitchen wasn't finished yet. So, on an agreed-upon Sunday in late August, Helga and I loaded six big boxes of food and gear into the trunk and backseat of my Buick, feeling very happy to be Muhammad's caterers as well as his dinner guests.

Smiles after the first dinner that Helga cooked at the South Woodlawn house.

Helga and I got to South Woodlawn around two p.m. Muhammad and Veronica were out. We unloaded the boxes in the kitchen and got to work. Helga was in the role of master chef, I was her very enthusiastic sous chef, and we got to work doing all of the prepping for dinner. By the time Muhammad and Veronica got home a couple of hours later, there were pots simmering on every burner and piles of sliced and diced ingredients laid out on the counters. Veronica couldn't believe her empty kitchen had been transformed into a restaurant-quality production line. She said we should consider leaving all our cookware there and just coming over for dinner every night.

Technically, our dinner was for a party of five. On August 6, Veronica had given birth to Hana Ali at the hospital in Benton Harbor, Michigan, near Muhammad's property in Berrien Springs. I thought little Hana was the cutest baby I had ever seen. Unlike some guys, I was always comfortable with babies—I was thirteen years old when my youngest brother, Kevin, was born, and I had put in plenty of time changing his diapers and rocking him to sleep. I wanted to hold Hana right away, but Muhammad didn't seem happy about another man holding his little girl. (When he stepped out of the room at one point, Veronica put the baby in my arms for a few moments before he came back. I would have many more opportunities to hold my dear Hana later.)

Helga and Veronica were meeting for the first time, and they liked each other right away. Helga saw in Veronica what I did—a beautiful, sophisticated young woman who was taking on the challenge of adjusting to a new home, a new baby, and the craziness of life with the world's greatest celebrity. Helga was beautiful and sophisticated herself, with the advantage of age and worldly experience. She took a great interest in Veronica and, starting right there in the kitchen, became a kind of mentor, confidante, and "older sister" to our new young friend.

When it was time for dinner we took our places at the dining room table. Helga had it set up elegantly with place settings of her grandmother's china and silver around a centerpiece of flowers. It felt like such an intimate, homey scene—four new friends gathering to share a meal.

The Muslim faith had some dietary strictures that Muhammad tried to follow, and when Veronica had heard that Helga would be cooking, she passed along some advice for the menu: pork wasn't allowed, and mushrooms were considered "unclean." But Helga had her heart set on making her wonderful cream of mushroom soup for Muhammad, and when Helga had her heart set on doing something, it was going to get done.

The soup was served. Muhammad took a taste.

"Oh, that's good," he said. "My aunt Coretta made good soups, but I don't remember her making any cream soups. This is delicious. What is it?"

"This is my cream of mushroom soup with cheese," said Helga. "I knew you might not want to eat mushrooms because of your faith, but I decided to take a chance and make you one of my favorites."

Far from being upset about the mushrooms, Muhammad asked for a second bowl of soup. "This tastes so good, you could convert all Muslims to think again about not eating mushrooms," he said.

I knew that the consumption of alcohol was definitely against the Muslim faith, and Muhammad never drank as far as I was aware, but Helga and I figured that if we were supplying the feast, we could at least partake of some fine German wine. We had brought four bottles of Helga's favorite Riesling. As Helga poured glasses for us and for Veronica, she explained that the wine came from the Rheinland-Pfalz region, close to her childhood home in the town of Wiesbaden, and that she had actually picked this very type of grape when she was in her teens.

"Give me some of that," said Muhammad.

We were all surprised, but Helga got him a glass.

"This is German wine, Muhammad," I said. "We didn't want to offend you by pouring you a glass. But if you really do want to try it, I think you might like it because it's a little sweeter than most white wines."

"I'll try it," he said.

I poured him some wine and he took a sip. He swished it around in his mouth a little bit like a professional wine critic, made a funny face, then put his glass down. "Oouuuhh, that tastes good. Let's get high."

You don't argue with the heavyweight champ, so the wine continued to flow. After the soup, Helga served beef tenderloin, salad, vegetables, French bread, garlic mashed potatoes. By the end of dinner, Muhammad had polished off exactly two sips of wine. He wasn't "high," but he did have a relaxed smile on his face. (I never saw him drink another glass of wine after this night—I think he partook mostly as a sign of respect for Helga's efforts.)

Veronica, Laila, and Hana at home in Chicago, 1977. My favorite photo of them.

The dessert was Helga's take on Black Forest cake—a triple-layer chocolate cake covered in whipped cream and sour cherries. She was ecstatic when Muhammad announced it was the most delicious cake he had ever tasted. The wine and all that good food put Muhammad in a reflective mood, and he began to talk about some of the time he'd spent and meals he'd had at his aunt Coretta's House of Goodies restaurant. But after reminiscing for a bit, he surveyed the table and the company and made another announcement: "This is the best home-cooked meal that I have ever had." I could tell Helga didn't fully believe him—it sounded like Aunt Coretta would be tough competition in the kitchen. But Muhammad sounded sincere, and we were delighted that we had been able to make him so happy (and I should probably add that Muhammad has looked forward to one of Helga's specially baked cakes on just about every birthday since that dinner).

After the table was cleared, Helga and Veronica talked at the dining room table, and Muhammad and I went into his den. There was a large rocking chair in there—a gag gift a friend had sent, along with a pipe and some tobacco, so that Muhammad might get a head start on retirement in the wake of the Thrilla in Manila. Muhammad actually loved that chair, though, and he sat in it now and picked up the pipe and pouch of tobacco from a side table. He dipped the pipe into the pouch, filled the bowl, and patted it down tight. He held a match to the bowl and puffed and puffed but couldn't get any draw. I told him that I had watched my father smoke a pipe for years and knew the trick to it. I took the pipe from him, tapped out half the tobacco in the bowl, gave it some air, and lit it right up. Muhammad looked at me as if I had done a magic trick and said for the first time a line I would hear a lot, "You ain't as dumb as you look!"

Muhammad rocked in his chair and puffed on his pipe and looked reflective again.

"Do you ever wonder what all the old people are thinking about when they're sitting in their rocking chairs on the porch just looking out at nothing? In forty years you'll come and visit me and you'll hobble up the stairs with a cane and sit on my porch in the rocking chair I'll have waiting for you and we'll rock together and stare at nothing and we'll finally know the answer."

"Let's make it fifty years, Muhammad," I said. "Forty sounds a little too soon."

"OK. It's a deal." He took a few more puffs of his pipe and then sniffed at the air. The aromas from Helga's cooking still lingered, and were now mingled with the pleasant scent of the tobacco smoke.

"This home finally smells like it has been *lived* in," he said.

I don't think anybody wanted the evening to end, but eventually it was time for Helga and me to be on our way. I got up and headed back to the kitchen to find Helga and Veronica. I thought Muhammad would follow me, but I saw him pick up a pad of paper that was on his side table and begin to write something.

The ladies and I talked about doing this again soon, and then Muhammad joined us. I gave him a handshake and Helga gave him a big hug and a kiss. Helga turned to Veronica and gave her a big hug and a kiss, and then I gave Veronica a hug. I turned to Muhammad and he suddenly put his hands firmly on my shoulders. Was giving a hug to his woman a wrong move on my part? No, he was smiling. He walked me back next to Veronica, pushed us together, and said, "Don't they make a good-looking couple?" There was no edge to it—he was just being playful. So I put my hands on his shoulders, pushed him next to Helga, and said, "I think you two make a better-looking couple—*both* of you are pretty."

Veronica's birthday, enjoying some fine German wine. She never drank except with Helga.

We all laughed, and then Muhammad handed me the note he had written while in the den. I read the note to myself, then read it out loud. Muhammad didn't say another word. What he had written was simple, heartfelt, and the perfect end to the perfect evening. It was all Helga and I could talk about on our ride home.

The note said:

To Helga and Tim Shanahan, From Muhammad Ali:

The Chef that prepares a good dish makes a greater contribution to Human Happiness than the Astronomer who discovers a new star. Thank you for the Good Dinner.

SIX

BIGGA

THE REMATCH WITH KEN NORTON was on. It was set to take place the night of September 28, 1976, at a fittingly dramatic and historic venue—Yankee Stadium. Norton was a tremendous athlete with an unorthodox, almost "awkward" boxing style. This was the third time that Muhammad would face Norton. During their first fight, in the spring of 1973, Norton—a former sparring partner of Joe Frazier's—not only won a split decision but fractured Ali's jaw. That had happened in the second round, and I could only imagine the pain that Muhammad endured for the next ten rounds as he was hammered by Norton's powerful blows. Even though Muhammad lost the fight, there were no doubts afterward that Ali was still one of the toughest fighters of all time. Muhammad had worn the jeweled "People's Choice" robe that Elvis gave him into the ring for that first Norton fight. But after losing the decision, Muhammad—always somewhat superstitious about his fight rituals—never wore the robe again. In a rematch with Norton just six months later, it was Muhammad who won the split decision after another grueling twelve rounds. Their third fight was going to be a fifteen-round match, and Muhammad knew he was going to have to train especially hard.

Just before Muhammad headed to Deer Lake to train, I had the opportunity to learn a lot more about his upbringing when his parents—Odessa and Cassius Clay Sr.—came to Chicago for a visit. Muhammad had always had a close, loving relationship with his mother, but he and his father had had a falling out when Muhammad became a Muslim, and they barely spoke at all during the years Muhammad was banned from boxing. From what I could tell, there hadn't been any great reconciliation between father and son. At some point they just started seeing each other again. But even now, tempers could still flair. One day Herbert Muhammad came to the house to say hello, and Cash wouldn't speak to him—he stayed in another room while Muhammad and Herbert spoke. After Herbert left, Cash asked Muhammad, "Is that guy still stealing your money?" and the two erupted into an argument over the Nation of Islam's interest in Muhammad's career. Odessa stayed out of it—she was also upset that her son had turned from the Christian faith he had been raised in, but her motherly love trumped her religious convictions.

Muhammad's mother and father—Cash Sr. and Bird.

The first direct encounter I had with Cash was a little unusual. I was alone in the kitchen of the South Woodlawn house. Cash walked in and, without a "Hello" or a "How you doin'," asked me for twenty dollars. Um—OK. I handed him the money and he headed straight out of the kitchen. I was actually kind of used to this, because a lot of times Muhammad would ask me for twenties to cover tips with valets or maître d's or anybody else who gave him any assistance. He rarely had cash on him so he would ask me to hand out twenties here and there— sometimes to guys who hadn't actually done anything for him—they just happened to be standing next to the valet or just looked excited about seeing Muhammad. It never occurred to Muhammad to pay me back for those handed-out twenties (and it never occurred to me to ask him to pay me back). So, I assumed that when I handed Cash his twenty, that was money I would never see again. I was right.

Odessa was as sweet as Cash was ornery, and I found myself sitting with her every chance I got so I could hear her stories about young Muhammad. Odessa told me she almost didn't get the chance to raise Muhammad—in the hospital, a few hours after the delivery, they brought her the wrong baby. That baby seemed too quiet to her, so she checked the newborn's wristband and saw that he was an infant named Brown. The nurses quickly corrected the mistake and brought her baby Cassius, who was kicking and crying.

"He was loud from the beginning," Odessa said. "In the hospital, when all the other babies were supposed to be asleep, Cassius would start crying and wake them all up. I was so embarrassed."

Odessa called Muhammad "GG" because she said those were his first words (Muhammad always claimed he was trying to say "Golden Gloves"). Odessa said that as a toddler Muhammad loved to sit on the kitchen counter and dip his feet in the sink water. He loved banging on pots and pans with a big spoon ("Nearly drove us nuts!"). If he had trouble sleeping, he'd sit in a wooden chair and bump his head against the backrest until he fell asleep. "To us, it looked like it hurt," she said. "We could not understand why he was doing that, but it always calmed him down."

Muhammad was walking at ten months, but Odessa said he never actually took a first step. His first step was three steps at once, then four steps, then five, then he just got up on his tiptoes and started running everywhere he went. "We could barely keep up with him," she said, laughing. "We would get out of the car to go to church and little GG would have to run ahead of us. We would go visit his aunt Mary, and he would have to run into every room, trying to get the lay of the land— like a cat. And he always ran up on his tiptoes—Cash told me that GG was imitating me in my high heels. I tell you—he was a strange kid. He was queer!"

By the time Muhammad was going to school he would eat the lunch she had made for him on the way there, so that he could spend his lunch period running around the school track. He sometimes raced the school bus to school—often beating it, as the bus had to make twenty-six stops along the way and Muhammad didn't.

Muhammad had inherited his fine, light skin from his mother, and Odessa told me that when he was little he had some difficulty figuring out what their complexion meant. "I remember when he was four years old we took a ride on a bus full of all kinds of people. Different shades of people. When we got home, he looked up at me and asked, 'Momma, are you a white lady or a colored lady?' I had to explain the whole situation to him. Then he asked me why all the bus drivers where white. That was a whole other conversation. He was a very curious little boy."

After four days in Chicago, Cash and Bird left with Muhammad to go to Deer Lake. I went to Deer Lake a few weeks later, but by then Muhammad's parents had already gone home to Louisville. There were a couple of other visitors to camp whose presence seemed to put a little extra spark in Muhammad's workouts—Sugar Ray Leonard and Floyd Patterson. Leonard had just won a gold medal at the Summer Olympics in Montreal, and had come to Deer Lake both to observe the champ in action and to ask Muhammad for some career advice (Muhammad counseled Sugar Ray to turn pro, and insisted that the only trainer he should consider working with was Angelo Dundee. Ray took him up on both suggestions). Muhammad had fought Floyd Patterson twice and defeated him decisively each time, but Floyd and Muhammad had become quite close over the years, and Floyd was very open about calling Muhammad the greatest fighter ever.

I again put up with dirty looks from the camp crew to run with Muhammad. He and I would usually run two or three miles, finishing with a punishing final sixty yards up "the monster," the 45-degree hill that led up to the camp. Knowing that Muhammad needed to push himself a little harder in training for Norton, one morning I decided to try to give him a little extra motivation. I stayed behind him most of the run, but when we got to the hill and he started grinding it out, I broke into an all-out sprint. I blew by Muhammad and got to the top of the hill. When he got up to the top, he acted as though he wasn't very impressed with my uphill speed. But as we walked toward the gym cabin together he said, "Why are you staying in such good shape, Shanahan? What are you training for?"

"Nothing, Muhammad. But I'm still playing a lot of tennis."

"You don't need those muscles for tennis," he said.

"Well, actually, I just read this new book by a runner, Jim Fixx. The whole book is about how running is good for your brain and your body. I think there's something in my chemical makeup that gives me a need to run every day."

Muhammad shook his head. "I wish I had that. My chemical makeup is I look at a bowl of ice cream and it attaches itself to my belly."

Even with the ice cream, by the night of the Norton fight Muhammad was in the best physical and mental shape he'd been in for some time. My work schedule made it impossible for me to travel to New York to be ringside, but this didn't bother me too much. Considering how much personal time I was spending with Muhammad, I really didn't mind missing the fights. Being part of that scene would mean that I would spend more time around Kilroy, Wells, and the rest of the characters I didn't get along with, and it was not my desire to be part of the limelight around Ali or to be seen as just one more hanger-on. I didn't want to be seen in photos or videos as just another face in the Ali entourage. I cherished the fact that my friendship with Muhammad was something we'd developed in private, and I didn't want to risk affecting that by becoming part of his public life. I also didn't want my own professional career to be affected by others looking at me as "the guy who knows Ali." I never told any of my coworkers or clients that I knew him, and while some friends and family knew that I had met Muhammad, I never told them how much time I was spending with him. Dr. Charles Williams and a few of the nurses at the University of Chicago were really the only people who knew that my relationship with Muhammad had progressed after the initial connection through Athletes for a Better Education.

Ali looked good physically in the Norton fight and he moved well, but he couldn't dominate a powerful foe the way he used to. Norton was in tremendous physical shape, and Muhammad was still bothered by Norton's off-kilter rhythms. Norton was a very hard puncher, and Muhammad took a lot of punishment, including one vicious body shot that had him doubled up on the ropes. I saw Muhammad flinch (I flinched, too, just watching it on TV), and I could tell that he was trying to cover up the fact that he was hurt as he walked back to his corner after the round. I thought he might have suffered a broken rib, but the punch actually landed on a kidney. When I asked Muhammad about that punch later, he told me that he had blood in his urine for days after the fight. A lot of observers thought that Norton should have gotten the win, but the judges seemed to feel that the contender didn't do enough in the last round to justify taking the title from the champ. Muhammad won by unanimous decision. So Muhammad now found himself in a strange position—even as his skills in the ring were diminishing, his fame continued to expand, and the money he was commanding per fight had never been better.

THE THIRD NORTON FIGHT MADE Muhammad almost two and a half million dollars richer (he received a six-million-dollar purse for the fight, minus taxes, management fees, and his standard donation to the Nation of Islam). He had received half of his earnings before the fight, and on a mid-December afternoon, in expectation of the second payment coming through, he was feeling flush and happy.

"Let's go shopping," he said to me.

"What do you want to shop for, Muhammad?" I asked.

"A Rolls-Royce. Where should we go?"

I had never shopped for a Rolls before, but I was enough of a car guy to know that the best place to buy one was at European Imports out in Lake Forest, a suburb about half an hour north of Chicago. So we got into Muhammad's Cadillac and headed north. I thought the purchase of a Rolls-Royce might be a big-enough deal that Muhammad would bring some others along on the shopping trip—perhaps Gene Dibble or Herbert Muhammad. But it was just the two of us. For me it was another of those "big moments" that was significant because it wasn't a big moment. Muhammad Ali wanted to buy a Rolls, and Tim Shanahan was the guy he asked to come with him. No big deal.

As Muhammad drove us north on the expressway, I asked him a question I had been pondering for a while.

"Muhammad, do you think you would have been a great athlete in any other sport?"

"I don't know." He shrugged.

"Well, in football, don't you think you would have been a tremendous wide receiver or tight end?"

"I guess so," he said. "But football never appealed to me."

"Why not?"

He made an expression like I was missing an obvious point. "Because you have to put a helmet on, man. Nobody can see your face. The fans only recognize you by a number. I want people to see *me* when I'm doing what I'm doing. And I want to be in control—me against my opponent. I don't want to depend on anyone else for me to win."

When we got to the car lot, we had the showroom to ourselves for a few minutes, and before long Muhammad had narrowed his choices down to a white Silver Shadow, a black Corniche, and a two-tone, kelly-green Corniche. A salesman explained to us that the green was a one-of-a-kind model, as that color was considered "experimental."

"Which one should I get?" he asked me.

I thought the black car was the best-looking, but I could tell Muhammad wanted to be talked into the green—he seemed to really like the fact that it had a tape deck already installed.

"I know you're liking that white Silver Shadow, Muhammad, but that two-tone Corniche is an eye-catcher. I haven't ever seen a two-tone color like that, especially in green. And after all, kelly green is a color made for a Black Irishman like you."

He took the kelly green.

Before the guy could begin the paperwork, Muhammad told him that he wanted to get "a cute little ladies' car," too—Veronica's birthday was coming up. She had told Muhammad that she was interested in a silver Mercedes 450SL hardtop, but they didn't have any on the lot. The salesman said he could give Muhammad a good deal on an Alfa Romeo Spider, and walked us over to show us the little Italian sports car. Muhammad liked the look of it with the top down, though when he attempted to sit in it he barely fit in the driver's seat. He pulled himself out and asked me to get in. I did, though it was a tight squeeze for me, too. I started up the engine so Muhammad could hear it purr. He liked the car—especially the fact that it was Italian—but he was still thinking he wanted the sporty Mercedes. The salesman told us that the Alfa Romeo's list price was $18,000, but that since Muhammad was also buying the Rolls (for $88,000), he could have the second car for $13,500. Whether the salesman was really giving us that much of a discount or not didn't matter—I would learn that Muhammad was a soft touch whenever a salesman gave him a good pitch. ("They have to make a living, too," he would say.) So our shopping trip was done. Muhammad drove home in his new kelly-green Rolls. I drove the Spider to South Woodlawn, then went back to the lot later with Muhammad's private chauffeur, Harold Hazzard, to retrieve the Cadillac.

Muhammad was very happy with his Rolls, but Veronica wasn't as thrilled with the Alfa Romeo. For one thing, it was small for her five-eleven frame. More important, she'd never learned to drive a stick shift.

Muhammad ended up getting her the 450SL, and the Alfa Romeo sat in the driveway, sometimes used by Harold Hazzard to run errands.

MUHAMMAD LOVED HAVING MONEY TO spend, but he was never happy just to spend it on himself. One of the errands I was running for him a couple of times a week was a trip to Western Union during which I would use a pile of his cash to wire money to the growing list of people that asked him for help—ex-wives, friends, associates, and members of his extended family. If they asked, Muhammad sent money, usually hundreds of dollars at a time and sometimes more, and never grumbled about it one bit. In fact, his attitude was "If I have it, why wouldn't I help the people who need it?"

There were times when I thought he was too generous to some of the people around him, but he constantly awed me with the generosity and compassion he could show to complete strangers. Driving around with him, I got used to the sudden stops he would make if he spotted somebody he thought he could help. It might be some old guy sitting on a stoop with a bottle. Muhammad would pull over, get out of the car, walk over to say hello, and then hand the guy a twenty-dollar bill (and, again, if Muhammad ran out of cash in his pockets, it would be my twenty-dollar bill).

On one cold day we were driving around the South Side of Chicago and saw a woman on the side of the road, carrying a small child and walking hand-in-hand with a little girl. It was a very cold day, and right away Muhammad noticed that the small child wasn't wearing shoes and had on just a sweater rather than a winter jacket. This really bothered him. He pulled up alongside the woman and rolled down his window. "Where are the baby's shoes?" he called to her. She seemed so weary and beaten down that she barely registered any surprise at who was speaking to her. And she sounded angry and embarrassed as she admitted that she didn't have shoes for her child because she couldn't afford them.

"Get in the car," said Muhammad.

We drove them to their home in a run-down two-level flat not too far away. Muhammad carried the older child up the stairs to the second floor. When we stepped inside the woman's apartment, we saw an awful picture of poverty. There was no heat, and the place was a mess. Muhammad opened the refrigerator, which was practically bare except for some juice, some milk, and a couple of Pop-Tarts. The woman told us that the freezer was broken and so was the stove and the oven. There was a pile of dirty laundry in front of a small washer, but there was no dryer. The woman glumly told Muhammad that she was a prostitute and a heroin addict and that her pimp boyfriend had recently left and taken all her money. Muhammad asked me to write down a list of everything the apartment needed and to price it out. I was no expert on appliances, but I figured that $1,200 would cover a refrigerator, stove, floor heater, dryer, and some clothes for the kids. Muhammad didn't always carry cash, but he sometimes traveled with a blank check in his wallet. He took the check out now, wrote it out for $1,500 and asked for the woman's name.

"You better not use this money on drugs or booze," he told her. She now had tears in her eyes. "This is my assistant, Tim Shanahan. He's going to come back here in three weeks and check up on you to make sure you bought all these things you need for your family."

I did make the trip back a few weeks later, and I was very pleasantly surprised to see that she had made all the home improvements on the list. The refrigerator was working, a small washer and dryer stood in the corner, a floor heater was keeping the place warm, and a new stove was scheduled for delivery. Her kids were in new clothes and had two new winter jackets. She had a new warm sweater for herself. She had spent her last bit of the money on a sweater that she wanted to give to Muhammad as a Christmas gift. She told me that she knew Muhammad had been sent by God to help her, and that she would never do drugs again.

I don't know if she followed through on that promise. I do know that when I told Muhammad what she said and presented him with the sweater, he said, "That makes *me* wanna cry."

• • • •

I TRULY DIDN'T WANT ANYTHING from Muhammad but his friendship, but sometimes it was impossible to escape his generosity. A week or so after Muhammad's Rolls-Royce shopping trip, Helga and I went car shopping for ourselves and bought a '76 black Cadillac Seville with black leather interior. We loved the car and so did Muhammad (the first time he asked to drive it, he got it up to 100 on the freeway). But we had it for only three months before it was stolen from our condo's underground garage. Instead of having a great new ride, we were dealing with insurance papers and looking at eating a $10,000 loss. I didn't say anything about the theft to Muhammad, but he picked up on it.

"What happened to your new car?" he asked.

When I explained, he simply handed me the keys to the Alfa Romeo and told me to drive that until we got a new car. So Helga and I started driving the Spider. And by the time we got our own new car, Muhammad didn't want the Spider back. In truth, it was not a very practical car and, given Chicago weather, we didn't often have the chance to put the convertible top down. But that little Alfa Romeo still ranks as one of our most cherished possessions.

THERE WERE LIMITS TO MUHAMMAD'S generosity. One night I was sitting with him in the South Woodlawn dining room. We had just finished dinner and were talking about nothing of much importance. The doorbell rang, and the houselady let in an unexpected visitor. It was a black guy about sixty years old, wearing dirty overalls and looking pretty ragged and down on his luck. He stood before us and took off his hat, looking very humble. Muhammad motioned for him to come take a seat with us, and almost as soon as he did, he started crying.

"Muhammad," he said, "I own the gas station on the corner of Halsted. You come in all the time to get gas."

"Yeah. OK," said Muhammad. "What's going on?"

"They're going to evict me," the man said between sobs. "I can't pay my bills. I need some money quick or I'll lose everything."

Right away, Muhammad reached in his back pocket, pulled out his wallet, and opened it up.

"OK, OK, take it easy now. How much do you need, man?" he asked.

"Ninety-three thousand dollars," said the old guy.

I don't think I've ever seen Muhammad's eyes go as wide as they did at that moment.

"Ninety-three thousand! Oh, maaaan. I can't give you ninety-three thousand dollars. Are you crazy?"

"That's what I owe, Muhammad."

"That gas station ain't worth ninety-three thousand. How did you get into so much debt?"

"I don't know how it happened," the guy said, crying quietly.

"Well, I can't give you that kind of money," said Muhammad. "I've got my own family to take care of. I've got family all over the country."

The guy stopped sniffling for a moment. "Well, can you give me half?" he asked.

Muhammad ended up giving him all the cash he had—probably a couple of hundred dollars—and wished him well as he walked him to the door. The old guy still had a long way to go to get his debts paid off, but he couldn't thank Muhammad enough for the time and generosity the Champ had extended to him.

THE HOLIDAY SEASON SOMETIMES BROUGHT out the playful side of Muhammad. On several occasions I would be sitting with him at home when he would say, "Let's call somebody." He would pick up the phone and dial any random seven- or ten-digit number. When he got an answer, he would say, "Merry Christmas! This is Muhammad Ali—the heavyweight champion of the world! Who am I talking to?"

Quite often, the recipient of the call understandably assumed this was a prank and would hang up. In those cases, Muhammad would stare at the phone in disbelief and say, "They were talking to Muhammad Ali and they didn't even know it!"

Occasionally, though, people would talk to him. Muhammad had some very interesting impromptu conversations over the years, and a few times those calls ended with Muhammad handing me the phone and telling me to get the address of the person on the other end so that he could send them a check for Christmas.

ONE MORNING, ON OUR WAY to the Southside Gym for a workout, Muhammad decided to stop at an elementary school we often drove past. He said he knew the principal of the school, a Mrs. Stone, and wanted to say hello to her. She was thrilled to see Muhammad stroll into her office and gave him a big hug, congratulating him on his win in the Norton fight. When Muhammad asked if he could surprise some kids, Mrs. Stone said, "Let's go into Miss Parker's fourth-grade class. She's a big fan of yours."

We walked down a hallway to the classroom, and Muhammad peeked through the glass in the door, watching the lesson in progress for a moment. Then he rushed into the room.

"Look who's here!" he announced to the startled Miss Parker and her students. "Muhammad Ali, the heavyweight champion of the world, has come to see you kids today!"

Miss Parker's lesson was immediately jettisoned as she jumped up and gave Muhammad a big hug. She gave the signal that it was OK for the students to leave their seats, and suddenly twenty little nine-year-olds let out a roar, rushed out of their desks to gather around Muhammad Ali, and started going crazy. Muhammad scooped up one little girl and gave her a kiss.

"Did you see me beat Ken Norton on TV?" he asked. She nodded her head yes, and Muhammad gave her another kiss.

All of Miss Parker's fourth graders were circling Muhammad, climbing on him, or just jumping up and down and screaming, "Ali!

Ali!" Everyone, that is, except for one little girl in the back of the room who stayed at her desk. She did not look happy.

Muhammad called out to her, "Don't you know who I am, little girl? Why don't you come up here?"

"She's not allowed to, Muhammad," said Miss Parker. "She's been a bad girl today and she's been told to stay in her seat until class is over."

Muhammad untangled himself from the kids climbing on him and walked to the back of the classroom. He settled his big frame on a tiny desk right next to the girl and bent over her.

"What's your name?" he asked her.

Silence. She wouldn't answer him. She just kept her chin buried in her hands and stared down sullenly at her desktop.

"Her name is Drucilla," said Miss Parker.

"Drucilla, don't you know who I am? I hear you've been having a bad day, but aren't you excited to see Muhammad Ali? I'm the heavyweight champion of the world and I came here today just to see you."

Drucilla didn't move her head an inch, but her eyes shot in Muhammad's direction. She said, "Aww, man, you're just another nigga tryin' to get bigga."

Muhammad laughed so hard that he fell off the desk and lay on his back with his arm over his forehead. The rest of the class took the cue to go even crazier and started climbing on him again.

When Muhammad finally caught his breath, he sat up and spoke to the little girl again. "Drucilla—where did you hear that? Did your daddy tell you that? Come on—you couldn't have made that up yourself! Maaan—tell me your daddy told you that."

Drucilla kept her chin in her hands and didn't say another word, but you could tell now that she was smiling just a little bit. Muhammad stood up, then lifted the little girl out of her seat. She resisted at first but he lifted her over his head, then cradled her in his arms and began playfully giving her kisses on the cheek. Drucilla, who had been having a very bad day, was now giggling and fully enjoying the attention of the heavyweight champion of the world.

•　　•　　•

MUHAMMAD HAD A SEVEN-MONTH LAYOFF between his battle with Ken Norton and his next match—a May 1977 fight that put him in the ring with another of his less-talented opponents, the Spanish heavyweight Alfredo Evangelista. During that time off, he seemed to enjoy domestic life with Veronica and baby Hana. He and Veronica and Helga and I would occasionally double-date and go to the movies or to a concert, but just as often there were nights in, when we would simply enjoy one another's company in front of a blazing fireplace. We were friends as couples, but Helga had her own relationship with Muhammad, and I had a real friendship with Veronica. Veronica told Muhammad that she liked having us around because we were the only "young people" in his life. In terms of age, we might not have been that much younger than the people around Muhammad, but in terms of spirit, she had a point. Muhammad even became more relaxed about my holding Hana, and

Helga's thirty-seventh birthday. She celebrated by cooking dinner for Muhammad and Veronica and baking her own cake.

there were many nights when I could not imagine anything more fun than crawling around on the floor of Muhammad's living room with that sweet little girl. Helga and I didn't have children, but for us Hana was the next best thing.

Toward the end of January, I got a phone call from Muhammad (I still called him a lot more often than he called me, so when he did call I always knew it was about something he considered important). The country had been riveted to its TV screens all week watching the groundbreaking miniseries *Roots*, and the big final episode was coming up on Sunday.

"Shanahan—you have to come over and watch the finale," Muhammad said. "We're going to have a big family dinner and then we'll start a fire. I'll move a TV next to the fireplace so we can watch it there after we eat. Can Helga cook dinner for us?"

"Sure—what do you want to eat?"

"Her schnitzel, garlic mashed potatoes, and peas and corn," was the answer.

Helga was always happy to cook for Muhammad and Veronica, and she had done this a few times by now, including a feast she had prepared for Veronica's birthday dinner. And by this point, we didn't have to bring our own pots, as Veronica had really transformed the South Woodlawn house into a beautiful home, using her eye for design in everything from the curtains to the carved wood dining room pieces to the white grand piano she set in the living room for Muhammad (he knew how to play a few simple chords, and boy, did he love to pound them out).

We had a wonderful night lounging in front of the fire and watching the story of Kunta Kinte and Chicken George come to its conclusion. Muhammad really liked the fact that the miniseries was based on the book by Alex Haley, who had done one of the first great interviews with Muhammad back in 1964, after the Liston fight, for *Playboy*. I was well over the shock of being welcome in Muhammad's home and never gave a second thought to why he might call us together, but looking back I suppose it might strike some people as odd that a black superstar athlete—a man giving a share of his income to the Nation of Islam—would invite a pair of white friends into his home to watch, of all things, *Roots* (then again, those white friends were bringing him his favorite chocolate cake). To me, it just underscores my long-held feeling that Muhammad has the biggest heart and most loving spirit of anyone I've ever met. He saw us as family, and race or skin color was not going to get in the way of a family night.

MUHAMMAD AND I HAD A slightly less positive experience in front of a TV a couple of weeks later. He was a huge fan of monster movies, and had a real fondness for mummy and vampire movies. He asked me what I thought was the scariest movie ever made. My answer was *The Exorcist*. I had seen it in a second-run movie house not long after my move to Chicago. I went to that movie with Walter Payton—the young Chicago Bears running back who I had also met through Athletes for a Better Education. Big, strong Walter told me he couldn't sleep at all after seeing the movie. Neither could I. Helga was out of town at the time, and as I lay alone in bed on that rainy, windy night, the branches of the big tree outside our bedroom kept scratching against the window glass and throwing creepy shadows across the room.

Muhammad was fascinated that a movie could be so scary, and not too long after I told him about the film, I got another of those rare Muhammad calls: "I've got *The Exorcist*. Come on over."

Muhammad had some new Hollywood connections through his participation in *The Greatest*, a dramatized film about his life in which he had starred as himself. He had called one of those connections, worked his magic, and had a copy of *The Exorcist* delivered to him. We made plans to watch it together on the big screen in his third-floor rec room.

Up to this point, the scariest thing I had watched with Muhammad was *Abbott and Costello Meet the Mummy*. For that film, Muhammad had fun talking back to the screen, mimicking some of the lines and laughing when the monsters showed up. For *The Exorcist*, he sat wide-eyed on the edge of the sofa, not making a sound. Not making a sound, that is, until anything scary happened on screen. Then he would jump back in his seat and yell, "Uhhhh!" or make a noise like he was strangling back a scream. Sometimes his noises and jumps startled me even more than what was happening in the movie. And after every scary, shocking moment had passed Muhammad would lean to me and ask, "Did that scare you? Did that scare you?" My answer almost every time was "Hell, yes!" to which he'd let loose a laugh and then focus on the screen again.

When it was over, we sat in silence for a moment and then he asked me again, "Were you scared?"

"Were you?" I asked in return.

"Yeaahhhhh," he said. "You were right. That's the scariest movie I ever saw. You know why?"

"Why, Muhammad?"

"Because it was real," he said. "That wasn't ghosts and gimmicks. When you've got the devil as a monster, it's real."

Once I made it home and got into bed, I tried desperately to remind myself that demons were not any more real than vampires and werewolves and mummies. It was a losing battle. I had cut down those scary branches outside the window, but I still couldn't sleep.

The next morning, Muhammad called once more: "Come on over. We're going to watch it again."

I really did not have any great desire to see that poor little girl's head rotate another 360 degrees, but I got in the car and headed over. When I arrived at the house, the door was open so I walked right upstairs to the rec room. There was Muhammad sitting in a chair near the couch. On the couch were two new viewers, the Williams brothers, ages nine and eleven. They were the sons of Muhammad's next-door neighbors, Tom and Mary Williams, and he had invited them over to watch a scary movie with him. The movie had just started, and Muhammad glanced in my direction.

"Shanahan—sit down and have some popcorn and be quiet."

I sat in a chair off to the side and, though I tried to focus more on Muhammad and the boys than on the screen, I still got as deeply involved with the movie as I had the first two times. When it was over, the boys didn't seem to react too much. They agreed with Muhammad that it was scary, said thank you for the special invitation to watch a movie with him. The next day, Muhammad called me yet again.

"What's up?"

"Mrs. Williams just called me," he said.

"What did she say?"

"She said the boys had nightmares all night long. She didn't know the movie was going to be that disturbing, and she hopes the boys aren't going to have psychological problems from it. I told her I was sorry. I just thought the boys would like watching a scary movie with me."

He sounded hurt. He had wanted to do something special for these young neighbors, and it had backfired. It probably would have been clear to most people that those boys were a little too young for *The Exorcist*, but to Muhammad's way of thinking he had gotten hold of something special and all he wanted to do was share it.

I happened to see Mrs. Williams just a few years ago. She told me that the boys, now grown men, considered that day with Muhammad to be one of the most memorable days of their lives. But she also told me, "My sons are in their forties and they're still having nightmares about that movie."

WHEN MUHAMMAD WAS OUT OF town, I sometimes worked out with Walter Payton. When I first met Walter through the Athletes for a Better Education charity, he was a phenomenal, record-setting player for Jackson State who'd become a first-round draft pick for the Bears. Coming to Chicago from Columbia, Mississippi, and suddenly being in the national spotlight was a lot for a young guy like Walter to adjust to. Despite the attention he was getting, he felt very much alone, especially as he was now apart from Connie Norwood, his college sweetheart. Helga and I became friendly faces to him, offering him both home-cooked meals and some guidance in adjusting to the big city.

During spring and summer—football off-season—Walter and I would sometimes run together. One of our favorite spots was a huge construction site where work was being done on the 90 freeway extension west to Elgin. There was a hundred-foot pile of dirt that sat there for months, and we worked up a regimen in which we did sprints around the pile and then ended by running to the top of it and back down ten times in a row, taking a short break after each round trip. Walter was built for short, fast, powerful runs—if you look at his career stats there aren't a lot of 60- and 70-yard breakaway plays. He was a full-contact runner who earned his reputation running through defenders rather than by outrunning them, and he always did seem a little self-conscious that the faster defensive backs could run him down. In our runs, I could equal him in the 40- and 100-yard dash and I could beat him up the dirt mountain (he hated that and warned me, only half-jokingly, not to tell anyone).

He didn't have to worry about competition from me. I had speed, but next to him, or Ali for that matter, I was a six-foot-one, 180-pound weakling. Sometimes Walter would ask me to rush at him, and he could keep me away with one hand, no problem. I couldn't touch him. Though he made his living primarily with the strength of his legs, anyone who ever saw him stiff-arm a linebacker on a run up the middle knows how powerful his arms and hands were. Walter could bench press 300 pounds, but as big and powerful as Walter was, he was acrobatic, as well, able to make a 360 flip in the air off a running jump. Once, when I saw him do a handstand on a practice field and told him I was impressed, he proceeded to flip himself back up in the air and walk on his hands for 60 yards. He truly was a physical wonder.

Walter told me that he got his nickname, "Sweetness," after a high school game in which he cut around a defensive back to score a touchdown and a teammate congratulated him by saying, "That was a sweet move." Walter was an athlete with astonishing size, speed, strength, and agility, like Muhammad. But in character, he was very different from Ali. While Muhammad was comfortable being Muhammad no matter how big a spotlight was on him, Walter had a tough time living up to the image that the media had painted of him as "the small-town sports hero who became the NFL's humble superstar." He really was shy and a bit insecure in the public limelight, and he could also be moody. While Muhammad wanted everyone around him to be happy, Walter didn't seem to really consider how he affected the people around him, as long as he did his job as a running back and kept the Bears fans happy. Muhammad wanted to make everyone's encounter with him a positive, memorable one. Walter didn't mind leaving people disappointed at times.

Without a doubt one of the best things Walter had going for him was Connie, one of the sweetest people I've ever met and still one of our dearest friends. She finished school at Jackson State during Walter's rookie year with the Bears, and once they married, the couple moved to Arlington Heights, just a few miles from the Rolling Meadows suburb where Helga and I lived. Walter was a tough character, and if Connie had trouble keeping him in line, Helga was always ready to supply some tough love. We had Walter and Connie over for my birthday in the summer of 1977. Helga made another one of her great dinners and baked a special cake. The evening started off wonderfully, with talk of training camp, some joking around, and a mutual admiration for the Chaka Khan records we were playing. But when we sat down to eat, Walter said he had to get something he had left in his car. He came back with a little portable TV and told us that there was a show he wanted to watch while we ate. Helga told him that was not permissible, and he reluctantly put the little TV under the table. We had a fine meal of Helga's seafood pasta, but when Helga and I cleared the dishes and got ready to serve the cake, from the kitchen we could hear a laugh track in the dining room. We stepped back out to see that Walter had turned the TV on and was watching his show.

Elite athletes are used to getting away with a lot, but not at Helga's dinner table. She was willing to cook for Walter and to wait on him, but there were some lines that couldn't be crossed. She gave him a very stern lecture on the manners of dinner guests, and on the value of respect. The star running back was not happy about following Helga's rules, but he listened quietly without a word of protest. And the next time we had Walter and Connie over for dinner, he did not have a TV with him.

A LOVE OF MUSIC WAS one of the things that Muhammad and I first bonded over, and during the years we were in Chicago, one of our favorite nights out was to go see a show at the Mill Run Playhouse in Niles, Illinois, about a thirty-five-minute drive from Muhammad's place. It was a great place to see national acts—an intimate theater in the round with a revolving stage. And it was set up so that there was easy side-door access for Muhammad—he always like to get to a seat after a show had started and leave before it ended so as not to draw any of the crowd's attention away from the people on stage. Not long after I met Muhammad—and heard what he liked to play on his car radio and cassette deck—I noticed that Eddie Kendricks was appearing at the Mill Run. I got in touch with the manager of the theater (a guy I eventually got to know quite well) and we made arrangements for Muhammad and me to attend. I left a message for Eddie with Ali's private number, and by the time I picked up Muhammad to take him to the show, Eddie had already called him to invite us backstage afterward (where we got to meet Pops and Mavis Staples). Then I noticed that Tony Orlando—the first of Muhammad's "million best friends" that I had spoken to—was appearing at the Mill Run, so we went to that show, too. We ended up backstage again with Tony and Dawn (Telma Hopkins and Joyce Vincent Wilson, Tony's beautiful backup singers), and were then invited back to the group's hotel suite for food and drinks.

Over the course of four years, Muhammad and I—frequently with Veronica and Helga—saw and spent time with some incredible talents: Dionne Warwick, Diana Ross, Lola Falana, Donna Summer, the Spinners, Lou Rawls. When we went to see the Chi-Lites, the group's lead singer, Eugene Record, who lived in Muhammad's neighborhood, showed up at South Woodlawn the next day and Muhammad put me on the spot by having me sing the group's big hit "Have You Seen Her" to Eugene. (Of course I was nervous, but I managed to make it through the "rapping" into and the first verse, after which Eugene jokingly invited me to come on tour with the band.) The only unpleasant moment I remember from all those Mill Run nights was when we went to see Bill Cosby. Cosby did a great set of stand-up comedy, but when I went to his dressing room with Muhammad and Veronica and was introduced to him, he barely acknowledged me. He was talking with Muhammad and Veronica and suddenly said to them, "Why do you need people like him hanging around you—you don't need hangers-on following you around wherever you go."

Veronica spoke up first and said, "Tim is not a hanger-on, he and his wife, Helga, are friends of both Muhammad and I."

Muhammad, usually so easygoing, now looked annoyed. "I don't *need* him with me," he said to Cosby. "I *want* him with me." Muhammad usually let people express all kinds of opinions around him without ever turning a conversation into a confrontation. This time, he proceeded to tell Cosby that he didn't like people telling him how to run his life, or who to spend his time with. Cosby got the point. When Veronica changed the subject, the tense situation eventually became a little more relaxed—though Cosby never did introduce himself to me or say a single word to me directly.

WHEN MUHAMMAD GRUDGINGLY BEGAN TRAINING for his Evangelista fight, I joined him for a few more morning runs around the park. After a run in which we pushed a little harder than usual, we lay on the grass and stared up at a cloudy sky.

Muhammad said, "To be a great champion, you must believe that you are the best."

I processed this for a moment, then sat up to take a sip of water from a paper cup.

"But what if you don't believe that?" I asked.

He paused until the cup came to my lips and said, "Then fake it." He loved the fact that he got me to do a spit-take.

A couple of days later, after a Saturday morning run, I came up with some words of wisdom of my own. Muhammad started talking about all he had done to help and inspire black people around the world. When he finished, I said, "Muhammad—you won the race on race."

He laughed and said once again, "You ain't as dumb as you look."

MUHAMMAD WAS STILL A MAGNIFICENT athlete and a great champion. But, especially after the punishment of the third Norton fight, every so often I thought I detected that all those rounds in the ring had taken their toll, and I began to wonder how long Muhammad would continue to fight. After his third Frazier fight, Muhammad had occasionally talked to the press about retiring, but it usually sounded like something that was off in the future, a few more big fights away.

He had always moved so gracefully in and out of the ring, but once or twice now I had seen an odd shuffle in his step. Nothing dramatic— just a slight misstep as if perhaps he'd caught his foot on the edge of a rug. And once or twice I'd heard his voice dip into a guttural slur. He worked hard and had trouble getting enough sleep—it was easy to think he might just be overtired at times. But when you added up all the punches that had landed on him, especially since his return to the ring and his adopting the self-punishing rope-a-dope tactic (which he was using now even with sparring partners), it seemed like he was getting close to the limits of what a healthy body could withstand. I knew that his hands were often in terrible pain now—the Thrilla in Manila was almost canceled because Muhammad's hands were so sore. Ferdie Pacheco had suggested some surgical treatments that might help heal Muhammad's hands, but Muhammad thought the healing process would take too much time. Instead, he was now taking cortisone shots in his hands just to be able to throw punches. It was a terrible shame that he had had nearly four of what would have been his finest years taken away from him when he was banned from boxing between 1967 and

1970 (as Angelo put it, "We were robbed of seeing the eighth wonder of the world—Ali at his best."). But Muhammad was thirty-five years old now and there was no way to get those missing years back. Everybody who loved him wanted him to start thinking of a future beyond boxing.

I HAD GOTTEN CLOSE ENOUGH to Angelo Dundee that he offered to pick me up at Allentown airport when I flew in to spend a few days at Deer Lake before the Evangelista fight. I had heard that for the last few camps, Angelo was there only for the last couple of weeks before a fight. As we drove, I asked him why he limited his training time with Muhammad that way.

"I don't enjoy being there as much as I used to," he said. "Ali needs his people around him and that's OK—they take up the slack while I am not there. I've had the very best times of my life with Muhammad, but now those days are over. I am hoping that these next fights are the last fights of his career. Nobody wants to see Muhammad get hurt trying to prove something that has already been proven. But if he decides to keep on fighting, I will be there for him." It was a touching testimony to Angelo's love for Muhammad.

Angelo continued, "I could tell right away you weren't one of those guys. I asked Muhammad about you, and he told Jimmy Ellis and me that he trusted you as much as he trusted his brother. That was good enough for me."

Good enough for me, too.

THE ATMOSPHERE AT DEER LAKE was even more sour than usual this time around. Muhammad was not taking his training very seriously, and his "people" had nothing nice to say about a big change that was coming in Muhammad's family status: he and Veronica were going to get married. I heard a couple of the guys bad-mouthing Veronica, and one time, when I spoke up in her defense, I ended up in a confrontation that would have turned into a fistfight if Jimmy Ellis hadn't stepped in to calm things down.

The more time I spent at Deer Lake, the more I knew that I really wanted to maintain only the "Chicago friendship" I had with Muhammad. I didn't enjoy the "fight" side of his life and didn't like what I saw around me at camp. Some of the camp hands would pass out flyers inviting people to come watch Muhammad train. Then they'd charge the people that showed up five dollars each, and insist that visitors also had to buy an Ali T-shirt they'd had printed up, or a hat or coffee mug. None of that cash made it to Muhammad—it went straight into the pockets of his "training staff." Muhammad knew about it and let it happen. The guys knew that Muhammad knew, and instead of feeling any shame, they just continued to take advantage of their position with him.

Apparently some of those guys expressed their own negative feelings about me to Muhammad, because one night when he and I were in the main cabin, Muhammad said, "Last night Kilroy and Wells were talking bad about you."

"Oh, really?" I knew Muhammad was jabbing me to see how I would react.

"Yeah," Muhammad continued. "They said you were only after my money. You're going to get me into bad business deals. I shouldn't trust you. You're not good for me."

I knew that Muhammad was well aware that this kind of talk came out of jealousy and insecurity. He knew the others didn't like that I was getting close with him. But he wanted to see how I'd respond to the charges.

Frankly, those guys weren't worth much of a reaction. "I know what you're trying to do, Muhammad," I said. "You're trying to get me riled up to see if you can start a fight! But, wise master, it won't work. I'm way ahead of you, you devil!"

He laughed. That was the end of that discussion.

I was back home in Chicago when Muhammad fought Evangelista in Landover, Maryland. The fight added another win to Muhammad's record, but it wasn't much of a win. Yes, in so many ways Muhammad was still a great champion. But in that fight, he seemed to be "faking it."

• • •

MUHAMMAD AND VERONICA'S WEDDING TOOK place in June in Los Angeles, where Veronica had been raised and where her parents still lived. The ceremony and reception were held at the Beverly Wilshire Hotel, and I was with Muhammad in the lobby when we encountered the man whom Muhammad considered "the greatest movie star of all time": Christopher Lee, star of so many of Muhammad's favorite Dracula movies and horror films. I hadn't realized Christopher was invited—he was one of just a few celebrities who were. Veronica wanted to keep the wedding small and intimate, with less Hollywood star power (though Warren Beatty was there, too).

By heavyweight champion standards, the event was elegant and understated. Muhammad and Veronica had already been living together for more than a year, Hana was nine months old, and Veronica was three months pregnant with a second child (Laila, who was born in December), so the fact that Muhammad and Veronica were starting a life together was not big news. I had the feeling Muhammad would have been content just signing papers at the courthouse in downtown Chicago, but he knew that his bride and his mother-in-law, Ethel Porche, had their hearts set on a "beautiful" event. So Veronica supervised every detail with her usual tasteful eye, and it really was a fine celebration. I know Muhammad was not so excited about dressing up in a white tux and tails (with white gloves!), but Helga and I agreed that we had never seen a more attractive couple than the new Mr. and Mrs. Muhammad Ali.

BACK IN CHICAGO, LIFE RESUMED its day-to-day rhythms. I was spending a few mornings a week in operating rooms, and often put in long hours training nursing staffs on new equipment. Helga was still busy doing expert restoration work at the Art Institute of Chicago. There were some more nights out at the Mill Run Playhouse, and a few more couples' dinners. Muhammad and I went for a few early morning runs, and Helga and Veronica went on shopping trips. Muhammad's next fight was scheduled for September, and it was going to be a tough one. He would be

facing Earnie Shavers—a big, brawny fighter who, after George Foreman, was considered the hardest puncher in boxing. There would be no
"faking it" this time—Muhammad was going to have to train hard and
fight harder.

One overcast afternoon, Muhammad and I were driving along
Lake Shore Drive in his kelly-green Rolls, with the radio on. I had just
purchased a new cassette of Curtis Mayfield's greatest hits, and I told
Muhammad that even though he knew Curtis's songs, if he listened
to all his hits in succession it would prove that Curtis was one of the
greatest songwriters of all time. Muhammad laughed and said, "Play it."
So, as we headed north along Lake Michigan, we listened to "People
Get Ready" and "Gypsy Woman" and "It's All Right" and all the great
Mayfield hits. I sang along with the songs, and we talked a little in
between them. When the tape ended, we continued driving in silence,
just listening to the hum of the traffic. After a while, Muhammad spoke.

"You know that you are good friends when you can sit in a car and
drive together for a long time and you don't have to say anything."

I let his words sink in, but didn't respond. Nothing more needed
to be said.

SEVEN

SIGNATURE MOVES

MUHAMMAD AND VERONICA WERE ON their way to Hong Kong. Muhammad had been invited to help celebrate the opening of a new casino on the island of Macau with an elite group of VIPs: Cary Grant, Gregory Peck, Kirk Douglas, and Telly Savalas (this was June 1977, when *Kojak* was one of the hottest shows on TV). I had just driven Muhammad and Veronica to O'Hare Airport to catch a flight to San Francisco, where they would meet up with the others and fly in a private jet to Hong Kong. Muhammad had asked if Helga and I wanted to come along on the trip, and it was a tempting offer. It would be a remarkable adventure to share with him. But I had no intention of making that group of VIPs uncomfortable by having us show up as Muhammad's guests. So I told Muhammad that while it was one of the best invitations we had ever received, work obligations forced me to respectfully decline.

Since I was staying behind, Muhammad asked me to stop by the South Woodlawn house when I had free time so I could answer the phones—this was in the days before answering machines, and Muhammad never took the time to hire a temporary answering service. He wanted me to take messages and leave word for him at the hotel in

Macau if anything important came up. I had just come back from the airport when the phone rang.

"Ali residence," I answered.

"Is Mr. Ali in?" asked a voice with a Southern lilt.

"You just missed him. He's at the airport on his way to Hong Kong. Who is this?"

"This is Elvis Presley's residence calling," the voice said. "I'm with Elvis right now and he'd love to talk to Mr. Ali but I guess that's not possible. Do you know where Mr. Ali will be staying in Hong Kong?"

The call seemed legit, and I loved the idea that Elvis might be right there next to the person I was talking to, but there really wasn't any way to know who was on the other end of the line (though whoever it was did have Ali's private number). If the call really was coming from Graceland, I certainly wasn't going to stand in the way of Elvis and Muhammad speaking to each other. I gave the caller the name of Muhammad's hotel and the phone number there. I explained that when Muhammad traveled by himself he almost always registered at hotels under his own name. But since he was now with a group of celebrities who might want to keep things quieter, he might be registered under his preferred alias, "Billy Boyd" (Boyd was his ex-wife Belinda's maiden name). The caller thanked me, and that was that.

A couple of weeks later, when Muhammad and Veronica got back home, the first thing I asked him was "Did Elvis call you?"

Muhammad looked at me. "What?"

"Did Elvis Presley call you in Hong Kong?"

"Noooo—"

I told Muhammad about the call I had received at his house, and Muhammad's eyes lit up. "You know, they did tell me I had a message at the hotel, but I never picked it up. I figured if it was somebody I knew, they would call back."

"I think that was Elvis," I said.

"Hmmm. Elvis Presley wants to talk to Muhammad Ali. I like that. I'm going to have to give Elvis a call."

"You have his number in your black book," I said. "Why don't you call him now?" I was selfishly hoping I might get to hear Muhammad's side of the conversation.

"Nah, not now," he said.

Even for Elvis, Muhammad was not the kind of person to worry about returning calls promptly. And he never wanted to make a call until he had a chance to think about what he wanted to say. He would call when he felt ready.

IN PREPARATION FOR THE SHAVERS fight, Muhammad decided to work out at his Berrien Springs property before opening camp in Deer Lake. So, in early August, I found myself in that two-tone kelly-green Rolls-Royce Corniche with Muhammad and Jimmy Ellis, barreling east on the Indiana toll road. Muhammad always wanted to floor the accelerator when the freeway was clear, and had gotten the Rolls up to 125 miles an hour once before. The road was clear now, and Muhammad started to gun the engine. Even with him at the wheel, I didn't feel safe being in a car going that fast, and I asked him if he would at least keep it under 100 mph.

Just as he was starting to slow down a bit, he spotted lights flashing in the rearview mirror.

"The heat is behind us," he said. "Be cool. Let me do the talking."

Muhammad pulled off to the side of the road, and we waited for the trooper to approach. I think Jimmy and I were a little surprised when we saw that the officer was black. The officer was even more surprised to see who he had just pulled over.

"How you doin', Champ?" he said with a smile. "I can't believe I just stopped Muhammad Ali."

"Hey, brother." Muhammad stuck out his hand to shake the officer's hand.

"This is a sharp car, Champ. I love the color. It looks like the kind of car that you would expect Muhammad Ali to drive."

"The heavyweight champion of the world's car."

"Well, Champ, do you know how fast you were going?"

"No, Officer. This car has such a smooth ride. Was I speeding?" he asked with a sly grin.

"I could barely catch up with you. I clocked you at over one hundred ten."

"Oh, maaan," said Muhammad. "This car has such a fine, smooth ride. It felt like we were doing sixty, didn't it, Tim?"

"Well—maybe seventy," I lied.

"I'm very sorry, Officer. I'll slow down. I'll be more careful. You're not going to give me a ticket, are you?"

"All right, Champ," the officer said. "But don't make me pull you over again."

"I won't."

"And if *you* don't mind—could I get an autograph for my son?"

"Give me that ticket book."

The trooper handed over the book he was holding and Muhammad wrote right across the cover of it, "Your dad is the Greatest. Peace, Muhammad Ali."

"How old is your son?" asked Muhammad.

"He's eight, and a big fan of yours."

"Well, you give him this and you tell him I said his dad's the Greatest. I wrote it, but you tell him I said it, too, and when he is eighteen years old he'll look back on this day and he'll tell all of his friends that Muhammad Ali thinks that his dad is the Greatest."

"I will. Thanks, Champ."

That was probably the sweetest ending possible to a speeding stop. But Muhammad wasn't done. He wanted to share with the officer his favorite joke, one I had heard him tell a number of times.

"This guy is speeding in a Rolls-Royce just like me," he began. "Cop stops him, just like you did. The cop says, 'Man—my police cruiser has a souped-up four-hundred-horsepower engine and I could barely catch you. What have you got under the hood?' Guy says, 'I'll show you.' Gets out of the car. Pops the hood. The cop looks in—and guess what he sees . . ."

"What?'" asked the trooper.

"Eight brothas in sneakers," said Muhammad.

The trooper burst out laughing and said, "That's good!"

I thought to myself, Muhammad Ali is the only person in the world who can tell that joke to a black police officer and not get arrested.

We had driven just a little farther when I asked Muhammad, "Why eight?"

"What?"

"Why eight brothas under the hood?"

"One for each cylinder, man," he said. "You can't go that fast with just six brothas."

MUHAMMAD WAS IN DEER LAKE when the world heard the news: Elvis was dead, just forty-two years old. Helga and I had gone to see Elvis in concert in October 1976 at the Chicago Stadium, and the first thing Helga said when he took the stage was "He doesn't look healthy." He was pale and out of shape, and seemed to be bothered a great deal by the stage lights. He still had his voice, though, and even in a big town like Chicago, an Elvis concert still felt like a must-see event. I had worried then about Elvis—some of the same worry I was starting to have about Muhammad: How far could a human being push himself trying to live up to a superhuman image? Now, with Elvis gone much too soon, I just felt an awful wave of sadness. As soon as I could I called the camp and spoke with Muhammad. I'd never heard him sound so down.

"I should have called him," he said. "He had some reason for calling me, and I should have called him."

I could tell the death was hitting him hard, but I wasn't sure how much he wanted to talk about it.

"I'm sorry you lost a friend, Muhammad," I said. "You lost someone you loved and admired. And I know it doesn't make it easier, but there are millions of people around the world who are feeling this loss, too."

Muhammad spoke quietly. "When I was fifteen years old and saw Elvis on TV, I wanted to be Elvis. Other kids in the neighborhood were listening to Ray Charles and James Brown, but I listened to Elvis. I admired him so much and I decided that if I was going to be famous I'd do it just like him. He's one of the reasons I wanted to entertain people and be loved by the people and make the girls admire me so much. I always wanted Elvis to drive me down Beale Street in a convertible, so his hometown could see that Muhammad Ali and Elvis Presley were great friends. Then I'd bring him to Louisville and do the same thing. I'm sorry I couldn't help him."

He paused a moment, then said, almost in a whisper, "I feel like I did when Sam Cooke died." He couldn't say any more than that.

We had talked about Sam before. I knew he had become a close friend of Muhammad's in the early 1960s and had been very interested in Muhammad's turn to Islam. They spent a lot of time together in 1963 and 1964, and Muhammad always said he was with Sam in '64 when the singer signed a recording contract that made him one of the highest-paid entertainers of the day, and one of the very few black entertainers to control his publishing and business affairs. In December of that year Cooke was shot to death at a cheap Los Angeles motel. He was only thirty-three. Muhammad said he missed his friend every time he heard one of his songs. Now that was going to be true of Elvis, as well.

Muhammad thought very seriously about heading to Memphis for Elvis's funeral, but training camp had just gotten started, and Muhammad didn't want his presence to be any kind of distraction at the service for Elvis. Instead, when I came out to the camp a few weeks later, we held our own sort of services for Elvis. The local TV stations had started showing Elvis movies almost every night. Muhammad and I would watch those in his cabin and talk about Elvis's music, and his life.

One night the movie being shown was *King Creole*. I told Muhammad that when I was eleven years old I took my first bus trip to downtown Milwaukee so I could see Elvis on the big screen. I was so mesmerized by the film that I hid in the bathroom twice to sneak into the later showings. The film had remained my favorite Elvis movie, and now Muhammad and I talked about how impressed we were with Elvis's performance: how natural he was on the screen and how serious he seemed to be about his acting. Watching the movie with Muhammad, I got excited about it all over again. As Elvis made his way to the stage of the New Orleans nightclub to transform from busboy to star in one big, showstopping musical number, I beat the King to the punch:

"If you're looking for trouble, you came to the right place," I sang before Elvis did.

Muhammad seemed to get a kick out of this, so I kept going.

"If you're looking for trouble, just look right in my face . . ."

I got into the groove of the band on stage with Elvis and sang a couple more lines. Muhammad laughed the way he always did when I burst into song. Muhammad and I quieted down and watched the King belt out the rest of the song.

When it was over, Muhammad said, "I should have taken that drive with him."

"You mean in Memphis or Louisville?" I asked.

"No, from Las Vegas to Los Angeles."

"What?"

Muhammad explained that when he had met Elvis in Las Vegas in 1973, before the Bugner fight, Elvis not only presented Muhammad with the famous "People's Choice" custom robe, but also invited Muhammad to drive back with him from Las Vegas to Los Angeles—Elvis was closing out his February run at the Las Vegas Hilton just a week after Muhammad's fight. The ride would be in one of Elvis's custom cars—a specially designed gold-plated Cadillac station wagon. Muhammad agreed to take the ride with Presley, but he then got word from his brother that his mother, Odessa, who suffered from diabetes, had suddenly become very ill. Instead of driving with Elvis, he had to fly back to Louisville.

"Can you imagine Elvis Presley and Muhammad Ali driving along the American highway together?" he asked. "Maaan, that would have been historic."

MUHAMMAD KNEW HE HAD TO be in good shape to take on Earnie Shavers, and he did try to keep a fairly rigorous training schedule at camp. Sometimes when we would run, he would have a few blasts of flatulence (don't forget—I was always running behind him). Sometimes I'd match him blast for blast, and a couple of times we synched our blasts in perfect rhythm with our run—a development that had both of us laughing as we ran. Muhammad was puzzled as to why this was happening—he was dieting to drop some weight and had cut out spicy foods. I pointed out that both of us were eating a lot more salads at this camp, and that the iceberg lettuce and radishes we were filling up on were low in calories but high in fiber, generating gas. He took my mini-lecture on the digestive tract as an opportunity to reuse one of his favorite lines: "White boy, you ain't as dumb as you look."

Muhammad was staying focused on training, and while he was doing that the usual shenanigans were going on around the camp. Muhammad had an expense budget for training, typically around $100,000, but whatever the budget was, somehow every dollar of it was always used up before camp broke. Muhammad didn't care that his training budget was being used by some of his crew to cover personal expenses, like putting up girlfriends in a nearby motel, or charging gas or meals to the account when away from the camp. When the camp went over budget, Muhammad simply covered it out of his pocket.

One day, I was concerned enough to bring this to Muhammad's attention.

"Muhammad, do you know that some of the people here are ripping you off?"

"Whoever took money must have needed it."

It was hard to argue with that, but I did. "Muhammad—these guys around you are taking advantage of you . . ."

"How do you know what they're doing?" he snapped at me. I had never heard Muhammad speak to me in that tone of voice. It shocked me a little that he would respond so angrily to an innocent question.

"You're not runnin' this camp, I am," he continued. "You don't know how we run the camp up here and it is none of your business, so stay out of it. Now, put on the fight tape."

And that was that. The matter was clearly not up for discussion, so I didn't say another word. Lying in bed that night, I realized that though I thought I was trying to help Muhammad, somehow I had overstepped my bounds. That was the way he seemed to see it, anyway. As close as we had become, it was scary to be talked to that way by him. I decided would never "meddle" in Muhammad's affairs again, no matter how frustrated I was with what was going on around him.

THERE WERE SOME NOTABLE VISITORS to the camp while I was there. I got to spend an afternoon with Muhammad and Andy Warhol when the artist came to stay for a couple of days so that he could take photos for a series on famous athletes he was putting together. Warhol was very much in awe of Muhammad, but Muhammad wasn't familiar with Warhol's work and didn't know what to make of him. Muhammad and Veronica had just flown in from London and the jet lag was hitting Muhammad hard. He was not a very cooperative photo subject, and he and Warhol

Muhammad and Andy Warhol at Deer Lake. There
was not a lot of chemistry between the two.

both seemed to be uncomfortable in each other's presence. Warhol was there only about three hours, then drove off in his limo. I don't believe the two ever crossed paths again after that one meeting, though the lithographs Warhol created from those Deer Lake photos still hang in Muhammad's home.

I came back to Deer Lake on a few different weekends, and a couple of times I heard about Muhammad spending time with friends with whom he was a lot more comfortable. Lola Falana was a Deer Lake visitor, looking even more lovely and sexy in person than she did in pictures. She had a great, fun-loving spirit and loved to joke around with Muhammad.

A couple of weeks later, Diana Ross was in camp. She was a long-time friend and supporter of Muhammad's who'd been in tears at his side in the dressing room after the loss to Joe Frazier in 1971. According to Jimmy Ellis, Diana and Muhammad spent a lot of time alone together at Deer Lake.

I knew that Muhammad loved Veronica and loved his family, but that wasn't going to stop him from being Muhammad. Veronica knew that, too. When Muhammad was with Veronica, he was absolutely devoted to her. When he was away, he lived by different rules. As close as I was to both of them, I didn't feel it was my place to interfere.

I SPENT A LOT OF time with Jimmy Ellis at Deer Lake—we both wanted to get away from some of the others as much as possible. Jimmy and I were both average golfers, usually breaking 100, and we enjoyed playing at a course a short drive away from camp. Muhammad had never tried golf before, but something about the way Jimmy and I talked about our games must have intrigued him, because one afternoon when Jimmy asked Muhammad to come along so that we could show him a little bit about the sport, he agreed to join us.

Muhammad was just going to ride along in a cart and watch us and maybe take a few swings. But as Jimmy and I began warming up by hitting some balls on the driving range, Muhammad felt he had already seen enough.

"Golf is boring," he called out to us. "If I were going to play golf, I would make up my own rules to make it more interesting. I would award points for who finishes first. You hit the ball, run after it, hit it again, run after it, and whoever finishes the hole first gets a stroke off his score. That's how you play 'Ali Golf.'"

He came over to us and said he wanted to hit a few balls. I cautioned him that the grass we were on was moist and slippery, and said he would be better off wearing golf shoes or at least tennis shoes rather than the leather-soled combat boots he was wearing. He wasn't interested in changing his shoes, so I teed up a ball for him. He took a huge swing and missed the ball completely. He took another swing and just grazed the ball off the tee. If Jimmy and I were going to teach him the game, we had our work cut out for us.

I told him that the club is like a pendulum in your hands, and that all he needed to do was to bring it straight back and then swing straight through while looking at the ball as he hit it. He did all that at half speed with a good follow-through that impressed me and Jimmy. The ball flew straight down the middle of the range. Pretty good.

He took a few more swings in my suggested pendulum style, slowing down to make solid contact with the ball. He started hitting consistently, sometimes flaring to the right or left but often driving the ball straight for a decent distance.

Muhammad placed another ball on the tee. Then he wound up big and tried to hit the ball even harder than when he had started. He squibbed the ball to the right off the toe of the club, then slipped on the grass with the force of his windmill follow-through. He let out a grunt of pain.

Muhammad limped back to the car with an ankle sprain. He was a little over a month away from a title fight with a ferocious opponent, and now he was going to have to train through an injury for which Jimmy and I felt partly responsible. Muhammad wasn't angry, though. And he didn't tell anybody else at camp why his ankle was bothering him. It was a mild sprain and he knew that the swelling would go down in a couple of days and that he could train through it. In the meantime, he could take it easy for a day.

"SHANAHAN, YOU'RE BUSY WITH THOSE doctors, aren't you?"

"What do you mean, Muhammad?"

"When I want to do something, you always have to check your schedule. Every day you're in surgery, dealing with these important doctors. Smart people." He paused a moment, then said, "No way you would want to work for me."

"I really do love my job."

"You wouldn't work for me?"

I thought about this man I had become so close to. I thought about the people that already worked for him, and what it would mean to become like some of them. It wasn't hard to figure out how to answer Ali.

"Muhammad, I can't tell you how much it means to me to have you ask me that. But, frankly, I don't want to work for you. I'll do anything for you, but I don't need you writing me a paycheck."

"Maan, maan, maan," he said. "That's disappointing. But now I like you even more."

THE SHAVERS FIGHT WOULD BE a fifteen-rounder and was set to take place at Madison Square Garden in New York. A few weeks before the fight, I was sitting with Muhammad and Angelo Dundee when Angelo asked Muhammad what kind of request he should put in for personal tickets. Muhammad said he wanted a block of fifty for private guests. Then he turned to me.

"Tim, you're coming, right?"

He'd never asked me that directly before. I started mumbling something about checking the date with my work schedule.

"Man, you're always working," said Muhammad. "Can you make this fight?"

When he put it that way, there was only one way to answer: "I'll be there."

So, on September 28, 1977, I met up with Muhammad in New York City. I made the trip with another athlete I'd met through my charity work, Wally Chambers, an all-pro tackle for the Chicago Bears. I brought Wally to meet Muhammad in his suite at the Statler Hotel, and it was interesting to see how relaxed Muhammad was before a fight. Rather than see all his visitors and well-wishers as a distraction, he really loved having new friends, old friends, and celebrity friends around him before a fight. You could see that this was a part of being "the Champ" that he really loved.

That night, we were alone in his room for a moment. Without the buzz of people around him, Muhammad let his energy drop.

"I'm tired," he said.

"Well, you should get in bed and try to get some sleep."

"No, I'm *tired*. Do you know how long I've been fighting? And this guy is the hardest puncher in the heavyweight division and tomorrow he's going to be pounding on me."

"Muhammad, if you win this one, will you retire?" I asked.

"I should," he said. "But if I don't, I'm going to take it easy, I'm going to line up a bunch of 'bums' to fight. Joe Louis had his 'Bum of the Month' club. That's what I'll do."

When it was time to head to the venue the next day, I walked there with Muhammad and Angelo—the hotel was just across the street from the Garden. In the lobby were a dozen or so people who had some connection to Muhammad but didn't have tickets to the fight. Muhammad told them to follow him. By the time we got to the employees' entrance at the Garden, another dozen were tagging along—following the heavyweight pied piper. Muhammad called for the Garden's manager and told him that he had a group of friends without tickets, but wanted the manager to find standing room for them. At first the manager refused to let the unticketed crowd in. Muhammad told the manager that unless he let them in, Muhammad wouldn't be fighting that night. Angelo had to help with the negotiation, but Muhammad did get all his "friends" in.

It was exciting to be a part of the crowd in the Garden as Muhammad made his entrance (to the theme from *Star Wars*) and stepped into the ring. For all the time we'd spent together, this was my first chance to witness Muhammad at work, doing what made him so famous in the first place. He seemed to be in great spirits, jawing at Shavers while they got their instructions from the referee, and making a great show of polishing Shavers's shiny, bald "Acorn" head with his boxing glove. (Muhammad had referred to Shavers as "Acorn" in prefight press conferences.) Earnie loved Ali and played along. But things got more serious when the fight began. Suddenly I was nervous, anticipating what would happen if one of Shavers's powerful haymakers caught Muhammad's jaw. In the second round, Shavers hit Muhammad with some hard rights. At first, Muhammad clowned his way through them, shrugging off the effect. But by the end of the round he looked hurt. Shavers was dangerous, and Muhammad wasn't going to win this fight by distracting his opponent with showmanship.

Muhammad was hoping that Shavers would tire by the later rounds, but it didn't happen. In fact, Shavers came on strong in the thirteenth and fourteenth rounds, landing some of the hardest punches I'd ever seen Muhammad absorb. I knew Muhammad was hurt, and certainly Shavers did, too. But Muhammad was still the master of the psychological game. By acting more hurt than he was, he tried to trick Shavers into attacking. Several times, Muhammad let his legs look wobbly, like he was going to fall. But instead of going in for the kill, Shavers held off. Muhammad weathered the storm, but could barely make it back to his stool after the fourteenth. Then, in the last round, Muhammad seemed to draw on every ounce of strength he had left and fought as great and courageous a three minutes as he had ever fought. In the last thirty seconds of the fight he unleashed powerfully on Shavers, and at the final bell, Shavers was reeling off the ropes. If the fight had gone another thirty seconds Muhammad might have scored a knockout. As it was, he fought what I consider to be the last great round of his career, and won by unanimous decision. The winner and still heavyweight champion of the world: Muhammad Ali.

THE MORE I GOT TO know Angelo Dundee, the more impressed I was with him, as a trainer and as a person of both warmth and integrity. So it was a quite an honor when Angelo asked me to be his guest at a dinner celebrating him as one of the first class of inductees into the newly founded Italian American Boxing Hall of Fame in Chicago. Of all the people Angelo worked with around Muhammad, I was the only one he asked to join him, his wife, Helen, and his daughter Terri at the event. It was a great, memorable night for me, and it was fascinating to get Angelo's perspective on Muhammad as an athlete. At one point we talked about the chances of Muhammad retiring, and I said something about Muhammad trying to make up for those years he missed when he was banned from boxing.

Helga playing Beethoven while Hana plays Ray Charles,
at the South Woodlawn house in Chicago.

Angelo got very emotional about that. "It's a godawful shame that the world got robbed of seeing the most beautiful athlete that has ever graced a boxing ring," he said. "We missed the three most dynamic years of a magnificent athlete performing in his prime. Oh, Lord, what we would have witnessed—watching the best heavyweight in boxing history at his peak—that would have been the greatest joy a boxing fan could imagine. Nobody was capable of what he was capable of back then. I've never seen any other athlete like him."

BACK IN CHICAGO THERE WERE some more "family" dinners at Muhammad's house (cooked by Helga, of course). One night, I brought along a special guest. When I had been put in charge of maintaining the base gyms back at Fort Sill, Oklahoma, I sometimes employed local college kids as summer help. One of those kids was a six-foot-five, 210-pound black guy named Ray Burris. When I first moved to Chicago, I learned that the same Ray Burris who had swept the gym for me was one of the four starters in the Chicago Cubs pitching rotation. I got in touch with him and recruited him to do some events with Athletes for a Better Education. He and his wife, Regina, became good friends of Helga and mine. So one night, having gotten the okay from Muhammad, I invited Ray and Regina to come along to dinner at South Woodlawn. Ray was actually giddy when I invited him, and made me promise that I wasn't playing a joke on him.

Dinner was great and everyone got along exceptionally well. It took Ray a while to relax in front of someone he idolized, but Muhammad's sense of humor eventually had Ray feeling right at home. Ray felt comfortable enough to explain that this wasn't the first time he had seen Muhammad in person. Ray said that he and his teammate José Cardenal had attended a sports convention at McCormick Place and had had the opportunity to see some truly great sports icons signing autographs at their own booths: Joe DiMaggio, Stan Musial, Ted Williams, Johnny Bench, Elgin Baylor. But at a booth across from Musial's was a crowd three times bigger than anybody else's. That was the crowd in front of Muhammad's booth. Ray said he and Cardenal just stood there and stared, awed that they were looking at their greatest athletic hero in person.

The real highlight of the night came after dinner when Muhammad decided to become Ray's pitching coach. The three of us were in the home's garden room. Muhammad asked, "What kind of windup do you have, Ray? Is it a standard windup or do you have your own style?"

"Well, it's just a tight, standard windup. Nothing fancy."

"OK, now check this out, you've got to do something that gets people's attention."

Muhammad stood up and went to the end of the room, where he had some space to move. "All the great pitchers have a signature move. Think about it. There's Satchel Paige . . ." Muhammad imitated the famous windmill windup of the great Negro League and Major League star, and Ray and I looked at each other and laughed.

"Then there's Juan Marichal," Muhammad continued, kicking his leg as high as he could in the style of the former San Francisco Giants pitcher, then followed through on a pretend pitch, looking like a graceful and powerful major leaguer. "Then there's Luis Tiant," said Muhammad, imitating the Red Sox pitcher's distinct, back-to-home-plate windup. "Now, if Muhammad Ali was on the mound, I'd really give the people something to watch. Something like this . . ."

Muhammad whirled his long arm through two full windmills, then did one windmill in reverse. He kicked his leg up and then held it as long as he could before following through explosively with his pretend pitch.

Ray was leaning over on the couch laughing. "You're right, Champ—that would get attention."

"I'm serious, Ray," said Muhammad. "You might be good now, and people know you, but if you have a unique style that people remember, you will be more famous."

As far as I know, Ray never put Ali's advice into practice. But I do know that Muhammad really did feel a strong appreciation for any athlete who was a one-of-a-kind figure in his sport. I remember asking him

After a family dinner in Chicago, we made a fire.
Evelyn, the nanny, is holding Hana.

once who his favorite football player was, expecting that he would name
Jim Brown, or O.J. Simpson, or maybe Walter Payton.

"Duane Thomas," he said without hesitation. Thomas had been a
Dallas Cowboys' running back and was the NFL Rookie of the Year
in 1970, but his career was marred by difficult relations with management, teammates, and the press that had him veering between outspo-
ken proclamations and vows of silence.

"Duane Thomas? Why him?" I asked.

"Because he was surrounded by controversy," said Muhammad. "I
love controversial players. Controversy is my middle name."

IN DECEMBER 1977 I WAS listening a lot to music from the soundtrack of a new
movie called *Saturday Night Fever.* I was a longtime Bee Gees fan—*Bee
Gees' 1st* (their third album) was the first record I bought for Helga
in Germany—and I enjoyed their reinvented sound for the disco era.

Based on the music I heard, I was eager to see the movie, and when I told Veronica about it, she wanted to see it, as well. One night I picked up Veronica and Muhammad and we drove to the new Water Tower movie theater on Michigan Avenue.

As usual, Muhammad had no concerns about getting in and out of a public place without being bothered by fans. He enjoyed being asked for autographs and making someone's day by granting the request as often as he could. On our way to the theater, he did just that quite a few times. When we got into the theater lobby, Muhammad had his priorities: he went straight to the concession stand and bought an Eskimo Pie, three Cokes, and a huge tub of popcorn (Muhammad never watched a movie without going through several boxes of popcorn). We made our way to seats in the back of the theater and waited for the lights to dim.

In conversations and especially in dealing with the press, if the person speaking to Muhammad didn't grab his attention in the first thirty seconds, he would tune out that person. But watching a movie—even a bad movie—Muhammad was very attentive, taking in every detail on the screen. When *Saturday Night Fever* began, with the iconic shot of John Travolta strutting down the street to the sounds of "Staying Alive," Muhammad, Veronica, and I were all glued to the screen.

"He walks like you," I said to Muhammad, which got a laugh out of him.

We stayed until the end titles were rolling. Muhammad leaned toward me and said, "Let's watch it again."

I got up to pay for another three tickets. The guy at the booth waved me off—Muhammad would be the theater's guest for the second showing (but I bought Muhammad a second Eskimo Pie).

The movie was just as much fun to watch the second time around. As the credits ran again, Muhammad asked me, "Do you know him—Travolta?"

I guess he thought I might have met him through my charity work, but I had not. "I know him from TV," I answered. "He's on a comedy series, *Welcome Back, Kotter.*"

"I bet he's a regular guy, just like me."

I thought, There's no way anyone would ever describe Muhammad Ali as a "regular guy." But I said, "I bet you're right."

"I'd like to meet him sometime."

I started planning right then how I might arrange that. I knew that Muhammad's name was magic, and with my experience rounding up celebrities for Athletes for a Better Education I figured I could at least get a call back from Travolta's people. The day after we saw the movie, I got in touch with Burbank Studios, where *Welcome Back, Kotter* was filmed, and left a message. Soon enough, I got a call back from a woman named Jeannie—she was John Travolta's personal secretary. We spoke briefly and—sensing that I was legit—Jeannie put me on the line with Joan Edwards, Travolta's personal assistant.

"You say that Muhammad Ali wants to meet John?"

"That's right," I said. "Muhammad, his wife, Veronica, and I saw *Saturday Night Fever* yesterday and we all were very impressed with John's performance. We even stayed for a second showing to watch it again and we were glad that we did. Muhammad would really like to get in touch with John."

I could tell that Joan wasn't entirely convinced that I wasn't just some nut pretending to be a friend of Muhammad Ali. I figured the best way to reassure her was through normal, pleasant conversation. I heard she had a British accent, so I asked her how long she had lived in the United States. She said she'd been working with John for two years—since *Kotter* began—but before that she'd run a dinner theater in Omaha, Nebraska. This rang a bell for me.

"The Edwards Dinner Theater?" I asked.

"Yes . . ."

"And do you ever remember the Creighton University basketball team coming to your theater?"

"Yesss . . ."

"I was on the freshman team. We came to a dinner show with the team physician, Dr. Bevilacqua, who I believe was a friend of yours."

We were both startled by this coincidence, but our connection didn't end there. When I mentioned to Joan that I was calling from Chicago but was originally from Milwaukee, she told me that she and her daughter Kate had once staged a production of *Fiddler on the Roof* in Milwaukee at a venue called The Scene. She wondered if I was familiar with the place. Was I ever. The Scene was owned by Frank Balistrieri, a Milwaukee mob boss who was sometimes referred to as "Mr. Big." In high school, I took Frank's daughter Benedetta on a date to The Scene to see Ray Charles play. For me, the evening was more tense than romantic, as Mr. Balistrieri had arranged for Benedetta (or Benny, as I called her) and I to be accompanied by armed bodyguards. One date like that was more than enough for me.

I told Joan that story, and suddenly we were talking like old friends. She was smart and charming, and I couldn't have imagined my Travolta cold-call going any better than this. We set up a day the following week for Muhammad and John to speak on the phone. John would be at the studio to do a read-through of a new *Kotter* script, and I would make sure to have Muhammad by the phone at his place. The next time I saw Muhammad, I gave him the news.

"I got in touch with Travolta's people. He wants to talk to you."

"Good," he said. "I should hire you as my manager. You've got the complexion for the connection."

The following week the phone rang at the appointed time, and Muhammad answered. "Joe's Bar," he growled out in a low voice.

Joan must have thought that after all our incredibly coincidental connections, she had been elaborately pranked. Right away Muhammad's tone changed and he sounded almost apologetic.

"No, no, this *is* Muhammad Ali. No . . . no . . . this is Ali." He handed me the phone. I straightened things out and explained to Joan that she really had been speaking to Muhammad. Answering with "Joe's Bar" was just a gag that he often played. Other favorite salutations included: "City Morgue," "Schwartzes' residence," "Clint Eastwood's residence," "Pope's residence," and "Hello, this is Superman speaking . . ."

Joan said she was handing the phone to John, and I handed the phone back to Muhammad.

"John Travolta!" he almost shouted. "Is this *the* John Travolta? John Travolta, man, you can dance. Tim and I have been listening to the Bee Gees, do you know them? I gotta meet those guys. This white boy here is showing me some of your moves on the floor, and by the time we meet I will be a dancing machine and we'll have a dance-off."

They spoke for a few more minutes and then Muhammad said, "My friend Tim Shanahan will let you know my schedule. We'll get together soon."

Joan and I stayed in touch, beginning a close friendship that endures to this day. A couple of times, she put me on the phone with John. He was only twenty-three at the time and had just gone from being the biggest heartthrob on TV to the biggest movie star of the year. I could only imagine how quickly his life was changing. But in our conversations he came across as a warm, sensitive, very sincere young man. He must have thought that if Muhammad Ali could trust me as a friend, then John Travolta could also, because he always seemed relaxed and candid. He joked that a year ago no one had cared about his opinion on anything, now everybody wanted his opinion on everything—from movies to sports to politics. At the end of one call he told me he liked talking to me because I seemed upbeat and happy. Apparently not everybody he dealt with in Hollywood had that attitude.

Eventually, Joan asked me when I might be coming to Los Angeles. I told her that I actually had a trip scheduled the following month to meet with a pacemaker company. She told me that I was welcome to stay with her at her home in Encino—a wonderfully generous offer to make to someone she knew only over the phone. I decided to take Joan up on that offer, and a few weeks later I was in the home she shared with her daughter, Kate—John's first Los Angeles girlfriend—and her mother, Ivy, the matriarch of the house and as direct and no-nonsense a woman as I have ever met. The three ladies welcomed me and served me a delicious homemade dinner of British-style chicken pot pie.

The second day of my visit we went to the set of *Welcome Back, Kotter* on the Burbank Studios lot to see John at work shooting an episode. During a break in the taping, John walked over and we finally got to meet face-to-face. In person he seemed just as sweet, sensitive, and sincere as he had on the phone. He told me that his father, Sal, had been a semipro football player and was a big Ali fan, as were his mother, his three sisters, and his two brothers. We didn't get to talk long, but he expressed how excited he was about the chance to meet Muhammad.

By the end of my L.A. trip, I felt I had new friends in Joan, Kate, Ivy, and John, and I was sure John and Muhammad would get along well when they met. The one thing that Muhammad hated in other celebrities was arrogance. He had no time for people that were full of themselves and believed their own hype. Ironic, I know, because there was no one better at hyping himself than Muhammad, but that was for the cameras. He didn't carry that persona into his private life. John Travolta was the hottest movie star in the world, but from what I could tell, he didn't have a trace of arrogance. He really was, as Muhammad would put it, "a regular guy."

BY THE BEGINNING OF 1978, there were some significant changes around Muhammad. Ferdie Pacheco was upset enough by Muhammad's latest medical lab results—particularly the state of Muhammad's kidneys—that he decided he would no longer be part of the Ali team. Ferdie thought it was important to take a stand and let Muhammad know that he would no longer support Muhammad if he continued to box. Ferdie believed that Muhammad needed to stop boxing in order to prevent long-lasting injury to himself, and I had heard Ferdie say at the last camp that even if Muhammad stopped boxing right now, it would take a year or two for the damage already done to begin to heal. Muhammad played down the loss of this important member of his team, commenting, "I don't need Pacheco's help."

With his thirty-sixth birthday approaching, it did seem like maybe Ferdie was right and that it was time for Muhammad to hang up the boxing gloves. The phenomenal final round of the Shavers fight would mark a great end to a great career. But even though Muhammad had conceded that he "should" retire, he wasn't quite ready. He was approached with an offer of $3.5 million to fight a young heavyweight named Leon Spinks. Spinks had fought professionally only seven times, but was part of the 1976 Olympic boxing team that also included Sugar Ray Leonard, and, like Leonard, he had brought home a gold medal. Muhammad took great pride in the fact that he himself was an Olympic gold medalist who had beaten every other gold medalist he had faced: Floyd Patterson, Joe Frazier, and George Foreman. Defeating yet another gold medalist—this one young and hungry—would be the perfect cap to his career. After a bit of negotiating, the bout was scheduled for February 15, 1978, at the Hilton Hotel Convention Center in Las Vegas.

For at least a little while longer, Muhammad's gloves would stay on.

EIGHT

ON THE ROPES

EVEN WITH ALL THAT HE had, and despite the fact that he could buy just about anything he wanted, Muhammad loved receiving gifts. He always got very excited at the prospect of opening a present, big or small. Depending on what that present turned out to be, he might not stay interested in it for very long, but he loved the receiving part. I always liked picking out a birthday gift for him, and would try to come up with something that I thought he would really enjoy. For his thirty-sixth birthday, on January 17, 1978, I presented him with a book of quotations.

One of Muhammad's great regrets was that he didn't feel he had gotten the full benefit of a higher education. He often put down his own ability to read and write. This seemed crazy to me because not only did he have one of the sharpest and most creative minds I had ever encountered, when he put that mind to a written work he was passionate about—the Quran, for instance—he not only had a deep understanding of the text but could memorize long passages of it. When it came to wit and wordplay, he was incredibly fast, and had come up with some amazing lines in interviews through the years that captured his showmanship, his humor, and his philosophy:

"If you even dream of beating me, you better wake up and apologize."

"Rivers, ponds, lakes, and streams. They all have different names, but they all contain water, just as all religions contain truths."

"Friendship is not something you learn in school. But if you haven't learned the meaning of friendship, you haven't really learned anything."

"Silence is golden when you can't think of a good answer."

Muhammad loved bits of wisdom that could be presented as sayings, and he often enjoyed putting his own spin on the sayings that he heard, so I thought he would appreciate a new book of quotations. His brother, Rahaman, was visiting Chicago this year on Muhammad's birthday, and when I presented Muhammad with the book, he and Rahaman began paging through it excitedly, looking for lines they liked. Muhammad was especially taken by a few that he found:

"The mountain in front of you is not as difficult as the pebble in your shoe."

"Service to others is the rent we pay on earth for our room in heaven."

That last line was originally ascribed to Wilfred Grenfell, a nineteenth-century British medical missionary, but Muhammad began using the quote so often in his interviews that it is often now credited to him. The words perfectly captured Muhammad's loving spirit: even though he made his living as a warrior in the boxing ring, he always wanted to be of service to people who needed his help.

RIGHT AFTER HIS BIRTHDAY, HE headed off to Deer Lake to train for the upcoming match with Leon Spinks. From what I saw in the time I spent at camp, Muhammad wasn't demonstrating much warrior spirit at all. He didn't run much, and he didn't put much effort into sparring. As usual, Muhammad encouraged celebrity friends to visit him, and this time he had two or three VIP visitors a week: Lola Falana, Diana Ross, Andre the Giant, Howard Cosell, Sammy Davis Jr., and the Jackson 5, among others, all stopped by Deer Lake at some point. Muhammad always put on a great show for these friends, but rarely did any serious training. He posed for plenty of pictures, but hardly threw any punches. It almost seemed like Muhammad was retiring without retiring. He was going to line up fights with lesser opponents and take the paydays that came with them, but he wasn't going to train hard before getting into the ring.

Leon Spinks was fighting Muhammad as a heavyweight but still looked and moved like a light heavyweight, the division he had fought in at the 1976 Montreal Olympics. He was more of a brawler than a polished fighter, but there was no guarantee that he would play the part of the "bum" that Muhammad was expecting. Jimmy Ellis and I spoke about trying to get Muhammad to train harder. I didn't feel that it was my place to push Muhammad, but he would at least listen to Jimmy, even if he would not always take his advice. Still, I wasn't going to lie to Muhammad. One day the guys around him were telling him how great he looked in the Shavers fight, going through all the usual lines about how he was the still the greatest and how there wasn't anybody out there that he couldn't beat. Muhammad listened to them for a while, then held up a hand to silence them and looked my way.

"Tim—what do you think?"

"Well, Muhammad. That last round was one of the most magnificent rounds that you have ever fought. You deserved the win. But I've got to say—it was not a great fight. You did not look your best."

There were groans of complaint from the others, but Muhammad silenced them and said, once again, "You ain't as dumb as you look, white boy."

If Muhammad thought I was speaking the truth, however, it didn't seem to make much difference in his training. He had come into camp with his weight up around 240, and it was hard to see how he would get down closer to the 225 he had been for the Shavers fight. Just a few weeks before the fight, I was sitting at a training table with Michael Dokes, a former national Golden Gloves heavyweight champion who had won a silver medal at the 1975 Pan American games (he was defeated in the finals by the esteemed Cuban fighter Teofilo Stevenson). Dokes had recently turned pro and had fought a nationally televised exhibition match against Muhammad. The younger fighter was grateful for that opportunity and felt honored to have been asked by Muhammad to come to camp as a sparring partner. But the lackadaisical training regimen and the lack of serious sparring sessions seemed to bother Dokes. It was hard for this young fighter to see his hero treating this fight so casually.

As Michael and I sat at the table, Muhammad appeared and joined us with a dish of ice cream in his hand. We had just seen him eat one of Lana Shabazz's great home-cooked meals—fried chicken, mashed potatoes and gravy, black-eyed peas, and a salad covered with ranch dressing. The ice cream—and the fact that Muhammad had skipped his morning run—really bothered Dokes.

"Champ, please take Spinks seriously," he said, almost pleading. "We have to train harder."

I was impressed with Dokes for speaking up. He felt it was partly his responsibility to get Muhammad prepared for the fight, and he

Walking the grounds at Deer Lake, with daughters Rasheda and Maryum.

couldn't understand why Muhammad would assume that Spinks didn't pose any threat at all.

Muhammad said, "I'll be ready for the fight like I always am. I won't let this amateur take my title away—he's too ugly to be champion of the world." With that, he dipped a spoon into the ice cream. I smiled, but Michael didn't.

MUHAMMAD DID MANAGE TO GET his weight down by the time he got to Las Vegas for the fight. I was very impressed that he still had that much willpower. He ended up three quarters of a pound lighter than he was against Shavers. He still seemed strangely relaxed about taking on his young opponent, but at least it wouldn't be extra pounds that slowed him down in the ring. Muhammad was booked into a suite at the Las Vegas Hilton, where in the days before the fight he held court for assorted well-wishers and a steady stream of Vegas-based celebrities. I flew into Las Vegas with my own special guest—a very close high school friend whose life had taken a terrible turn.

Peter Gingrass graduated fourth in our class at Marquette University High, then went on to graduate second in his class at the University of Michigan Medical School. He trained as a surgeon, and quickly became a highly regarded figure in cancer research. While he was performing surgery, Peter became dizzy and collapsed in the operating room. After a barrage of tests were run, the most horribly ironic diagnosis came back: Peter himself had an inoperable, cancerous brain tumor. He went through repeated rounds of treatment, but nothing was proving to be effective. At the age of thirty-one, Peter had been told by his doctors that he probably had only a few months to live. Having thought hard about what he would want to do with those finals days, Peter allowed himself one indulgence. He was one of the very few people I had spoken to about my friendship with Muhammad, so Peter contacted me and asked if it might be possible to speak with Ali. I told Peter that I could introduce him to Muhammad in person, and that I would fly to Las Vegas with him.

I had explained all this to Muhammad beforehand, and he was truly moved. When Peter and I got to the Hilton, we called up to Muhammad's room and he told us to come up directly. We got to the suite, where Muhammad was entertaining a group that included Eddie Kendricks of the Temptations, the actor Hugh O'Brian (star of one of Muhammad's favorite classic TV westerns, *Wyatt Earp*), and the promoter Butch Lewis—the key figure in putting the Spinks-Ali fight together.

As soon as we walked into the room, Muhammad stopped talking and shouted out those words I always enjoyed hearing: "My main man—Tim Shanahan."

The room went silent, and stayed that way as Peter and I walked over to Muhammad. I introduced Peter to him, and began to remind him of Peter's story. The others sensed that this was a more personal matter than usual and stepped away to give us some privacy. As I finished talking, Muhammad looked like there was nothing that concerned him more than Peter's situation. Peter had an expression that was a mixture of happiness and disbelief that this was really happening.

"Are you in pain?" asked Muhammad.

"No," said Peter.

"Do you fear dying?"

"It's not fear—it's an anguish." I thought that word really defined Peter's circumstances, and the feelings of his friends and family.

"I know you're a smart doctor," said Muhammad. "And you know that if you are determined to fight against the cancer, you could beat it. We both know the impossible can happen. They said it was impossible for me to beat Sonny Liston. This ex-convict was going to kill me in the ring, and nobody gave me a chance. I had fear, but I was determined to prove everyone wrong. I had the confidence to do the impossible. You can do this, too, Doc. The world needs you and your knowledge, so don't give up. Keep fighting. Tim will give you my phone number and you call me when you need to talk. You will prove everyone wrong when you beat this disease."

Peter was indeed a brilliant doctor, and as he stood before Muhammad he may have been quite certain that his situation was hopeless, but the look of comfort and relief on his face as Muhammad spoke is something I'll always treasure. It was one of those moments when I realized how the title of "the Greatest" wasn't just hype, and it wasn't just a description of Muhammad's boxing skills. That line about service to others being the rent we pay on earth for our room in heaven was not just a saying to him. Anytime he had a chance to serve others, he did.

A NIGHT BEFORE THE FIGHT, Muhammad, Howard Bingham, Jimmy Ellis, and I took a cab over to Caesars Palace to catch a performance by Lou Rawls. As we walked toward the casino's main entrance, Muhammad and I saw something that startled us—at the top of the steps in front of the glass doors was an older black man in a wheelchair who was shaking hands with arriving guests.

"Maaan," said Muhammad softly. "That's Joe Louis."

Louis had been a hero of boxing fans everywhere, but he had been a particular symbol of success and achievement for Muhammad. Before Muhammad came along, Louis—the Brown Bomber—was the most influential boxer in the world, reigning as heavyweight champion for more than a decade in the 1930s and '40s, and almost single-handedly changing the image of boxing from that of a corrupt backroom attraction to a legitimate athletic competition. Muhammad's father once took his young son to visit a tree in Louisville simply because it was the tree Joe Louis had leaned against during a visit to the city. Louis had made it to the top in every way, but poor financial decisions and awful tax problems robbed him of his wealth, and hard living had damaged his health. Now he was parked in front of Caesars as an official greeter. He looked happy enough, but it was a sad way to see him. We had no idea how much Caesars was paying the former champ for shaking hands and signing autographs, but we all knew that the Great Joe Louis deserved better than this.

We made our way over to Joe, who beamed as soon as he saw Muhammad. They spoke for a few moments and Muhammad got a couple of good laughs out of Joe. They posed for some pictures making fists at each other, then Muhammad wished the ex-champ well and we headed in to see our show.

As soon as we were through the lobby doors, Muhammad said, "That man is my hero, but I don't ever want to end up that way. You hear me? I don't ever want to be broke and in a wheelchair. That's not going to happen."

"Of course not," I told him.

When something did make an impression on Muhammad, he would think about it for hours and hours. During the show that night, I looked over at Muhammad a few times and saw that he wasn't paying much attention to the stage. I knew he was still thinking about Joe Louis, his hero, shaking hands from a wheelchair.

That night, on the ride back to the Hilton, I thought about Louis, too—a perfect example of a superstar who had let his physical gifts and his hard-earned wealth slip away. I decided to raise the idea of retirement again with Muhammad.

"Muhammad, do you ever think about all those great fights in which you went the distance? Those incredible fights against Frazier and Foreman and Norton? Don't you think that when you add those up they have taken a toll, and maybe it's time to think about retiring?"

"Those big fights took a lot out of me," he replied. "But what most people don't know was that all my training and all my sparing sessions took even more out of me. I lay against the ropes and let the sparring partners pound on me because I was training for a fight where I couldn't dance anymore. When I came back to boxing, after not training for three and a half years, I was older and not as fast anymore. I had to figure out a way to beat the younger opponents and I knew I had to use my brains more than my skills. I couldn't dance for fifteen rounds anymore, so I had to figure out a way to pace myself for the fifteen rounds, entertain the crowd and win the fight in the later rounds, where the judging was always more important, If I had kept up the training routine for those three and a half years, I believe that I would have been much more prepared for the big fights as I got older. But I can't get those years back, and I don't regret any of it.

"I'm thinking about retiring because I don't want to train anymore. I have to have a reason to get up at five a.m. and run three miles and spar for two hours every day. When I fought Joe Frazier, George Foreman, or Ken Norton, I had that reason. I wanted to train hard so I could beat them. Now that desire is gone."

I had never heard him talk in such detail about his evolving boxing style and his own diminishing competitive fire.

"When do you think the ideal time would be for you to retire?" I asked.

"After this fight. You're going to help me start a foundation to help people and I will become an ambassador to the world."

I wasn't sure what exactly Muhammad's foundation would do, or how exactly I would be involved, but I was very happy to hear that he wanted me to be a part of his life after boxing.

UNFORTUNATELY THERE WERE FIFTEEN ROUNDS to get through before that life could begin, and those rounds against Spinks added up to the fight that many of us around Muhammad had been fearing. Spinks was not a masterful boxer by any means, but he was a young, strong, aggressive brawler whose only fight strategy was to keep swinging with roundhouse punches. Against Shavers, Muhammad's fight plan had worked. Shavers got tired in the later rounds, and Muhammad ended the fight scoring big. But Spinks never got tired. He came after Muhammad right away in round one, and stayed just as aggressive through round fifteen. Rope-a-dope no longer looked like a tactic—it was a means of survival. Every chance that Muhammad had, he would grab Spinks and try to keep him close, but Muhammad's reflexes seemed noticeably slower and he never seemed able to unleash a counteroffensive against Spinks's flurries. By the thirteenth round, Muhammad was getting hit with poorly thrown punches that he once would have easily avoided. When Muhammad finally put together a last-ditch attack in the final rounds, it didn't go the way it had against Shavers. Spinks landed the last big blows of the fight. There was a split decision, with one judge generously giving Ali the edge by a point. But the other two judges scored the fight decisively for Spinks. "The Greatest" was no longer the heavyweight champion of the world.

The mood in Muhammad's dressing room was somber. He sat on a stool with his head hung down. Nobody was talking. Then Michael Dokes burst into the dressing room, looking angry.

"I told you, Ali," he shouted, his voice cracking with emotion. "I told you that you needed to train harder, I told you not to take this lightly. I told you that you can't let this ugly punk-ass middleweight take the title away from you. You let this amateur who had no business in the ring with you take the crown away from you and now he is the heavyweight champion of the world? How could you do it, Muhammad?"

Dokes was standing over Muhammad. Muhammad looked up at him, and it was easy then to see that there were tears streaming down

The troops gather in Muhammad's Las Vegas Hilton suite the morning after the loss to Leon Spinks. I'm in the coat and tie to the left. Ali is pointing at the screen, to the post-fight interview.

his face. As soon as Dokes saw that, he began sobbing. He knelt down next to Muhammad and put his arm around him. He whispered something to him and walked out. Muhammad sat still on the stool and hung his head again, not saying a word.

THE NEXT MORNING A LARGE group of us gathered in Muhammad's hotel suite to watch TV coverage of the upset. Muhammad was in a subdued mood, but he was not in denial—he was very open with all of us that he had done wrong by not taking the fight seriously enough. He was also gracious enough to give Spinks full credit for the win. In fact, in a postfight interview with Brent Mussberger, Muhammad said, "I was so impressed with Leon, I'm going to be his new manager." (To Leon's credit, his response was "Ali's the Greatest, I'm just the latest.")

The one thing Muhammad said over and over again in the days after the Spinks fight was "Gotta get back to Deer Lake." He said he wanted to start training for a rematch right away, and that nothing was more important to him than getting in shape and getting the title back. It was good to hear him talking that way, and I think I was as hungry for the rematch as he was. I wanted Muhammad to stop fighting, but I didn't want to see his boxing days end with this lousy loss. Before we all left Las Vegas, I asked Angelo Dundee if he felt the same way.

"We're not going to end his career with that fight," he said. "We'll get camp opened and get back in training for a rematch. I don't know when, but sooner rather than later."

ABOUT A MONTH AFTER THE Spinks fight, I got a call from Dr. Peter Gingrass's fiancée, Elizabeth. Despite the valiant efforts of all his own doctors, Peter was in the last days of his life. Her wish was that she and Peter would spend as much time together as they possibly could, while they could. They were going to spend his last days together at a quiet getaway spot in Florida—Peter had decided that one of the last things he wanted to do in this world was to take a walk on the beach with the woman he loved.

When I relayed this sad news to Muhammad, he insisted that I come over to his house so that we could get in touch with Peter right away. I called Peter and asked if it was all right for Muhammad to speak to him again. Peter still sounded strong, and he said it would be wonderful to speak to his hero. Muhammad picked up the other line and gave Peter a beautiful pep talk, telling him he had lived a meaningful life doing God's work with his hands, and that even if it was a brief life, it was a great life.

"Champ," said Peter, "the only good thing about my situation is that there is no more guessing. I know *when* I am going to die."

"Then take comfort in that, Peter," said Muhammad. "We all have to die someday. We can't beat death. We just have to face it the best we can and hope that we are prepared. And you are prepared."

Muhammad and Peter said goodbye to each other but I stayed on the line. "I can't tell you how much this call has meant to me, Timmy," said Peter. "I can't believe that Muhammad Ali is concerned about Peter Gingrass, but I can hear in his voice that he really cares."

Two weeks later I got the word that Peter was gone. When I told Muhammad the sad news and said how much his call had touched Peter, Muhammad looked awfully sad. That really hit me. This was not a good time for Muhammad: he had lost his title in an embarrassing fashion and he certainly had plenty else to think about. Yet he was grieving for one of my best friends as if that person were one of his own. It reminded me once more of just how big and pure this man's heart was.

BACK IN CHICAGO, MUHAMMAD STAYED focused on setting up a rematch with Spinks and made a commitment to getting back into shape. Suddenly the fire was back and he wanted to run three or four miles every morning.

"Everybody loses, it's how you handle the loss that counts," he would say. "I want to make this a loss that will motivate me, like my other losses have. I've done everything that I wanted to do in boxing, but now I will shake up the world again and be the first heavyweight champion to regain his title for the third time. Can you imagine? Jack

Johnson, Joe Louis, Gene Tunney, Rocky Marciano, none of them were in a position like I am in now. So let's get out in the snow right now. I am not going to leave boxing a loser. I am going to win the title a third time. Let's go."

In losing to Leon Spinks, Muhammad was stripped of his titles by the WBC (World Boxing Council) and the WBA (World Boxing Association). By the summer of 1978, those losses were greatly overshadowed by problems with another agency—the IRS.

I went over to South Woodlawn one day and found Muhammad looking extremely pensive.

"Muhammad, what's the matter?"

"I never had any trouble with my white brothers around me. It's always my black brothers who try and screw me."

"What happened?"

As careless as Muhammad could be with his money, he had been very determined about one thing—paying his taxes. Mindful of Joe Louis's tax problems, Muhammad wanted the money that actually came to him personally to be pure after-tax profit, so that he wouldn't have to worry about a tax bill later on. Through the Nation of Islam, he was put in touch with a black lawyer whose main job, as far as Muhammad was concerned, was to pay Muhammad's taxes when Muhammad was paid for fights. The lawyer was supposed to put $2.5 million in escrow to cover the taxes due on the earnings from the Jimmy Young, Richard Dunn, and Norton III fights. When the taxes came due, however, there was no money in the account. The lawyer claimed he had spent the money on legitimate expenses and investments, but this was less than clear. In any event, with the taxes now overdue, Herbert Muhammad informed Ali that he would not be receiving any of the second million-dollar-plus payout that Ali had expected.

"I need a new lawyer—one with your complexion," he told me. "You know a good lawyer who can help me protect my money?"

"I know that the chairman of the top bank in Chicago is interested in helping you manage your money."

"Call him," said Muhammad.

No matter what was going on around Muhammad, he always maintained his dignity. He didn't seem angry or vengeful, just depressed that he had been taken advantage of. I knew how these things went, though. No matter how bad the situation turned out to be, Muhammad would be willing to forgive those who had cheated him. This time, I was not ready to forgive. I had not ever wanted to get involved in the business side of Muhammad's life. But, as a friend, it seemed the right time to get involved. I knew I wasn't the only one concerned about the many ways in which Muhammad seemed to be taken advantage of by the people around him—Ferdie Pacheco, Howard Bingham, and Angelo Dundee had all expressed similar concerns.

I had recently read an article in the *Chicago Tribune* about Robert Abboud, chairman of the First National Bank of Chicago. Abboud had heard that the Cubs great Ernie Banks had lost a lot of money through a business agent and was worried about other star athletes falling prey to bad management. He was particularly worried about Muhammad. So now, at Muhammad's house, I quickly tracked down a phone number for the bank's main office. As usual, Muhammad's name worked its magic. We got an appointment with Mr. Abboud that week. We would meet with him just before he left town for a business trip.

Three days later Muhammad and I got into the kelly-green Rolls—Muhammad behind the wheel—and started to make our way up Michigan Avenue toward the First National Bank building. But after a few blocks, traffic came to a near standstill. There must have been a bad accident farther ahead, because the cars on Michigan were just barely inching along, and the side streets were just as jammed. I began to think there was no way that we would get to Abboud's office before he had to leave.

"What time do we have to be there?" asked Muhammad.

"One thirty, but it's getting tight," I said. "Why don't I just get out and make a call. We can reschedule."

Muhammad considered this for a moment, then said, "No, we'll make it."

He inched the Rolls toward the curb, then drove up over it. He carefully maneuvered the car, and soon we were rolling down the busy sidewalk at about three miles per hour—considerably faster than the cars in the street. Muhammad was gently tapping the horn every few seconds to warn the pedestrians ahead of us, and while people were at first shocked and frightened at the sight of a car coming toward them, as soon as they saw who was driving, they began walking and jogging alongside the Rolls and cheering Muhammad. Some got right up to the driver's window and asked for his autograph (this was the rare occasion when Muhammad declined, explaining that he was in a hurry to see his lawyer). When we got to the end of a block, the Rolls would bump-bump over the curb, drive along the crosswalk, and then bump-bump back up the next curb.

I have to admit, even with an ever-growing crowd walking with the car, we made good time. We rolled off the sidewalk into the beautiful pedestrian plaza of the First National building with minutes to spare. But there was no place to park, so Muhammad simply drove to the nearest No Parking red zone and left the car there. Muhammad joked that since he was Chicago's most prominent citizen, Mayor Michael Bilandic had awarded him many specially reserved parking spaces—all painted red so Muhammad could easily spot them. (In truth, Muhammad racked up about ten parking tickets a month, and the mayor had a staffer who would periodically collect Muhammad's tickets and come to the South Woodlawn house so that Muhammad could settle up, usually paying about half of what he was fined.)

As we walked into the First National building, Muhammad wasn't worried about parking tickets. He had a problem even more pressing than his finances: he had to urinate. The kidney damage he suffered in the third Norton fight had not completely healed, and it had become difficult for him to go very long without having to relieve himself. He had been sitting in the Rolls and feeling uncomfortable. We quickly got into an empty elevator car, and I pushed the button for the top floor of the sixty-story building. I told Muhammad I was sure that as soon as we got up to Abboud's office there would be facilities for him to use. But sixty stories must have sounded like too long a wait, because the next thing I knew, Muhammad pulled out his business and began to relieve himself against the carpeted walls of the elevator car. He still had a steady stream as we got close to 60 so I stopped us at 59 to let him finish (luckily no one was waiting there to get on). When he was done, we went up the last floor and stepped off. I made a note of which car we were on—we would be sure to take a different one on the way down.

We were shown into Abboud's office, and the bank chairman gave Muhammad the full royal treatment (Muhammad introduced me as "my administrative assistant—my cousin Tim Shanahan"). Abboud did most of the talking, explaining that he was a big fan of Ali the boxer and Ali the human being, but that through what he had read in the press, he was worried whether Muhammad was being treated fairly about his money. Abboud knew about Muhammad's arrangements with Herbert Muhammad and the Nation of Islam. He felt that he could put together a team of expert lawyers, accountants, and advisers that would get Muhammad's tangled finances in order, steer his investments, and ensure that Muhammad stayed a wealthy man once he retired. Abboud said that he wanted to make sure that Muhammad lived out his life after boxing in peace and with financial security.

"After all, Muhammad," Abboud said, "I don't want you to end up like Joe Louis."

That hit Muhammad hard, and he decided very quickly to become a client of Abboud's. Muhammad wasn't going to sever his business ties with Herbert Muhammad, but from my perspective (and I believed also from that of Veronica, Bingham, Angelo, and others), Muhammad's hiring some real professionals to look out for him was the best business decision he had made in a long time.

On the way out of the building, I stopped at the security desk to let them know that somebody might have had an "accident" in elevator number 4. Out in the plaza, I took Muhammad over to see Marc Chagall's massive *Four Seasons* mosaic, one of Helga's and my favorite works of public art (she and I had actually been in the plaza just a few years before when Chagall personally dedicated the work to the city). Muhammad and I were talking about the artwork and all the skill and passion that went into it when he noticed a tow truck pulling up behind his Rolls. He jogged over to the truck driver and politely asked if he might get a break. Muhammad explained all about being late for an appointment with his attorney and—maybe to make the appointment sound more urgent—said he was setting up a rematch with George Foreman. The driver didn't need to hear any explaining—he was so excited to be talking to Muhammad Ali that all he wanted was an autograph before he drove away without touching the Rolls.

MUHAMMAD DID NOT FIT ANY stereotype of the uneducated, gullible athlete. I thought of him as being childlike, but never childish. He approached life with a sense of wonderment, but he was no fool. Still, the practical matters of financial responsibility were not his strength. This wasn't so unusual—I worked alongside plenty of wealthy doctors who didn't know how to handle their money. The difference was that those doctors hired smart, capable people to take care of their money for them. Not only was Muhammad not interested in managing his own money; he had never been concerned enough to hire trustworthy professionals to do the job. He had trusted Herbert Muhammad to manage his career simply because Herbert was Elijah Muhammad's son. Herbert cared for Muhammad, but his business experience was in running Nation of Islam ventures such as bakeries, laundries, and restaurants, not managing a world-class athlete. He had not had to master the art of negotiating contracts because, as Muhammad Ali's manager, he had leverage over everyone he dealt with.

Throughout his career, the investment advice Muhammad had received had mostly resulted in disasters. During the first wave of his success in the 1960s, he lost money on a poorly managed chain of Champburger restaurants and a licensed Mr. Champ soda. He was still licensing his name to all kinds of odd products that would turn out to be low quality or otherwise unmarketable, and he would "invest" money into projects and business ventures that would have little chance of providing him with any real return. If losing his money wasn't bad enough, the contracts for these businesses created a mess of obligations and commitments for Muhammad that had to be resolved through round after round of litigation.

Over the last couple of years, Muhammad had been convinced to open an Ali's Trolley chicken-and-burgers joint in Hyde Park that was about to go out of business. Muhammad got excited at first about the concept—I went with him to look at the refurbished street trolley car being converted into a diner just before it opened. When it did open, I took Helga to dinner at Ali's Trolley once and the meal was OK—the place made a decent burger. But poor planning and poor management took its toll, and Muhammad hardly did anything to promote the project. After about a year and a half, Ali's Trolley ran off the tracks.

The biggest obstacle to Muhammad's financial security was not his advisers, though, but Muhammad himself. The world's greatest fighter hated confrontation. He was ferocious in the ring and could be aggressive in his speeches, but in his personal life he wanted things quiet and easy. He just didn't want to admit that anything was wrong or that he had made a bad judgment of someone's character. No matter what was taken from him, he was still living well and he wasn't interested in going after anyone who had wronged him. Muhammad was now willing to hand his financial troubles over to Robert Abboud's team. Muhammad could feel the weight of the world on his shoulders sometimes—he said that was what fueled his chronic insomnia. But, given the choice, he wanted to joke around and be carefree, and wanted to see that the people around him were having fun. He was not interested in grudges, accusations, or criminal proceedings. He was quite open, though, about being an easy target.

"I have an easygoing nature," he would say. "I'm a soft touch. I don't always see what's happening around me, so anybody could take advantage of me." (I remember trying to hush him up when he said this in front of some of his inner-circle guys—it didn't seem wise to announce such a thing.)

Another part of the financial problem was the amount of money Muhammad willingly gave away. He was still asked constantly for money by relatives, and he never said no. One time when I tried to help sort through a pile of Muhammad's bills, I was shocked to discover that during a single month, in addition to his personal expenses, he was spending $64,000 on insurance, mortgages, rents, and car payments for a long list of relatives. It may have been an unusual month, but still, even for a heavyweight champion, that was a large nut to cover for other people.

Muhammad was certainly not stupid, and he wasn't blind. But in his mind, he was not being victimized—he was simply supporting people who needed support. He had a tremendous desire to take care of people and to solve problems, and if his fame and money could solve other people's problems—so be it. He didn't see what was happening around him as "bad behavior." Instead, he felt he was making life better for other people and giving the gift of happiness. And I think he felt he was atoning for his own bad behavior, like having two daughters outside of marriage.

"Who am I to judge anyone else?" he would ask. "Allah's watching me, and he wants to see how I treat people who have less than I do. There's a tally sheet that God is keeping every day, and I want to put more in the 'Good Deeds' column than the 'Bad Deeds' column."

It was honorable and admirable that Muhammad was so concerned with God's tally sheet, and it said a lot about his loving nature. Still, I was very happy that Robert Abboud and his team would now be keeping tally sheets of their own.

THE REMATCH WAS ON. ACCORDING to the complicated boxing ranking system, Leon Spinks was supposed to make his first title defense against Ken Norton. But the promoters involved knew there was much more money to be made on a Spinks-Ali rematch. The contract for a Spinks-Norton fight would have earned Spinks $250,000. For the Ali fight he would get $3 million. Spinks-Ali contracts were negotiated and agreed to, but bypassing the rankings caused the World Boxing Council to strip Spinks of his WBC title, which was then awarded to Norton. Spinks still had the WBA belt, though, so while a rematch with Ali would not produce an "undisputed" champion, it would still be a heavyweight championship bout. Contracts were signed, and the fight was scheduled to take place at the New Orleans Superdome on September 15, 1978.

Even before the arrangements were finalized, Muhammad was training hard—harder than he had for the Shavers fight. It was inspiring to see him so focused and determined to get back into the shape he knew he needed to be in to take on Spinks again. It was clear that for this fight—possibly his last—he wanted to show the world that he still deserved to be a champion. He knew he had disappointed his fans by letting a lesser opponent take away his title.

Resting after a run in Deer Lake. Muhammad
chopped down those trees himself.

When I arrived in Deer Lake for my stay this time, it felt like there was going to be a much different atmosphere in the camp: more punches thrown, fewer limos, no distractions. Well—a few distractions. As Muhammad and I walked through Pennsylvania's Allentown airport after our arrival, we spotted a college-age kid in one of the waiting areas performing magic tricks for everybody. He didn't have a hat or a tip jar out. He seemed just to be practicing his tricks and entertaining anyone around him who cared to watch. Muhammad loved magic—everything from close-up sleight-of-hand tricks to bigger stage illusions. In his trips to Las Vegas, he had become friends with Siegfried and Roy, who had given Muhammad and Veronica a behind-the-scenes look at how they accomplished some of their illusions with their beloved big cats. We stood and watched the kid in the airport for a while, and Muhammad was impressed with the guy's talent. When the boy took a step, he had a distinctive limp, but his hands moved smoothly and gracefully and were clearly capable of all kinds of misdirection.

Muhammad nodded his approval to the young magician, and we moved on. A few days later, we made a trip to the Allentown mall to pick up something for the camp, and I spotted that same young magician again. This time he was putting on much more of a performance for the shoppers around him, and—to my eyes—he was really good. Muhammad agreed. Whatever we were there to buy could wait until after the magic show. When the young guy was finished and began packing his bag, Muhammad approached him and asked if he would be willing to teach Muhammad some of the tricks we had seen. The magician obviously recognized Muhammad, and seemed very excited about the chance to be his magic instructor.

"Do you know where my training camp is?" asked Muhammad.

"Sure," he responded. "Everybody knows where your camp is."

"Come to my camp tomorrow at three p.m. How long will it take me to learn what you do?"

"It's harder than it looks, Mr. Ali. We can take one trick at a time, then you have to practice for days. It could take weeks to learn all of the tricks."

The magician came to Deer Lake the next day and stayed for four nights in his own cabin, giving Muhammad intensive tutorials and coaching him through the new tricks whenever Muhammad took a break from training. It turned out that the young man was Terry Lasorda—nephew to Tommy Lasorda, manager of the Los Angeles Dodgers. Terry had grown up in Allentown and was studying metallurgy at nearby Lehigh University. Terry had suffered from polio as a child—magic became a passion of his in part because of the escape it offered from the physical limitations the disease caused. At the end of his four days at camp, Terry presented Muhammad with a big black case containing a variety of magic tricks. Muhammad reacted as if it were the greatest gift he had ever received.

"Maaan, maaan—now you've got me hooked," he said. "I'm going to be the next Houdini. I want to learn every trick in this set, and then after the fight you're coming back with me to Chicago to be my house magician."

That's exactly what happened. Over the next year, Terry was Muhammad's private magic mentor. In addition to being a talented magician, Terry was a very sweet-natured guy, and he and Muhammad got along great. For once, Muhammad had set up a business deal in which he was getting his money's worth.

At Deer Lake, magic was a much better distraction for Muhammad than celebrity visits. The concentration Muhammad put into his tricks seemed to fit well with the mental focus he needed to apply to his training. And I will say this—Muhammad really mastered those tricks. I don't know if Muhammad had what other magicians would consider "natural" ability, but whenever he really focused on something that he wanted to do, it was amazing what he could accomplish. Watching him learn tricks from Terry, I saw the same level of concentration he put into memorizing those forty-five-minute "off the cuff" speeches he gave at college campuses. And when Muhammad performed the tricks, I could follow some of the simple things he did, but there were many times when he completely amazed me by making things appear or disappear. The amazement usually didn't last too long, though. Muhammad loved magic, but he was worried about Islamic beliefs that "illusion" was the work of the devil. So any trick he performed for you, he would perform twice: once to fool you, and then to reveal exactly how he had just fooled you.

Muhammad trained hard this time, and considering what he had told me about all those rounds of training in the ring taking their toll, I knew he was summoning every bit of willpower to push himself the way he did in the ring at Deer Lake. I knew he was in pain when he was hit, and that his hands were in tremendous pain with every blow he landed on a sparring partner. But he kept pushing himself, and soon the results began to show. He didn't go through the same battles he had before to get his weight down, and when his weight was closer to what it had been for his most memorable fights, his hand and foot speed started to pick up again, as well. All of that meant his confidence was up, too. By the end of training camp, he looked strong and fit and ready.

He had once said, "My only fault is that I don't realize how great I really am."

Maybe in his first fight with Spinks, and in some of his lesser fights, he had forgotten how great he really was.

He was not going to make that mistake again.

NINE

TRIPLE CROWN

"HEY, SHANAHAN!"

Having by now spent quite a bit of time with Muhammad in public situations, I was used to a kind of happy invisibility. Wherever we went, his presence turned ordinary moments into events. He got noticed—I did not. There was a world of experiences centered on him—not me. I liked it that way. So it was a little strange to be walking through the crowded lobby of the New Orleans Marriott Hotel just days before the second Spinks fight and hear someone call out to me. Almost as soon as I heard my name there was a tap on my shoulder, and when I turned to see who could possibly be so interested in my presence, I was surprised to see an old high school friend named Johnny Alioto.

The Aliotos had quite an interesting place in Milwaukee history. Johnny's grandfather "Papa John" Alioto was the reputed boss of the Milwaukee mob through the 1950s. When Papa John decided to become less active, he turned the reins over to his son-in-law, Frank Balistrieri. Johnny's father, Joseph, had run a very popular restaurant, Alioto's in downtown Milwaukee. (The Milwaukee Aliotos were cousins of the San Francisco Aliotos, who established their own well-known restaurant on Fisherman's Wharf.) My parents were best friends with

Joseph and his wife, Florence, so our families spent quite a bit of time together. Johnny was a year behind me in school, but I came to consider him a good friend when we both attended Marquette University High School. Joseph dropped dead of a heart attack a few years before Johnny graduated, but my parents stayed close to Florence. I hadn't seen Johnny for a few years. Looking at him now, in the lobby of the Marriott, it seemed that those years had been good to him. He wore an expensive-looking suit, and was standing with an older, dapper gentleman in an even more expensive-looking suit.

"Johnny! What are you doing here?" I exclaimed.

"I'm here with Mr. Marcello," said Johnny, nodding toward the older man. I shook hands with both of them. "Mr. Marcello put up some money for the fight and he wanted to meet Muhammad. What are you doing here, Timmy?"

"Well, it's a long story, but I'm here with Muhammad Ali," I said.

Johnny looked both surprised and impressed. "Timmy, do you think you could get us an introduction to Ali?" he asked.

This made me a little uncomfortable. Introducing Peter Gingrass to Muhammad had been a special situation. Here was yet another high school classmate I would be bringing up to Muhammad's suite. But I liked Johnny, and I thought Muhammad might like meeting Mr. Marcello. I called up to the room and asked Muhammad if he wanted to meet one of the "big money men" behind his fight. He said to come on up.

Up in the suite, Mr. Marcello and Muhammad began to talk, and Johnny and I stepped aside and spent a few minutes talking about old times. We shared a little about what our lives were like now, but it wasn't until a few days later that I fully understood how well Johnny had done for himself. "Mr. Marcello" was Carlos Marcello, the "Godfather" of the crime syndicate in New Orleans. Johnny Alioto was now a lawyer with one primary client, Mr. Marcello.

The reconnection with Johnny Alioto turned out to be very useful for Muhammad. The fight was attracting so much attention that the hotel was in almost constant chaos and it became increasingly hard to control the number of people going in and out of Muhammad's suite. As usual, some of the Deer Lake guys found a way to profit from the situation, sometimes charging people a hundred bucks for the chance to come up and meet Muhammad. I was warned not to say anything about this to Muhammad, and I didn't—not for their sake, but because I knew Muhammad had enough on his mind. I still managed to earn the Deer Lake guys' wrath, though, because when I knew Muhammad was in the mood to have visitors, I brought people like Johnny Alioto and Carlos Marcello up to the suite for free before the other guys could ask for money.

Muhammad usually enjoyed being at the center of all this kind of attention, but for this fight he had worked so hard to get himself into the proper physical and mental shape that he didn't want any prefight distractions to interfere with his focus. He talked to the fight promoters about moving out of the hotel to a private home, and word of that request made its way to Mr. Marcello. Within hours, Muhammad, Howard Bingham, and I were in a limo with a Marcello family "consultant," on our way to a plain-looking home in a quiet residential neighborhood of tree-lined streets. The move to the private house was supposed to be kept quiet, but Muhammad wanted to let one special guest in on the change in plans. John Travolta was coming to town to finally meet Muhammad in person, and was planning on staying in a suite at the Royal Orleans Hotel. In the limo, Muhammad asked me to pick up Travolta at the airport when he arrived and to bring him to the house to stay with us. No problem. I especially liked hearing that Muhammad assumed I was making the move to the house with him.

The older couple that owned the house were either friends or relatives of Marcello's, but in any case they were happy to be loaning it out for Muhammad's use. They were there when we arrived and gave us a tour of the place. The older guy thought it was important to show us where his liquor cabinet was, and encouraged us to "entertain" as much as we wanted to (though the whole point of our being there was *not* to entertain). The house was a modest three-bedroom home that looked like it hadn't been updated a bit since being built in the '40s.

Muhammad would take over the master bedroom. Travolta and I would share a guest room that had twin beds.

Travolta was coming in from London, where he had been part of the promotions around the UK release of *Grease*. The movie marked another great success for him in his young career, but it also pushed him to a new, crazy level of celebrity. On the phone he had told me that events around the London premiere had led to one of the scariest moments of his life—his limo had been surrounded by a mob of screaming fans that, in their enthusiasm, almost managed to roll the car over. Then again, celebrity had its perks—John flew private jets provided by Paramount Studios from London to New York to New Orleans, and two days before the fight I picked him up at the airport in a limo and brought him to Muhammad's new, secret house.

Well, as with anything around Muhammad, it didn't stay secret for long. Word had gotten out in the neighborhood about who was staying there, and as John and I pulled up, we saw people sitting in front of their houses up and down the street, waiting for a sighting of some sort. Muhammad himself had been at a window watching for our car and he immediately came out on the porch and started shouting, "John Travolta—my friend John Travolta has come to see Muhammad Ali! Everyone, come on over here and meet my friend John Travolta. Maaaaan, John Travolta is here to see me, I can't believe it. Come on, everyone—John Travolta and Muhammad Ali are standing right here on your street! Did you ever think that could happen here? Girls, can you believe that this is John Travolta standing so close that you can touch him? Get his autograph, too!"

So much for keeping things quiet. A few giggling girls shyly came forward with pens and paper, and just like that, the man who had wanted to get away from all the distractions was cheerfully shaking hands and signing autographs. Travolta did his best to keep up with Muhammad. They kept at it until just about every autograph book had been signed, then said goodbye and headed into the house.

Inside, Muhammad went straight to his room and I took John to the room he would be staying in. Between his jet lag and the excitement of meeting Muhammad, John was buzzing.

"What's going to happen now?" he asked, sounding as nervous as any other Ali fan would. "What do we do? Does he want to talk some more or does he need his rest? Is he going to talk to me some more?"

"Well, he said he wanted to come out here to get away from that feeling he had of having no control over the hectic pace in his suite. He's probably in his room sitting on his bed, watching TV and thinking about what he needs to do to get mentally prepared for the fight. When he's ready to do something with us he'll let us know."

John and I tried to give Muhammad as much quiet as he desired in the last couple of days before the fight, but it must have seemed a little too quiet to Muhammad—he started inviting people to come by the house, just the way they would have come by his suite. John and Muhammad got along great, and I put that liquor cabinet to use, pouring vodka tonics for such visitors as Lee "Six Million Dollar Man" Majors, John Y. Brown (soon to be the governor of Kentucky), and Hugh O'Brian.

BY THE NIGHT OF THE fight the atmosphere in the Superdome was wild—the crowd was as pumped up as any I'd ever heard. Howard Cosell was there to call the network broadcast of the fight, and Sylvester Stallone sat with Frank Gifford to provide ringside commentary. I had met Stallone in the lobby of the Marriott while I was with John. Sly seemed surprised that Travolta was a fight fan. (John said he was more "an Ali fan.") Stallone asked John if he wanted an introduction to Muhammad, then seemed even more surprised—maybe even a little jealous—when John told him we had been staying in a private home with Muhammad.

The fact that this fight was a special event was made clear even in the singing of the National Anthem—a duty that fell to Joe Frazier, of all people! John, Veronica, and I arrived together and we took our seats in the third row ringside, in front of Johnny Cash, Kris Kristofferson,

Victory dinner paid for by John Travolta the night that Muhammad beat Spinks in New Orleans to regain the heavyweight championship for a record third time.

and Liza Minnelli (who would give John and me a limo ride back to the Marriott after the fight).

Stepping into the ring, Muhammad looked more focused and intense than he had in a long time. Unlike the Shavers fight, there was no clowning around, and once the fight started, Muhammad stayed focused. He had told the press that there wouldn't be any rope-a-dope in the rematch with Spinks, and he made good on that promise. From the opening bell he was on his toes, moving and dancing and ready to really box his way back to a title. Spinks was just as aggressive as he had been in the first fight, but this time Muhammad knew how to neutralize him. In the early rounds, Muhammad's defense was more impressive than his offense, and knowing how to use his weight as an advantage, he leaned heavily on Spinks and threw off his rhythm with clinches. As the fight went on, rather than showing any signs of tiring, Muhammad seemed to pick up energy and find his own rhythm—he started landing punch after punch, and Spinks seemed incapable of any real counterattack. In the last five rounds, far from looking like a champion, Spinks looked, as Cosell put it, "befuddled." The fight was no masterpiece, but at thirty-six years of age, Ali showed the world he was still Ali, still capable of speedy jabs, powerful uppercuts, and even a bit of the fleet-footed Ali shuffle (he told me before the fight that if I saw the shuffle, it meant he had the fight under control). At the final bell, there was no question about which fighter had prevailed. By unanimous decision, Muhammad Ali became the first fighter in history to win the heavyweight championship three separate times. Veronica and I hugged each other, joyful and relieved.

Later that night, Travolta, Muhammad, Veronica, and I went to the Jonathan restaurant in the French Quarter for a celebratory dinner that John had arranged. There was a group of about ten of us that included Joan Edwards and her daughter Katie; Jerry Wurms, a Travolta high school buddy who had become a business associate; and John's longtime friend Marilu Henner—a very pretty, very upbeat woman who had just landed a role in a new TV show called *Taxi*. (I spent the day before the fight with John and his guests taking a tour of New Orleans—I have to assume we were one of the rare tour groups that drove to the Louisiana swamps in a limo.) We were shown to a private dining room on the second floor of the restaurant, a spectacular Art Deco–themed place that served gourmet-quality Creole food. John was extremely excited to be hosting a dinner for Ali, and just about everybody else shared that excitement. Muhammad himself was as cool as could be—laid-back and low-key. I knew how much winning back the title meant to him, but I also knew that he was dead tired. While the room buzzed with laughter and high spirits, Muhammad fiddled with a plate of food and didn't really engage with the party around him.

A fifteen-round heavyweight fight took a lot out of him physically, but he seemed exhausted on an even deeper level. I hoped Muhammad would see this fight as the proper ending to an incredible career. Muhammad had achieved his great goal of becoming a three-time heavyweight champion. Now he had the rare opportunity to be the first heavyweight since Rocky Marciano to go out on top, as reigning world champion.

IN THE MONTHS BEFORE THE Spinks match, to my pleasant surprise, Muhammad had started to get more and more serious about setting up a charity foundation that he could run. He had asked me once, "Do you ever think about the poor people in the world?"

"Not as much as you do," I answered.

Then he said, "I want to figure out a way I can help all the poor people in the world with my fame."

From that starting point, he came up with the idea for WORLD—World Organization for Rights, Liberty, and Dignity. Muhammad wanted the foundation to have strong, ongoing antipoverty programs, but he also wanted it to be able to help people who were in immediate crisis around the globe—people dealing with earthquake, flood, fire, and famine. His idea was that the foundation would recruit a roster of his entertainer friends—Diana Ross, Lola Falana, Kris Kristofferson, Stevie Wonder, the Temptations, James Brown, and so on. In the wake of a natural disaster, the foundation would arrange a slate of WORLD talent to put on a benefit concert to raise money for relief. The idea seemed wild back then, but it was the same idea that would lead to Live Aid, Farm Aid, the Concert for Sandy Relief, and others. Muhammad was ahead of his time.

To launch such a foundation would take a lot of legal and financial planning, and Muhammad asked for help from a couple of the attorneys that Robert Abboud had put in charge of his business affairs, Michael Phenner and William Sutter. The foundation was also going to need some serious outside funding, so Muhammad put Gene Dibble to work tracking down potential financial partners. I was happy that Muhammad was finally taking some real steps to set up something he would do after boxing, so I offered to do anything I could to help get the foundation going. Through Dibble, I was put in touch with what at first sounded like an unlikely lead—the Christian Crusade, an evangelical organization based in Tulsa, Oklahoma, that was founded by the anti-Communist preacher Billy James Hargis. I flew out to Tulsa to meet with the Christian Crusade business manager, Lonnie Rex, and an attorney, Craig Blackstock, and found both of them to be very enthusiastic about getting behind Muhammad's foundation. Lonnie Rex's idea for coming up with funding was simple and direct: he proposed sending a newsletter to everyone on the Crusade's five-million-member mailing list that would ask for one-dollar donation to Muhammad Ali's favorite charity. Even if only half the recipients responded, there would be enough money to set up the foundation. Muhammad's WORLD dream was starting to feel like a reality.

HOLLYWOOD OFFERED ANOTHER OPTION FOR Muhammad's life after boxing. In November 1978, he headed off to Natchez, Mississippi, to begin work on *Freedom Road*, a Zev Braun–produced TV miniseries in which Muhammad played the lead role of Gideon Jackson, a Civil War–era slave who eventually becomes a U.S. senator. Chet Walker of the Chicago Bulls was a coproducer on the project, and Veronica had a small role as a senator's wife. I flew out to the film shoot a couple of times to see how Muhammad was taking to the acting life.

He wasn't. He had always liked the idea of becoming the "Dark Gable" as he put it, but—as he had once discussed with Warren Beatty—the painfully slow day-by-day mechanics of making a film were not easy for Muhammad. The first time I walked onto the set, just before a lunch break, I was excited by what looked like a place of great activity. But when I found Muhammad at his trailer, his heart didn't seem to be in the work.

"How's it going?" I asked.

"OK," he said flatly.

"What scene are you working on?"

"Mm—we've been sitting around all morning."

"Doing what?"

"We're sitting at a table, and the maid is supposed to come in and pour me a cup of tea. We had three or four lines of dialogue. It took an hour and a half to pour me one cup of tea. That's all we got done this morning."

Muhammad learned some new pranks from his *Freedom Road* costar Kris Kristofferson, with whom he began a close and enduring friendship. One prank was something Kris said he had learned from Willie Nelson. The idea was to walk up behind someone, put your hand close by the person's ear, and rub your thumb and index fingers across each other to create a fluttering sound like a moth or fly. The finger and thumb had to be dry, and if you got the sound just right, people would start swatting at their ear to make the mysterious insect go away. Kristofferson, following Willie's advice, would do this once to an unsuspecting victim and then walk away, maintaining the mystery. Muhammad, being Muhammad, would continue to do it until the person caught on to what was going on.

The long days wore on Muhammad, but we had some good times toward the end of the shoot, when I flew back to Natchez with Travolta on John's DC 3, which was decked out with its own lounge and dancefloor. John actually flew the plane, with a private pilot serving as co-pilot. Muhammad made another big loud fuss over the fact that "Superstar John Travolta" had come to visit him, and enjoyed introducing Travolta to Kristofferson. After dinner the first night, John gave Muhammad a tour of his plane, which he had landed in a nearby open field. He offered to take Muhammad up for a flight, but Muhammad's response was "No thanks. I don't like flying, and I would like it even less if the pilot is somebody I know."

Muhammad was always talking about how much he loved to watch John dance, so one of those nights I made arrangements for Muhammad,

John, and Veronica to go out to a little disco that was next to the motel we were staying in.

Before we left the motel, I asked John if he could teach Muhammad a simple step from *Saturday Night Fever* that he could use on the dance floor. John agreed to try, and Muhammad put in a decent effort, but it was not a pretty sight. After about five minutes of struggle, John rested his head on Muhammad's chest and said, "This is going to take longer than I thought."

"I told you," Muhammad said with a shrug, "I only dance in the ring!"

Most of the locals at the disco knew that Ali and Kris were in town, but when Muhammad walked in with Travolta, you could feel the excitement ratchet up. We got a table in front right on the dance floor and as soon as we were seated the disc jockey put on "More Than a Woman," a song from *Saturday Night Fever.* John asked Veronica if she would like to dance, and Veronica said "yes" with a big smile on her face. They started dancing, and looked terrific together (to me, Veronica looked better with John than any of his partners in *Saturday Night Fever*). Muhammad also got a great kick out of watching them dance together, especially when they did some of the moves from the movie ("She's good," he commented). Muhammad waited until the DJ slowed things down with "How Deep Is Your Love," put his arms around Veronica, and shuffled along with her to the beat. He didn't get close to the fancy footwork of the famous "Ali Shuffle," but he did look happy and very much in love.

When the shoot finally came to an end, Muhammad seemed to have decided that he was not interested in becoming the Dark Gable.

"My whole life is a movie," he told me. "I star in it every day. I don't want to be anyone else except Muhammad Ali."

MUHAMMAD AND I WERE IN the kitchen at the South Woodlawn home one night in December when Muhammad asked me a question that caught me off guard.

"How much do you make a year?"

"Twenty-four thousand salary, with commissions thirty," I said. (That seemed like decent money at the time.)

"I'll pay you fifty."

"It's a deal!" I answered quickly, with a laugh. But I saw right away that Muhammad was not joking around.

"Tim," he said, "why don't you come work for me? You work hard, you help a lot of people, but I need you to help me start WORLD. You've got the experience with the Athletes charity. I need you to help me set this up."

"Muhammad—why would you want me to work for you? I'm in medical sales. What I did for Athletes for a Better Education had nothing to do with running the organization. I just helped recruit people to contribute their time. Whatever you need help with in business, you can always find somebody better at it than me."

"Look. I trust you as much as I trust Rahaman and Veronica."

I had never heard him express his trust in me so strongly and directly. It took me a moment to respond. I said, "Well, that puts a little pressure on me, doesn't it?"

He laughed.

"Muhammad, I'll do anything for you—as a friend. If I start working for you, everything changes. Our friendship would be affected by that. I wouldn't want to work directly for you and have you pay me a salary. If I ever did that, I would have to know and be confident that I was the right person for that job. Even then, I would be so worried about doing a good job for you, I would live that job twenty-four hours a day trying to do it right. So I hope that you understand, Muhammad, right now I would rather just be your friend, and as a friend I can help you find the right person for the job."

He looked thoughtful for a moment, then said, "So what if I don't sign your paycheck? What if you don't work for me directly? You did a good job with the Athletes organization, and you'll do a good job working for WORLD. The lawyers are setting it up right now, and you'll have a role helping to run the foundation. You'll work for the foundation. Not for me."

Working for the foundation sounded a lot different from being one of the guys on Muhammad's personal payroll. If I could be involved in an organization close to Muhammad's heart and serve a good cause without getting in the middle of his personal business decisions, I could work closely with him without having to strike some balance between thinking of him as a boss and a friend. Frankly, whenever I spoke with Lonnie Rex or Mike Phenner, they seemed to assume I was already working for the foundation, so why not make it official?

"You know what, Muhammad? That sounds pretty good to me," I said.

"All right. Richard Durham will be president, Dibble's going to be vice president, and you'll be secretary. You'll coordinate everything between the board and the officers and the money people. Keep it running smooth. It's the perfect position for you."

"Well, I've never been a secretary before, but I think that I can handle that."

And that was that. Not long after that kitchen conversation, the legal papers for the foundation were drawn up. Durham was a black writer who did pioneering work in radio and had also coauthored Muhammad's 1975 autobiography, *The Greatest*. He and Dibble assumed their roles as president and vice president, and I officially became secretary of the World Organization for Rights, Liberty, and Dignity. I didn't quit my day job, and my day-to-day routine didn't change much, but I was ready for a new adventure with Muhammad.

FOR A WHILE NOW, MUHAMMAD and Veronica had been contemplating a major change in their lives—a move to Los Angeles. Veronica had been raised in Los Angeles and had never acclimated to the cold weather and snow. Muhammad loved the city of Chicago, and still liked being close to the Nation of Islam headquarters, but he had never been a big fan of the cold weather, either. Veronica's parents were still in Los Angeles, and she wanted to be closer to them and her five siblings (her parents, of course, loved the idea of having the grandkids Hana and Laila nearby).

Los Angeles also made sense for the future Muhammad was planning after boxing. Helga and I were going to miss having Muhammad and Veronica so close to us, but we also felt that at this point, no matter what happened, we would remain a part of one another's lives.

In anticipation of the move, the four of us took a trip to the West Coast in December 1978 and celebrated Christmas in Los Angeles with Veronica's parents. Right after the holidays, Muhammad was hosting the second annual Muhammad Ali Invitational Track Meet in Long Beach, and Muhammad and Veronica were going to spend time after the track meet to look at a new home that they were planning on buying in Hancock Park. For the track event, Helga and I stayed in luxury suites on the *Queen Mary*, and as we lazed around on the deck of the great ship in 70-degree sunshine—thinking about the snowfall back in Chicago—the appeal of Southern California seemed pretty obvious. The event itself was a lot of fun. Muhammad enjoyed being the beloved

Veronica and me at an "Urban Cowboy" party in Calabasas, California, 1980. I would have taken a chance on the mechanical bull, but she wouldn't let me.

and celebrated center of attention there; the AAU-sanctioned athletics competition was world class, and there was even a celebrity run that featured Jimmy Ellis, the jockey Angel Cordero, and U.S. Senator Alan Cranston.

Veronica took me along one day to show me the house she had picked out for her and Muhammad. I always enjoyed spending time with Veronica, and while Muhammad could definitely have a jealous streak when other men were around her, he seemed to trust my being alone with his beautiful wife. Even she was sometimes a little surprised that our friendship didn't bother Muhammad. I told Veronica that I believed the trust was there because we had a strong friendship between two couples. Muhammad could see that I loved Helga and he knew also that we both loved him. All four of us were always laughing, joking around, and having fun together as equals, and Helga and I knew how lucky we were to be a part of Muhammad's life. There just wasn't any reason for jealousy.

Muhammad's friend Lou Rawls was living in Los Angeles, and he asked June Eckstine—the Realtor ex-wife of the great swing bandleader Billy Eckstine—to help Veronica find a home near his on Fremont Place, a gated community of seventy-five homes in the well-to-do Hancock Park neighborhood. It was the wealthiest area in Los Angeles before being superseded by Beverly Hills. The houses on Fremont Place were still often used as exteriors in movies and TV series, and Fremont had a reputation for being home to L.A.'s black elite (Mayor Tom Bradley was a current resident). June found a beautiful house just a block away from Lou Rawls's place. It was breathtaking—a stunning, ivory-colored Italian Renaissance-style mansion sitting atop a rolling lawn. I watched Veronica's eyes light up as she walked inside, through the nine bedrooms, four bathrooms, and 10,000 square feet of living space. She knew immediately that this was what she and Muhammad wanted, and I knew, given her creativity and great sense of design, that she was already imagining how she would transform this big empty house into a beautiful home for the Muhammad Ali family.

• • •

MUHAMMAD AND I WENT ON a different kind of shopping trip a day later. We were driving down Wilshire Boulevard in a brand-new Cadillac that he had just bought for his father-in-law, when Muhammad decided that he wanted a new car for himself. Not just any car—but a new Rolls-Royce that would be waiting for him when he flew back to move into his new house. He asked me where we should go to buy a Rolls, and I suggested we head into Beverly Hills, where there were plenty of luxury car dealerships. We passed quite a few—Porsche, Jaguar, Ferrari, Lamborghini—before stopping at a Rolls/Bentley dealership. The place looked like it had just gotten a fresh shipment of vehicles. There still was a ramp attached to the showroom floor where new cars had just been placed, including a two-tone beige-and-brown Rolls Corniche convertible that was at the window closest to the street. Outside, employees were still moving cars into place around the crowded lot.

As soon as we parked, Muhammad stepped out of the car and headed straight inside to the two-tone Corniche. The three salesmen in the showroom stood and stared at Muhammad, not sure if they should approach. Muhammad stayed focused on the Corniche and seemed impressed that it had a new feature none of his other cars had—a car phone. He was also happy to see that the Corniche had a top-of-the-line cassette player and sound system—even in a Rolls, we had to be able to sing along to his favorite Temptations and Smokey Robinson tapes. Muhammad got behind the wheel and asked the manager for the keys. The manager told the Champ that they were not allowed to start up any cars on display in the showroom.

"What if I wanna buy this car right now?" asked Muhammad. "I have to hear the engine."

The manager handed over the keys. Muhammad started it up and let it run for a couple of minutes. He started asking the manager questions about the car's specs: how many cylinders?; how much horsepower?; how fast could it go? (the answers were 8 cylinders, 218 horsepower, and 130 mph). Muhammad also wanted to see how the automatic convertible top went up and down, which took a few minutes.

The staffers had just finished closing the windows and were about to move the ramp away from the dock when Muhammad said, "Wait a minute. Don't move that ramp—I wanna take this for a test drive. I'm gonna buy this Rolls."

The manager looked stricken. "Right now?" he sputtered. "Mr. Ali—I'm not sure if we can do that. We'll have to do this another time. We're simply not equipped—"

Muhammad cut him off sharply. "Call my lawyer," he said, handing the manager a business card. One of the strict conditions Robert Abboud had instituted in taking on Muhammad as a client was that if Muhammad was considering a decision involving business or money, he was to consult with his attorney Mike Phenner. To make that easy, Muhammad had been supplied with a few of Phenner's business cards. The manager tried to keep his smile in place as he looked at Phenner's information.

"Call him and tell him I'm going to buy this car right now. Have him give you all the information you need for me to buy this car. But before I buy it, I want to take it for a test drive."

The manager looked at Ali, looked back at the card, and then shrugged. Suddenly the whole sales staff kicked into action again, reopening the showroom and moving the cars around so that Muhammad could take his test drive. I got in the passenger side, and as soon as there was a clear path, Muhammad drove the Corniche out of the showroom and right onto Wilshire Boulevard.

I didn't bother asking Muhammad where we were going—I was just going to enjoy the ride. We drove out to the beach in Santa Monica and up the Pacific Coast Highway to Malibu and on to Pepperdine University's campus. We had the top down and the radio blasting the Bee Gees' "How Deep Is Your Love." It felt like a perfect California dream to me.

I don't think Robert Abboud had imagined that "consulting" with Mike Phenner would mean using the lawyer's card to buy a Rolls-Royce—but it sure was a nice ride. So our "test drive" became a new owner's first pleasure drive. When we finally drove back to Veronica's home, her brother Tony and I drove back to the dealership to pick up

Muhammad's Cadillac. Mike Phenner, back in Chicago, apparently handled whatever paperwork the dealership needed.

The Ali home at Fremont Place in Hancock Park, Los Angeles.

The next day, Muhammad told Veronica and me that he wanted to take the new Rolls on a real road trip over the next few days, before we all flew back to Chicago. I knew that John Travolta had just purchased an 86-acre ranch in Santa Ynez, in the hills above Santa Barbara, and I called him to see if the timing worked out for us to come up for a visit. John was planning on flying to Vail to go skiing that weekend with some friends, but, to accommodate us, he put the trip off until Monday. He told me he would be honored to have Muhammad as a guest and told me to contact Joan Edwards to get the exact directions to his ranch.

That afternoon Helga, Veronica, and I climbed in the Rolls and, with Muhammad at the wheel, we joined the stream of Friday traffic on the 101 North headed out of town. Helga and I were very excited to be taking a road trip together with Muhammad and Veronica—especially in the new car—and for the first hour or so of the trip there was a lot of animated conversation. But it was a rare rainy day in Southern

California, and after a while, the slow progress on the freeway and the wet weather had put everyone in a more reflective mood. The car became very quiet and then silent. For a good fifteen minutes, the only sounds were the radio and the steady beat of the windshield wipers.

Muhammad finally broke the silence, repeating a point he had made to me back on Lake Shore Drive. "See, this is why we are all friends," he said. "We have been driving for miles, nobody has said a word, and we're all happy. We understand each other."

I quoted back to him a line from the book of quotations I had given him as a birthday present: "Friends listen to what you say. Best friends listen to what you don't say."

"Heavy," came the deep-voiced reply from the front seat.

We drove in comfortable silence a while longer, when suddenly a big red "generator" light lit up on the dashboard.

"Tim, what does that mean?"

"I'm not sure, Muhammad, but that red light looks serious. Let's find a gas station."

We spotted one almost immediately off the freeway. As we pulled in, a guy in dirty overalls came out of the station and approached. As soon as he saw who was driving—and what he was driving—the guy let out a little hoot.

"I'll be goddamned! Muhammad Ali in a Rolls-Royce!" he said. "What are *you* doing *here?*"

"We're visiting friends," said Muhammad, "but this warning light came on a few minutes ago. Do you know what it means?"

The guy looked at the light, then told Ali to pull the car into the garage. We all went inside the station to get out of the rain. I bought two Kit Kats and split them among the four of us. About fifteen minutes later the attendant came in and said, "I fixed it. And, if you don't mind, can I ask how much you paid for that Rolls?"

"One hundred and sixteen thousand," Muhammad said.

"Well, that hundred-and-sixteen-thousand-dollar Rolls won't go very far without this four ninety-five fuse I just replaced."

We all thanked the guy, and Muhammad asked, "How much do I owe you?"

"No charge, Champ, but could you please sign my notepad so I can show my dad? He's a big fan and he won't believe you were one of my customers today."

Muhammad signed the pad and handed it back to the guy with a twenty and a ten.

The rain finally let up a few miles from the turnoff to Travolta's property near Gaviota State Park. Even after we made that turn, there was a mile of winding road leading to the main ranch house. Along the way, we saw groves of lemon, lime, and avocado trees. At one point, we saw fifteen or twenty Mexican laborers up on ladders picking fruit.

With mock astonishment, Muhammad said, "Tim—you didn't tell me Travolta owned slaves."

It really was great for the four of us to spend some perfectly relaxed time with John (though Muhammad, in typical fashion, got antsy and impulsively cut our stay short from two nights to one). I

Ali and Travolta, the weekend we drove Muhammad's brand-
new Rolls-Royce up to John's Santa Barbara ranch.

knew how much John was looking forward to this visit. For all that was going well for him, he was also going through some tough times. His run on *Welcome Back, Kotter* was ending, and I knew it had to be hard for him to say goodbye to the cast and crew he had been working with for years. The transition from steady TV work wasn't helped by the fact that John's latest movie, *Moment by Moment*, with Lily Tomlin, was the first major flop of his career. Most significant, John was still devastated by the death just weeks earlier of his mother, to whom he had been extremely close. I told Veronica and Muhammad about all this before we arrived, and Muhammad said he would talk to John when the time was right.

That night at the ranch we had an Asian-themed meal prepared by John's private chef. John wanted to keep the mood light, but Muhammad knew what was on John's mind and decided to be open about it. He offered Travolta some beautiful words of consolation about his mother's passing, and then added some words of encouragement about the actor's career.

"How old are you?" Muhammad began.

"Twenty-four," John answered.

"I was twenty-two when I shocked the world and became the heavyweight champion. I wouldn't let anyone convince me not to believe in myself. But when you achieve worldwide fame everything in your life changes and nothing will ever be the same. People are going to want your opinion on everything: politics, religion, sex, drugs, cars, movies. They will want answers to all their questions. You have to adjust to that and love what you're doing. Remain true to yourself and never doubt yourself. When the press is telling the world that you are finished, prove them wrong. The people who wrote negative things about me are the people who motivated me the most. You are already a great actor, John, and the fights in your life are just going to make you stronger. Always look to the future with dreams and forget about the negatives in the past."

We had just been served dessert, and with perfect timing Muhammad finished his advice to John and dug into some chocolate mousse.

John was beaming like he had just received a blessing (which, I suppose, he had).

The phone rang and John took the call in the kitchen, speaking for about ten minutes. When he hung up he told us that the caller was Veronique Peck, Gregory's wife. She had invited John to a small dinner party at their home in Holmby Hills the following Friday. The other guests at the party would be Cary Grant, Kirk Douglas, Jimmy Stewart, and their wives. Apparently the Hollywood "old guard" wanted to meet the new star and give him whatever guidance they could. John was ecstatic. And Muhammad was blown away.

"See, good things are going to happen for you," he said. "And one day you will be calling some young rising star to give him guidance on his career."

ON ONE OF OUR LAST nights in Los Angeles, Muhammad, Veronica, Helga, and I went out to dinner at the Red Dragon Chinese restaurant on Wilshire Boulevard. The restaurant was very busy, and, of course, everyone in the place took notice when Muhammad walked in. As we settled in to our table, Veronica gave Muhammad some explicit instructions.

"Now, Muhammad," she said, "I don't want you signing any autographs before dinner. Let's have a nice meal together—with hot food. After we eat, you can sign as much as you want."

Muhammad nodded in agreement. But not long after we had ordered our food, a pretty little ten-year-old girl came up to the table with a pen and paper and asked for an autograph. Muhammad talked with her and gave her an autograph. Then an older man came over to shake hands and ask for an autograph. Muhammad signed for him. Pretty soon there was a line of fellow diners snaking around our table, made up of smiling people who wanted a moment with the Champ. Muhammad kept talking to these fans and signing autographs, even as our dinner was brought to the table. Veronica just shook her head—she had been in this situation many times before—and with smiles we all started eating our food while it was still hot. After fifteen or twenty minutes Muhammad had spoken with everybody in line and began to eat with us.

I asked the question that seemed to be hanging in the air: "Muhammad, I know you don't want to turn anybody down, but why wouldn't you wait until after you'd had your dinner?"

He answered with a story I had never heard him tell before.

"When I was sixteen years old in 1958, a buddy and I were in New York for the Golden Gloves competition," Muhammad explained. "Sugar Ray Robinson was my hero, and I found out that he had a restaurant in New York about twenty blocks from where we were staying. I heard he was at the restaurant on weekends, so on Friday night we walked over there, even though it was raining like crazy. I was so excited about the chance to meet my hero. I was going to ask him to sign an autograph to me: 'To Cassius Marcellus Clay Junior, the future heavyweight champion of the world.'

"We waited under the restaurant's awning for about forty-five minutes, and then I saw the car I knew to look for, Sugar Ray's maroon Cadillac. Sugar Ray got out of the car and walked around to open the passenger door for a beautiful blonde in a white fur coat. They walked toward us, and I held out my pen and paper and started to speak. But Ray just walked right past us and said, 'Not now, kid—can't you see I'm busy?' Then he was through the door of the restaurant and gone. No punch ever hurt as much as that did. I sat down on the curb right there in the rain and cried like a baby.

"People will forget what you said, and they will forget what you did, but they will never forget how you made them feel," Muhammad told us. "I will never look down on the people who look up to me. This isn't the only Chinese dinner I'm ever going to eat, but it might be the only time these people ever get a chance to meet me. If I can make that moment special for them, I'm going to do it, and they'll never forget how I made them feel."

•   •   •

WHEN WE FINALLY FLEW BACK to Chicago, we were welcomed home by a bitter January cold. During our sunny week in California, Chicago had been hit by one of the heaviest snowfalls in thirty years. Muhammad and Veronica were met at the gate by a driver, and headed home in Muhammad's Rolls. Helga and I trudged to the airport parking lot to get our car, but the snow plows working around the lots had managed to pile so much snow over and around our car that there was no way to get to it. Helga and I, shivering in the icy wind, finally managed to hail a taxi for the ride home.

As we struggled to regain feeling in our fingers and toes in the backseat of the cab, a move to a warmer place didn't sound like a bad idea. I repeated to Helga something that I had heard Muhammad say a couple of times: "We have got to get out of this city."

TEN

STAR POWER

ONCE AGAIN, I STOOD IN Muhammad's kitchen. It was January 18, 1979, the morning after his birthday, and he was coming in for breakfast after a short morning run. Again, he asked a question that caught me off guard.

"When are you going to sell your condominium?"

"What do you mean, Muhammad?"

"We're moving to L.A. You should sell it before we move."

This was the first time that he made it sound like the "we" in "We're moving to L.A." actually included Helga and me. "Well—when are *we* moving to L.A.?" I asked.

"March or April."

"That's short notice, Muhammad. Let me talk to Helga."

"She'll come," he said with a shrug.

I was still wondering whether I had made the right decision in becoming a part of Muhammad's foundation, and the thought of pulling up stakes to join him in Los Angeles felt a little risky. But the foundation was starting to come together. Through Lonnie Rex's connections, sixty-four different nations had agreed to become sponsors of Ali's charity, and Dibble and I had lined up a roster of fifty-two top entertainers who had pledged to perform at WORLD events. Additionally,

Lonnie Rex's fund-raising newsletter was starting to get results. Christian Crusade members were sending in their one-dollar donations, and that drive alone would eventually add up to $3 million of funding. My job as secretary of a multimillion-dollar foundation certainly sounded substantial enough to justify a move to California.

Still, I couldn't shake thoughts of Ali's Trolley and Champburger—other "surefire" Ali endeavors that had fallen apart when he grew tired of them. Helga and I spent a long time talking things over, and we decided we would make the move to L.A. with Muhammad and Veronica if I could secure a second job there in my own field. Not long after that discussion, I was playing a friendly game of handball with one of Chicago's top heart surgeons, Robert Gasior, and when I explained my situation, he told me that he had just spoken with an associate who was looking for a manager for a new pacemaker company in Los Angeles. I quickly put together a second West Coast exploratory trip. I called Joan Edwards, John Travolta's personal assistant, and she was kind enough to put me up for a week. After two days of extensive interviews with the executive board of American Technology Pacemakers, I was offered the position of regional manager for California, Arizona, and Nevada. Whatever happened with WORLD, I would still have a steady job, doing work I was familiar with. Helga and I would make the move.

By April Muhammad, Veronica, Helga, and I, along with most of our earthly possessions, were in Los Angeles. In the rush to make the move to L.A., Helga and I still hadn't figured out where we were going to live. Muhammad took care of that. On one of those first days at the house on Fremont Place, he took me upstairs and pointed at one of the guest bedrooms.

"That's your and Helga's room," he said.

So we began our new life in Los Angeles as housemates with Muhammad, Veronica, Hana, and Laila.

IN CHICAGO, MUHAMMAD WAS INDISPUTABLY the biggest celebrity in town. In L.A., he was a superstar living among superstars—one of his neighbors on

Fremont Place was Donna Summer, who was then at the top of the pop charts. But on one of our first nights out in the city that was our new home, I saw that Muhammad was still in a class of stardom all by himself.

He and I arranged to have dinner with John Travolta's business attorney, Fred Gaines, to discuss John's possible participation in WORLD foundation events. Fred got us a table at one of the hottest restaurants in town, L'Orangerie. He told us he had selected the restaurant not only because the haute cuisine there was exceptional, but also because the owners, Gerard and Virginie Ferry, made a point of being very discreet about their clientele. A-listers such as Frank Sinatra, Warren Beatty, Cary Grant, and Ronald and Nancy Reagan could dine there without any fear of having their privacy compromised in any way. It seemed important to Fred to make sure Muhammad understood that at L'Orangerie he would not be bothered by the public. (I didn't have the heart to tell Fred how much Muhammad enjoyed being "bothered" by the public.)

We got to the restaurant, and the maitre d' ushered us toward a VIP table on the back, outdoor patio. As soon as we stepped onto that patio, one of the diners spotted Muhammad and immediately stood up and began to applaud. Another couple stood and joined in. Then another and another. Within seconds, Muhammad was receiving a full standing ovation from this poshest of crowds. By the time we sat at our own table, Fred was looking a little flustered.

"Well, Muhammad." He sighed. "Didn't I tell you this place was discreet about celebrities?"

Muhammad laughed—he loved it. And no sooner had we been handed menus when someone called over to congratulate Muhammad on his victory in the Spinks rematch and on being a three-time champion. Muhammad thanked the man, then waved him and his date over to our table and signed an autograph for them. Once that happened, others were emboldened to approach, and so all through dinner Muhammad kept signing. At one point our waiter actually looked upset that the restaurant's protocol of "leave the celebrities alone" had fallen apart around Muhammad.

"I'm so sorry," he whispered. "This has never happened before."

Muhammad said, "It's all right," and just kept smiling and signing and shaking hands. By the end of the dinner Fred began apologizing again. Muhammad responded by telling him the Sugar Ray Robinson story he had told us at the Red Dragon. This time, he ended by asking Fred, "Wouldn't you sign your name if you knew it could give that much happiness to someone else?"

Fred replied, "I guess now I know why they call you the Greatest!"

IN JUNE, MUHAMMAD HELD A press conference in which he made the announcement that many of us had been waiting for: he was officially retiring from boxing. I suspected that stepping away from the boxing ring—the place that had made him a champion—might be a difficult psychological adjustment for him. But I also knew how tired Muhammad was of his training regimens, and he truly seemed excited about focusing his attention on the foundation and other business interests. I felt a great sense of relief, because by this point it had become impossible to ignore some of the physical damage that had been done to his body. Those very occasional stumbles in his walk happened more frequently now—not often, but more frequently. For a while I had been watching him closely for any signs of telltale changes, and I was certain that he had been slowing down physically and athletically from the day I had met him. Now that his fighting days were over, maybe he would have a chance to heal.

One of the first steps Muhammad took in his new life as a businessman was to set up an office. Lonnie Rex had suggested to us that having an office for WORLD outside Muhammad's home would not only seem more professional, it would make for a nice tax write-off. We found a place in an office building on the 3600 block of Wilshire Boulevard, just a few blocks away from the famed Ambassador Hotel. In Chicago, Robert Abboud and Mike Phenner had found a wonderful woman named Marge Thomas to work as an administrative assistant and executive secretary on Muhammad's accounts, and she was dedicated enough to make the move to L.A. and begin running the office there. Marge was extremely competent, but she had her work cut out for her. The WORLD foundation was taking shape, but Muhammad's finances were still tangled up in a mess of poor previously made business and endorsement deals, and he was sometimes still making financial commitments without running them past his team of advisers at First National Bank.

Muhammad loved the idea of being successful at business and talked a lot about being the kind of businessman who would use his money to make more money. But, rather than master the art of contractual fine print, Muhammad's first big goal was to *look* the part of the prosperous businessman: the thing he really wanted to do most in retirement was to wear a suit and tie and carry an attaché case. So he had a wardrobe of beautiful suits custom-tailored for him, and purchased a fine leather attaché case that he carried with him whenever he went to the office. The contents of that case were usually a Quran, a yellow legal pad for copying passages from it, and a few of the magic tricks Terry Lasorda had given him. But Muhammad did indeed look like a smart, distinguished executive.

He also wanted to be seen by other executives. One afternoon I dropped by the office and Muhammad told me he wanted to go to the bar at the Cocoanut Grove nightclub inside the Ambassador Hotel—he had heard somewhere that L.A.'s downtown businessmen had a cocktail at the Grove after work. I knew the place was a celebrity hangout and I wasn't crazy about dealing with the hassle of getting our cars in and out of the Ambassador parking lot, so I suggested a closer location. The ground floor of Muhammad's office building was home to a popular hot spot called the Red Onion. We could go down there and have a drink with some of the businessmen who worked in his own building. Muhammad agreed. We dropped off his attaché case in his Rolls, then headed into the Red Onion's bar area, put some money in the jukebox, took our places at a cocktail table, and ordered a drink. In keeping with his Muslim faith, Muhammad almost never consumed any alcohol, but for now, to play the role of a businessman, he would sip a cocktail with me. He asked me what I was going to order, and I suggested a whiskey sour. There were a few other guys in suits in the bar area—they said hello to Muhammad and were excited to hear that he was working in the building. There wasn't much of a scene there, though, and after about half an hour I could tell Muhammad was ready to go. I finished my whiskey sour—and finished most of his—and we took off. One time on the bar scene was enough for Muhammad. The five p.m. executive cocktail did not become a regular part of his schedule.

I WAS ENJOYING MY WORK with both the foundation and the pacemaker company, and Helga soon had a position managing the upscale Pratesi linen store on Rodeo Drive in Beverly Hills (the kind of place that supplied Elizabeth Taylor, Barbra Streisand, and Cher with silk sheets and Italian cotton pillowcases). Veronica was busy taking care of Hana and Laila and decorating the new home with her impressive designer's eye, and Muhammad spent some time at the Wilshire office, though after just a few weeks he began working most of the time out of his home office.

There was more than enough room in the big new house for all of us to live comfortably, and it was wonderful to be able to spend that much time together so easily. I especially enjoyed the extra time I got to spend with Hana and Laila. One day I walked into the kitchen at Fremont Place when three-year-old Hana startled me by shouting "TIM SHANAHAN" just the way her father might. She let out a big laugh and then shouted it again, which made me laugh. It sure felt good to have two members of the Ali family who enjoyed shouting my name.

I loved to put on music and teach Hana dance steps. She would try hard to copy whatever I was doing, and even at three she moved with a natural ease. It wouldn't take long before she got silly, though, exaggerating all the moves to be funny and then losing interest entirely (again, like father, like daughter). Eventually she would decide that she was the star of the show and would cut loose with her own moves.

Hana was a snuggler, and no sooner would I sit down in that house than I would have her climbing into my lap. Little Laila, at only one

"Uncle Tim" with Hana Ali. I'm teaching her the words to Harry Belafonte's "Jamaica Farewell"—Laila eventually learned the lyrics, also.

and a half, had a very different temperament. While Hana looked more like Muhammad, Laila looked more like Veronica, and she had a personality more like her mother's. She was shy, reserved, and didn't want to be held by anyone, not even her father—though when she saw Hana sitting in her dad's lap she would want to compete for that seat of honor.

THE MOVE TO LOS ANGELES marked a wonderful new phase of life for all of us, but some things stayed the same—like Muhammad's sense of humor. Not long after Muhammad opened his office, he had a press conference there with French, British, and Australian reporters. I happened to walk in during the group interview.

"Tim Shanahan!" Muhammad called out. Then, to the reporters, he said, "This guy looks white, doesn't he?"

The members of the foreign press looked thoroughly puzzled.

"Well," continued Muhammad, "he's my cousin. His name is Tim Shanahan and he's a nigga like me, but he's been passing for years."

The reporters looked like they were desperately trying to work out whether Muhammad was teasing them or whether I had lied to him about my heritage. Muhammad didn't say another word about it—he just went right back to answering whatever the last interview question had been.

Now that Muhammad wasn't fighting, there wasn't any reason for many of his Deer Lake hangers-on to be around, so there were a lot more chances for us to do things together. I still ran every day on my own and tried to play as much tennis as I could—one of the joys of Los Angeles weather was that it was so easy to be active outdoors. Muhammad, on the other hand, did not work out at all. He had put his training days behind him and didn't seem to miss them. He did love the California sunshine, though. He told me that as a kid he had helped his father paint mosaics on the outside of churches, and that in the winter they could work only twenty minutes at a time before they would have to climb down their ladder and warm up in his father's truck. He said, "If my dad lived in California he could have got a lot more churches painted a lot faster."

We did take long drives together just the way we had in Chicago. He loved getting out on the Pacific Coast Highway in his Rolls or in his new silver Stutz Blackhawk, driving alongside the beautiful blue ocean from Santa Monica to Malibu and beyond. When the surf was in sight and we hit cruising speed, he liked to crank up the cassette player to blast his favorite songs. He loved playing the same trick on me he had played on Chicago drives—encouraging me to sing along with the highest falsetto parts, then cutting the volume to see if I was on pitch or not. With a laugh, he would screech out his own mocking falsetto, knowing it didn't come close to whatever Brian Wilson or Eddie Kendricks had been singing.

Muhammad also took advantage of L.A.'s car culture to interact with the public in new ways. When we pulled up to a stoplight, he loved to see the shocked looks on the faces of the drivers in the cars next to us when they happened to look our way. If that driver was a good-looking woman, Muhammad would mouth the words "I love you," just before we drove away. He would do the same thing when he spotted a good-looking woman driving on the freeway. Occasionally, after he was recognized, other freeway drivers would follow us to our turnoff. Muhammad didn't mind—he'd find a place to pull over and would give the pursuing motorists as many autographs as they asked for.

I NEVER MADE THE MISTAKE of thinking that I was special just because I was around Muhammad, but as his friend I was confident enough to feel comfortable around the many celebrities that were now part of our lives in Los Angeles. I was friendly with our Fremont Place neighbors: Lou Rawls, the actor Lou Gossett Jr., and Donna Summer. Eventually I became close enough to Donna to be one of the few men invited to her baby shower a couple of years later. Through Donna I got to meet two of her close friends, Natalie Cole and Chaka Khan, and I was together with all of them backstage at the Universal Amphitheater when Donna performed there. One of Muhammad's oldest celebrity friendships is with Chubby Checker. (Muhammad liked to say that they had both become famous as "dancers," and that Chubby looked like his blood brother.) Muhammad first met Chubby in Louisville when they were teenagers—Muhammad was an up-and-coming Golden Glover and Chubby was just about to launch his career with "The Twist." Chubby became famous before Muhammad, but he always treated Muhammad so kindly that Muhammad never forgot it. They stayed friends through the years, and whenever Chubby came through town on tour, he spent time with Muhammad.

Muhammad became friendly with Sylvester Stallone after the success of *Rocky* (he memorably snuck up behind Stallone as the actor was presenting an award during the 1977 Oscar telecast, and the two did some friendly onstage sparring). In L.A., Stallone invited Muhammad to a special screening of *Rocky II*, so one night Muhammad and Veronica (with Hana), Howard Bingham, and I went to the MGM lot together. I remember that Hana fell asleep in Muhammad's lap, was passed to my lap, and then spent most of the movie in Veronica's lap. I also remember being fascinated by Muhammad's running commentary on the boxing scenes. He had always recognized (and enjoyed) that he was the inspiration for the character of Rocky's opponent, Apollo Creed. At the end of the film, Muhammad said, "The acting is a good impression of me, but the boxing isn't right. Any boxer would recognize that isn't how I fight."

For all the ferocity of their Rumble in the Jungle, George Foreman and Muhammad had developed a mutual love and respect and become very good friends. In 1977, George stopped boxing after a particularly grueling loss to Jimmy Young (George claimed he had actually felt his soul leave his body during the fight). He became an ordained minister and dedicated himself to work as a preacher in Houston. One day I popped by Muhammad's house and took a seat on the couch in his office. He told me he was going to call George. Muhammad didn't have a speakerphone at the time, so I heard only his side of the conversation, which turned out to be some career advice for his friend: "George, think about this. You have a small church in Houston and you preach every Sunday to a small congregation. Why don't you try and get your own TV show like Billy Graham? Then everybody could hear what you have to say."

AS MUCH AS HELGA AND I enjoyed our time at Fremont Place, the plan had been for us to stay there temporarily until we found a place of our own. Muhammad would not have cared if we'd stayed there forever, but it seemed to me that after having made a stand about how I wouldn't work directly for him, it wasn't quite right to live under his roof. In July, Helga and I moved to a place in Northridge, in the San Fernando Valley, closer to the office of the pacemaker company. Our neighborhood wasn't quite as star-studded as Fremont Place, but we did find out that Richard Pryor lived just around the corner.

The first dinner guests we had over at the new place were, of course,

Muhammad and Veronica. We were enjoying another one of Helga's great meals when the phone rang and I got up to answer.

"Hello, is Muhammad there?" a rather gruff voice asked.

"Who's calling?"

"This is Frank Sinatra."

"Just a minute."

I had given our phone number to Howard Bingham and told him that Muhammad and Veronica would be with us that evening. Apparently he had been contacted by Sinatra's people and he told them where the Champ could be reached. I whispered to Muhammad who was on the line and handed him the phone. Muhammad had a brief conversation with Ol' Blue Eyes, then sat back down at our table. When we asked him what the call was about, he said, "I was supposed to meet Frank Sinatra tonight, but I'd rather stay here and have dinner with you."

He explained that Sinatra wanted to welcome him to Los Angeles, and there had been talk of Muhammad attending some kind of event Sinatra was hosting. But apparently Muhammad preferred our company, and Helga's cooking, to whatever Sinatra had to offer.

Muhammad didn't hold a lot of grudges, but he never warmed up to Sinatra, even though Sinatra had tried to get close to him several times over the years. Muhammad's antipathy stemmed from an incident after he fought and defeated Floyd Patterson in their 1965 Las Vegas matchup. Sinatra had been a vocal supporter of Patterson's before the fight, and Floyd was in Sinatra's suite after the fight. Muhammad had been invited to the suite, also, but when he arrived he didn't see Sinatra at first. Instead, he saw Floyd, sitting with his trainer at the bar and being ignored by everyone else. Muhammad approached Floyd to offer some friendly words, but Sinatra quickly appeared to congratulate him and steer him away from Floyd—the fighter who just the night before had been "his man." Muhammad was really bothered by the humiliating treatment Floyd was being subjected to, and he thought Sinatra was arrogant—a trait Ali couldn't stand in anyone. Muhammad never forgave Sinatra for that, so I suppose his opting for a night in Northridge over one in Beverly Hills was an easy call.

It was another great night for the four of us to be together, and at the end of the evening Helga and I walked Muhammad and Veronica to the door to exchange hugs and kisses. Rather than hug Muhammad, I gave him the fist and the mean face, which made him laugh. He turned to Helga and said, "You know why Tim acts a fool with me? Because sometimes you have to act a fool to be a friend."

Moving out of the Fremont Place house changed our daily routine, and Helga and I had fewer opportunities to spend time with Muhammad, Veronica, and the kids. I was working six days a week for the pacemaker company and filling in extra hours with work for the WORLD foundation. But I was at Fremont Place enough to witness some amazing moments. One afternoon Muhammad and I were both stretched out in his home office with the house to ourselves when Muhammad got a call from the security gate at the end of Fremont. Three young men had driven up and were asking if they could come through to Muhammad's house.

"What's their name?" asked Muhammad.

"They say that they're the Jacksons," came the answer.

Muhammad got up quickly and I followed him to the front door. We peeked out a window and saw a white Rolls-Royce Silver Shadow pull up. Michael Jackson was driving, and his brothers Randy and Tito were with him. Muhammad had met the Jackson 5 before—he had appeared on their TV variety show and they had visited Deer Lake—but I don't think they'd ever all had the chance to spend some private time together. Muhammad told me Michael had called earlier that day to ask if they could come by.

The brothers came toward the house, and just as Michael bounded up the front steps, Muhammad swung the front door open and shouted to anyone who could hear him, "Michael Jackson! Look, everybody! Michael Jackson and his brothers are right here. The Jacksons have come to visit Muhammad Ali! Everybody—come on out of your houses and say hello!" This time, the only response he got was nods from a couple of gardeners working across the street.

Muhammad wrapped his arms around Michael, then gave Randy

and Tito a hug. As we moved inside, Muhammad introduced me the usual way, "This is my cousin Tim Shanahan. He looks white, doesn't he?"

The brothers were handsome, great-looking young guys, and despite their own superstar status, they seemed humbled to be in Muhammad's presence. They told us they were back in town between legs of a worldwide tour in support of their *Destiny* album (Muhammad hadn't ever heard the term "legs" used this way, so Michael explained that they had broken up their tour into a run of international dates, a rest, and then a run of U.S. dates). We settled in to talk, and right away Muhammad seemed very interested in exactly how big the Jackson clan was.

"How many brothers and sisters are in your family?"

"Six brothers and three sisters," said Tito.

"Three sisters? Do any of them sing with you?"

"Janet does," said Michael. "She's the baby of the family. She's only thirteen."

"And where are the rest of your brothers?" asked Muhammad.

"They're home, in Encino. Except for Jermaine," said Michael. At this time Jermaine had left the group and had been replaced on the tour by the youngest brother, Randy.

We sat there talking some more, and Muhammad was just looking at them and smiling the biggest smile I had seen on his face in quite a while. Then he looked at Michael and said, "Sing a couple of bars of 'I'll Be There.' That's my favorite."

"No, Muhammad—I have to be in the right mood," said Michael.

Muhammad began asking the brothers another barrage of questions. He wanted to know how the group wrote their songs, whether they got up in the middle of the night to write down song ideas, whether they had to train as hard for a concert tour as he did for a fight, and how much trouble they had from the swarms of girls that surrounded them. The brothers answered all Muhammad's questions politely, then Muhammad looked at Michael and pointed over at the white baby grand piano that had made the move from the Chicago house.

"Look at that beautiful piano. Can you play?"

Michael took his place at the piano, played a few chords, and sang the first verse of "I'll Be There," then switched to "ABC." Hearing that distinctive voice singing out right there in Muhammad's living room gave me goose bumps. Muhammad wanted to see Michael show off some of his dance moves, so I set up a great big portable cassette player and then helped Muhammad roll back a big Persian rug so that Michael had a wooden dance floor to work with. I hit PLAY and turned the sounds of James Brown's "I Feel Good" up to full blast. Michael starting moving, showing us some of the signature dance moves he'd been doing since he was a little kid. Then he surprised us with a few steps that made it look like he was gliding backwards (what would become known as the Moonwalk). Muhammad made Michael stop and repeat that move in slow motion a few times, and both Muhammad and I tried to copy what he was doing.

"Muhammad," I said, "why don't you show them your Mashed Potato."

Muhammad got up and began to do the one dance move he had mastered—a simple, rhythmic twisting on the balls of his feet that he had learned with his cousin Charlotte back in the '60s. Michael got a great kick out of it—he laughed, clapped, rolled on the floor, then hopped up and joined Muhammad with his own version of the Mashed Potato.

When the music was over, we moved back to the office to talk. After a while, Michael asked to use the bathroom, and Muhammad pointed it out across the hall. Once Michael had been in there awhile, Muhammad quickly tiptoed over to the bathroom door and leaned against it with all his weight. This was another prank he had learned from Kris Kristofferson and Willie Nelson—one he'd gotten me with several times. The doorknob started wiggling, and then started wiggling a little more intensely. You could hear Michael trying to bump the door open from his side.

"Muhammad?" Michael's voice called out. "The door's stuck."

The doorknob kept wiggling, but when it stopped for a moment, Muhammad ran from the door and jumped back to his desk chair. In a final desperate effort, Michael hit the door hard from inside and this time came flying out into the hall.

"Muhammad—there is something wrong with that door."

We all burst out laughing, and Michael quickly realized he had been pranked. He just started laughing along with the rest of us. "You got me, Muhammad—you got me . . ."

Muhammad wanted to offer his guests something to eat, so he called out to one of the members of his new household staff—a woman named Edith Bell, who had come to work as a cook for Muhammad and Veronica after many years of cooking for Bill Cosby's family. Michael had met Edith before and greeted her warmly. Even though Michael was living a life of privilege, he clearly understood how hard someone like Edith worked and how important she was to the Ali household.

The Jacksons were on their way to a tour production meeting and couldn't stay to eat. Michael turned the invitation around, though, and asked if Muhammad would like to come to the Jackson house sometime.

"OK. When?" asked Muhammad.

"Saturday afternoon?" said Michael.

"Give Tim the address."

And so, a few days later, we were in Muhammad's Rolls-Royce headed to the Jackson home on Hayvenhurst in Encino. When we got there we were greeted by five brothers: Michael, Tito, Randy, Jackie, and Marlon. If the parents and the sisters were around, we never saw them. Michael and Tito began to lead us on a tour of the beautiful house and grounds. Then Michael told us he wanted to show us something "really special." He and Tito led us to a cottagelike guesthouse off to the side of the main house. Inside, was the "something special" that Michael wanted us to see—a display of dozens and dozens of dolls, all dressed in the native attire of countries around the world. Many were porcelain and all of them looked expensive, more like collectible works of art than toys.

"Wow, Michael," I said. "These are beautiful. Are they Janet's?"

"No!" he said. "They're mine. I love dolls, and I've been collecting them since I was a little boy."

Muhammad didn't say a thing, so I spoke up. "It's a beautiful collection, Michael."

I thought about the fact that Michael had begun performing when he was seven years old and was a superstar by the time he was eleven. He had never really had the chance to be a child, and if collecting dolls now gave him some childlike happiness, so be it. But I think Muhammad was as relieved as I was when we went back outside, away from the gaze of all those little glass eyes.

We went back to the main house, but this time there was no singing and dancing. In fact, it felt a little awkward, with the brothers just looking at Muhammad and waiting for him to ask questions or tell stories. After about thirty minutes, we all said our goodbyes. I didn't see the brothers back at the Fremont Place house again, but Muhammad did take Veronica to the closing night of the *Destiny* tour at the L.A. Forum.

IN SEPTEMBER, MUHAMMAD WAS AT the Forum for a different event—his own retirement party. Lou Rawls served as the emcee, and performers included Richard Pryor, Billy Crystal, Lola Falana, Diana Ross, and Melissa Manchester. I did some work to help line up performers and to contact VIP guests, so it fell to me to call Paul Newman and invite him to attend. Muhammad had met the actor years earlier in New York, and Newman's number was in Muhammad's black book. When I called, I recognized the voice that answered as belonging to Newman's wife, Joanne Woodward. I explained who I was and told her that Muhammad wanted to invite her and Paul to attend his party.

"Just a minute," Joanne said. "Paul's in the shower but I'll get him."

I was a bit surprised. I couldn't imagine there were too many calls important enough to interrupt Paul Newman's showers, but that was the power of the name Muhammad Ali. He got on the phone a minute later, and when I explained the purpose of the call, he sounded disappointed. He and Joanne were going to be at a family event in Vermont the weekend of the retirement party and he wouldn't be able to attend. He was touched to be invited, though, and said he wanted to pass a special message on to Muhammad. Just then, Muhammad walked into the room, so I asked Newman to hold his thought and handed the phone to Muhammad. They stayed on the phone a few minutes, and when Muhammad finally hung up, he had a great big smile on his face.

I had to know.

"What was Paul's message?"

"He told me that he wanted me to know that he thinks I am one of the greatest human beings he has ever met. I say I'm the Greatest, too, but *Paul Newman* thinks I am one of the 'greatest human beings' that he has ever met!"

It was great to see the outpouring of affection toward Muhammad at the Forum retirement event. Helga and I sat in a special VIP section off to the side of the stage, and we were among a group of Ali insiders that included Muhammad's mother and father and brother, Aunt Coretta, Bill Sutter, and Mike Phenner. Sutter and Phenner had done a lot of hard work to make this night happen, and I had really come to appreciate how conscientious they were about protecting Muhammad and setting him up for a healthy financial future beyond boxing.

Up on the Forum stage, Lou Rawls was as smooth as always, Richard Pryor did a fantastic half-hour set of stand-up, and Lola Falana sang a special song she had written called "Muhammad Ali." Tributes were presented by a variety of folks including Mayor Tom Bradley, Jane Fonda, Kris Kristofferson, and Kenny Rogers. Even Muhammad's heartbreaking hero—Sugar Ray Robinson—was in the house to pay his respects. The entertainment ended with a very funny and moving piece Billy Crystal created called "Fifteen Rounds," in which he acted out fifteen landmark moments from Muhammad's life. I don't know how much time Billy spent writing and rehearsing that piece, but it was an incredible and truly heartfelt tribute to a friend. At the end of the event, Muhammad got up onstage and spoke off the cuff beautifully, thanking each of the performers and the crowd of 12,000 paying attendees for all the support he'd had through the years. He got very personal at times, talking about his Muslim faith and also pointing out to this very mixed crowd that he had been married three times "to three beautiful black women." The proceeds of the night were donated to support the U.S. Olympic boxing team, and by the end of the night it really did feel like we had marked the end of the Greatest's boxing career in the greatest way possible.

IT WAS AFTER THE RETIREMENT event that I began to notice some shifts in Muhammad's general demeanor. As long as I had known him, Muhammad had been a happy, outgoing person in public. Now, at times, he didn't seem as interested in being as quick and funny as he used to be, and he began to be ornery in ways I had not seen before. I remember being in the office and talking about some far-fetched business ideas that were being presented to him.

I said in passing, "Muhammad, I know you and that's not something you would do."

He fixed me with a cold stare. "How do you know what I would do?" he said with a much harsher edge than I was used to. "How do you know what I'm thinking? You don't know me, and you don't know what I'm thinking. Only I know what I'm thinking and what I want to do."

I let that moment pass, but things got a little tense again about a week later. I was in the home office at the Fremont Place house and answered the phone for Muhammad. It was one of his lawyers, wanting to talk to him about the status of some new deal. Muhammad put Hana down to take the call. Hana started crying, "Daddy, Daddy—you said that you would take me for ice cream."

Muhammad spoke to Hana very sharply, "Hana, be quiet, I'm on the phone with an important call." Then to me, just as sharply, "Tim, take her away."

I scooped up Hana and walked out of the room. Earlier, Muhammad had asked me to make a trip to Western Union to wire money to one of the mothers of his other children, and if Hana wanted ice cream, it made sense to me to combine the errand with a trip to a nearby 31 Flavors. As soon as I told her where we were heading, the cries and sniffles stopped and she was as happy as could be. I got the wire transfers done first, then had the joy of watching little Hana dig into a dish of vanilla ice cream with chocolate sauce.

We were gone for about an hour, and when we got back to the house Muhammad was angry. Veronica was out with Laila at her mother's house and Muhammad was in charge of watching Hana. Apparently when he finished his phone call, he thought that I had just left on my own and that Hana had gone missing.

"Why didn't you tell me you were taking my Hana?" he shouted. "Are you crazy? You can't just take my baby! I don't know what you're going to do with her. You can't do that!"

The idea that Muhammad would think that I would put Hana in any danger was shocking to me. Wasn't this the man who told me that he trusted me as much as Veronica and his brother, Rahaman?

"Muhammad," I said quietly, "Hana just wanted some ice cream . . ."

I wasn't really trying to defend myself. I could understand the raw emotion of a father who thought his child was in peril. Hana hadn't been in any danger, but Muhammad had gotten himself worked into such an angered state that he wasn't going to back down.

"GET OUT," he shouted. "I don't want you around my family anymore! I don't want you coming around the house! Do you hear me?"

I left, feeling a lot worse than if I had actually been punched in the nose by one of Ali's straight jabs. My head was spinning, and I just couldn't figure out how such a misunderstanding could lead to such a blowup. I felt terrible that I had caused him to worry about Hana and had put him in this awful state of mind, but how could he not know how much I loved that little girl, too? How could he be banishing me from his home—his life—just like that? My stomach was churning and I started to feel physically ill.

When I got home, Helga was there to greet me with a hug.

"Muhammad called twenty minutes ago," she said. "Just after you left his house. He wants you to come right back."

I was physically drained and didn't really feel like getting back in the car for a drive back to Fremont Place. I called first.

"Tim—I'm sorry," said Muhammad. "I didn't know where my baby was and I was crazy with worry. I didn't mean what I said. I want you to come back. I want you to come back to the house right now."

"I just got home, Muhammad."

"Come on back, Tim."

"Muhammad, I know how much you love your sweet Hana, and I might have done the same thing in your situation. But I don't need to drive back to you to tell you this: As far as I am concerned, our friendship is forever, and once you love someone you never forget why you loved them in the first place."

Muhammad thought this over, and answered with, "Maaaaaan, maaaan!" Then all he said was "See you tomorrow"—his way of settling the most emotionally trying moment we had ever had in our relationship.

ROBERT SHANNON CAME TO VISIT Muhammad and Veronica that fall, but I ended up being the one to take him around town. Robert was a very talented bantamweight boxer who had been a guest at Deer Lake and was a sweet-enough kid that Veronica and Muhammad had joked about adopting him. He was going to miss his first shot at Olympic gold because the United States was boycotting the 1980 Moscow games, but he was still training with an eye toward 1984. Robert told me he was a huge fan of Burt Reynolds and asked if there was any way we might meet the actor. Burt was shooting a movie called *Paternity* on the Paramount lot, and I used Muhammad's name just enough to get us an invitation to visit the set. My conversational "in" with Burt was that when I was in Munich for the 1972 Olympics, one of my handball teammates was a guy named Harry Winkler, whose older brother had been a high school football teammates of Burt's in Florida. Burt was great to us, and seemed happy to talk about his old football days and excited to be meeting an Olympic hopeful.

The *Mork and Mindy* show was also shooting on the Paramount lot, and, with a little more wrangling, I got us in there. The show had been on the air for two years and had turned Robin Williams into a huge star. I wasn't sure how open he would be to saying hello to us, but when he heard that a friend of Muhammad's and an Olympic athlete were on the set, he made a point of coming over to speak with us. It turned out that he was a big boxing fan who loved going to the local Friday-night matches at the Olympic Auditorium in downtown L.A. He asked Robert and me if we might want to go with him, so just a day later the three of us were in the crowd at the Olympic watching some very talented amateurs slug it out. I got the feeling that Robin really was a Friday-night regular—a few people around us gave him a nod or wave but generally left the TV star alone to enjoy the fights. The three of us went to a pool hall after the fights and Robin beat us both pretty easily. Luckily we bet only five dollars a game.

THROUGH THE END OF THE year, and into 1980, Veronica and Muhammad did a lot of traveling. There was a European "farewell" tour organized by Barry Frank of the IMG agency, which was working with First National Bank to oversee Muhammad's commercial interests. Muhammad also traveled to India and, at the request of the Carter administration, went to several African countries to try to help raise awareness and understanding of the U.S. boycott of the approaching Moscow Olympics.

In Los Angeles, I started making some interesting connections through my love of tennis. Because of my connection to Muhammad, I met Mike Franks, a former Davis Cup player, who, with his lovely wife, Gloria, organized the Carl Reiner Pro-Celebrity Tennis Tournament to benefit a number of special-education schools in L.A. I joined Mike and Gloria in trying to round up celebrities who could commit to this Memorial Day event, and through that work I met Charlton Heston.

The teaching pro Gebre Wallace was giving Heston lessons, and I became Gebre's partner, showing up at Heston's backyard court to volley with "Moses" and his son Frazier. The Heston home was on the crest of Coldwater Canyon, with a beautiful view of the city below. The tennis court had its own guesthouse, which functioned as Charlton's "man cave." The refrigerator in there was always stocked with Heinekens and gourmet snacks, and the most prominent picture on the wall was a shot of an attractive nude woman playing Ping-Pong—a gift from Chuck's pal Richard Crenna. (I mean the picture was a gift—not the woman.)

The mix of tennis and charity led me to one of the most storied Los Angeles institutions: the Playboy Mansion. I had almost spent New Year's Eve there. Muhammad was invited to Hugh Hefner's party and asked me to come with him. But Muhammad was attending as Sammy Davis Jr.'s guest, and Sammy told Muhammad that security at the mansion was strict—a guest could not bring another guest. A couple of months later, though, I was on those fabled grounds as the organizer of a UCLA Cancer Research charity tennis event at which celebrities and tennis pros were matched against bikini-clad playmates. Most of the girls looked fantastic but didn't move all that well on the court. Nobody minded, of course. However, the newly crowned Playmate of the Year, Dorothy Stratten, was not only stunningly beautiful, with unbelievably perfect skin, she was also clearly a good athlete with some tennis-playing days behind her. She was such a lovely vision that spring day—it's awful to recall that just a few months later she was murdered by a jealous, unhinged boyfriend.

Toward the end of the day, I spotted Burt Reynolds at a table and went over to reintroduce myself. Burt was sitting with a couple of playmates, but he didn't seem to mind my interrupting whatever they had been talking about. He remembered me from the visit to the *Paternity* set, and said he had seen me playing on the courts that day. He introduced me to the girls and told me to have a seat at the table. He and I began to talk again about the Winkler brothers, which led to a discussion of Burt's college years playing football for Florida State and the serious knee injury that ended his athletic career but put him into drama classes.

After a while, Burt said out loud, "This is over soon. Do you want to come over to my house and use my court?"

"What do you mean, 'you'?" I asked, not sure if the pronoun included me.

"You and the girls," Burt said. "Get a partner and you and the girls will play doubles on my court."

I couldn't say no to this offer. He gave me his address, then took off and told us to give him a little time to get things set up. I found a tennis pro friend of mine at the event, explained the situation, and not long after that, I was at the wheel of my Oldsmobile, driving my partner and a couple of *Playboy* centerfolds over to Burt Reynolds's house.

When we arrived, we were instructed by staff to help ourselves to freshly made margaritas and then head down to the tennis court, which was almost hidden at the bottom of the canyon behind the house, accessible by about sixty steps that led down the canyon wall.

Burt came to the court and said to us, "You four are going to play tennis and I'm going to watch."

So we played mixed doubles for Burt. These girls were good enough players to hold their own, although at this point they were offering a little less to look at—the sun was down and they had put wraps on over their bikinis. We played one friendly set and then we all sat down and had some more margaritas. I told Burt that if he had any interest in picking up his tennis game, I'd be happy to come by anytime to hit some balls with him.

"No, I'm not really into tennis that much," he said. But he told me I could come by anytime to use his court, so long as I called ahead.

That sounded good to me. I left Burt's house after my second margarita. I don't know how the Playmates got home.

MUHAMMAD WANTED TO FIGHT AGAIN. After he returned from his travels and settled back home, offers were being floated to get him to return to the ring. To the shock of all of us close to him, he began to take those offers seriously. There were so many reasons for him to leave the boxing gloves off. He was thirty-eight years old and, after a year of not training, his weight was up over 240 pounds. His speed and reflexes were clearly in decline. The chances of the WORLD foundation ever really taking off would be terribly compromised if Muhammad pulled away from it now—one of the conditions of the foundation's tax-free status was that Muhammad had to be CEO actively, not just in title only. He was still the Champ to everyone who loved him, and none of us wanted to see him fight again. But the people who did want to see him fight were willing to put up a lot of money.

Mike Phenner and Barry Frank argued that in returning to the ring, Muhammad would make liars and fools out of all the people who had worked to set up his retirement tour and his postboxing business deals. They believed that the return would not only damage Muhammad's health, but, maybe even more important, his reputation. Muhammad had been called a lot of things in his day, but he had never been called insincere. This decision might make him look like a phony.

"No it won't," Muhammad said calmly when I asked him about these objections. "I made a mistake. I'm not ready to stop fighting. The world will forgive me. People will understand. Tim, if someone asked you to come out of retirement for eight million dollars, wouldn't you do it?"

I hated to admit it, but I had to answer honestly: "Yup."

Maybe it was just the money. Even with the help of Phenner, Sutter, Barry Frank, Robert Abboud, and the whole financial team, Muhammad was still being taken advantage of by a lot of people he trusted, and he still found ways to spend whatever money he had.

Maybe it wasn't just the money. Maybe in those travels around the world—hearing all those people in all those places cheer for him—he realized he wasn't ready to give up the spotlight he had earned in the boxing ring. Maybe he just wanted—despite the risks and the odds and the weight of time—to do once more what everybody told him he couldn't do.

In any event, a contract was soon in the works. Muhammad was to receive $8 million for an October title bout against the reigning WBC heavyweight champion, Larry Holmes (who had once been an Ali sparring partner).

Muhammad was right—I didn't know what he was really thinking. All I knew was that I was worried for him.

ELEVEN

FINAL ROUNDS

IT CAME DOWN TO THIS: Veronica and I had two hours to change Muhammad's mind.

Through the spring of 1980, as details were finalized for our October fight with Holmes, the topic of Muhammad's return to the ring was not open to discussion. Once he had announced his intentions, his attitude was "If you're not with me, you're against me." I quickly figured out that voicing my concerns about the fight directly to him was not going to go over very well, but that didn't stop me from talking with everybody else who was worried about him. Veronica was dead-set against him fighting, and she and I had several long, emotional talks about the unnecessary risk we thought Muhammad was taking with his health. Muhammad's mother, Mama Bird, was so against the fight that she told Muhammad she would not be there to watch it. Cash Sr. saw the fight as another reason to dislike the "damn Muslims," who he felt were persuading his son to "unretire" just so they could get another cut of his payday. Helga and I had quite a few sleepless nights trying to figure out whether we should stand up to Muhammad or support him.

We all assumed Muhammad's decision to fight again was final. But he was aware enough of all of our worries that he made this deal: the night before he left to open the training camp in Deer Lake, he would give Veronica and me two hours to talk him out of it. We were free to unload all of our concerns and make all our arguments. If he couldn't come up with solid answers, he would tear up the contract and cancel the fight.

Veronica and I knew that if Muhammad had really made up his mind, we would just be going through the motions of trying to convince him otherwise. We suspected the two hours were going to be less about his hearing our arguments than about him proving to us that he was making the right decision. I spoke to Veronica on the phone, then drove to Fremont Place about nine p.m. and the three of us sat in Muhammad's office. Veronica did most of the talking, but, sure enough, with every point she or I raised, Muhammad would listen carefully and then dismiss it with a counterargument. The money was a big part of it—Muhammad was focused on the astounding paycheck he would receive from this one night's work. When Veronica asked him not to think about himself but to think about his family, he responded that he was. He was going to provide for his family by earning that great sum of money.

I brought up the questions of his health. I had been with him when he went to the UCLA medical center for a full physical work-up after the second Spinks fight. The official report said that there were no signs of brain damage, but there were a few troubling signs of dips in his cognitive abilities and his reflexes. My feeling was that Muhammad was lucky to be as healthy as he was in comparison with the average thirty-eight-year-old male, but he was in no shape to defend himself against a younger, faster opponent in a professional championship boxing ring. I told him that I wanted him to stay healthy and live long enough so that we could make it to those side-by-side rocking chairs we had once talked about. Muhammad had been pretty calm so far, but he got angry at the talk of his physical condition.

"You're only worried about your position with the foundation," he said to me. "If you don't want to support me, then stay away from camp. I don't need you."

Ugh. I felt the sting of Muhammad accusing me of putting my own personal gain over his welfare. Muhammad then launched into his "I am the Greatest" mode, trying to convince us, and maybe himself, that his decision was based on more than money. He told us that his main goal was to become the heavyweight champion of the world for the fourth time (he had vacated the crown when he retired), and he believed that his fans wanted to see him win another title and would celebrate his return. As a four-time champion, he would set a record that might never be broken. We told him that he didn't need any more records—he was already the world's only three-time heavyweight champion. Muhammad said nothing. The two hours came to an end, and his mind was not changed.

Veronica and I had both said what we wanted to say, but predictably it was an exercise in futility. In spite of what had just happened, though, I knew that Muhammad was still assuming I would be visiting him in Deer Lake and would be supporting him for this fight. I felt torn. As much as I hated his decision to fight again, I had to support him. I think I had known that all along, even as Veronica and I tried to talk him out of the fight.

Muhammad was leaving for camp very early the next morning, and I went home for a few hours of fitful sleep. Just before dawn, I was back up, with Helga at my side. The fight with Holmes was going to happen—there was no way around that now. But at least I could see Muhammad off in person, to let him know my feelings about the fight didn't affect my feelings about our friendship.

"He's going to do this anyway," I told Helga. "I can't stop him so I may as well let him know I'm still behind him."

She took my hand. "We love Muhammad," she said. "Do what you have to do."

I was back at the Fremont house at 6:15 a.m. Muhammad already had his bags ready by the front door. As I walked in, he was coming down the stairs. I knew he didn't expect to see me—I had told him that because of my work schedule I couldn't give him a ride to the airport—but he didn't look surprised at all.

"Hey, Champ, how are you feeling?" I asked.

No answer.

"Do you want me to drive you to the airport?"

"Bingham's coming," he said.

I wanted to tell him again that the people who loved him wanted him to stay retired. That the people who loved him didn't care about the money he might make for one more fight. But the moment just didn't seem right for more of that kind of talk.

Little Hana had gotten used to listening for her father's early morning comings and goings, and she appeared at the top of the stairs. When she spotted the packed bags, she started climbing down toward us.

"Daddy, Daddy, I want to go with you," she said.

Muhammad was sitting in a chair in the hallway with his attaché on his lap looking for his plane ticket, so I picked up Hana.

"You can't go with Daddy right now," I told her. "He's going to his training camp. Your mother will take you to Deer Lake later, but you can't go with him right now."

Muhammad put his attaché on the floor and I handed Hana to him.

"Daddy—I want to go with you," she sobbed.

"Hana, listen to me," Muhammad said softly. "I want you to understand something—I am Muhammad Ali, the heavyweight champion of the world, and all the people in the world who are my fans look up to me and millions of these people are children, they look up to me, also. I'm not only your father—I'm a father to the children of the world and I have to fight for them as much as I do for you and Laila."

Hana calmed down a bit, but she was still crying. Muhammad gave her a kiss on her cheek, but she wouldn't kiss him back. She pushed his face away, jumped off his lap, went to the staircase, and started climbing up the stairs one at a time. I picked her up and took her back up to her room, hoping she would calm down after Muhammad left. I was trying to get her back into bed when Muhammad called upstairs to me, "Tim, bring Hana down here."

I carried her back down the stairs, but she was not a willing passenger and began kicking and screaming. Muhammad sat in his chair and I managed to put her back in his lap. With a low, soft laugh, Muhammad pulled her close and said, "Stop now, Hana. Give me some jaws. Come on, give me some jaws."

Hana just kept crying and struggling to get away.

"Hana—I won't go until you kiss me," Muhammad said to her. "Give your daddy a kiss."

"You're not my daddy," Hana wailed. "You're Muhammad Ali."

She wriggled out of his lap again, ran into the living room, put her head down on the cushions of the couch, and began sobbing loudly. It was heartbreaking to hear that awful, sad sound come out of such a little body. I had seen Muhammad get hit hard, but I had never seen the look of pain I saw on his face now—like he had gotten an arrow through the heart. We didn't say another word. He left me with Hana, and he picked up his bags and headed out the front door.

BY THE MIDDLE OF SEPTEMBER, Muhammad was training intensively at Deer Lake, and I finally gave in to my nagging conscience and went out there to spend time with him. I simply showed up one day, and when I saw him I gave him a hug and intoned the Catholic greeting I had once taught him—the phrase used to introduce a prayer or a hymn: "Dominus vobiscum, et cum spiritu tuo" (The Lord be with you and with your spirit). As always, he responded quite seriously with his Muslim greeting: "As-salaam alaikum." He said nothing else and, just like that, it was as if the uncomfortable prefight confrontation at Fremont Place had never happened.

I had to admit—Muhammad looked great. He had been training hard and had gotten his weight down to around 220. I watched him jump rope, work the heavy bag, and spar with Jimmy Ellis, and was surprised to see how sharp and fast he was. I had created a mental picture of a slow, heavy Muhammad unable to defend himself in the ring. That's not the Muhammad I was looking at in camp. Holmes didn't have a reputation as a very hard puncher, and watching Muhammad move in the ring with Jimmy, I actually saw some flashes of the Ali of old. I was very surprised to find myself thinking that Muhammad might really pull off this comeback.

I was in camp four days, avoiding the people I wanted to avoid, spending time with Jimmy Ellis and Lana Shabazz, and catching a couple of late-night movies with Muhammad. One night Muhammad and I were watching *High Plains Drifter* when I decided to fire a few questions his way.

"Muhammad, what is your favorite movie?"

"*Shane.*"

"Who is your favorite movie star?"

"Clint Eastwood."

"Who's your favorite singer?"

"Sam Cooke."

"Who's your second-favorite singer?"

"Elvis."

After a run the next morning, we were having breakfast in the kitchen cabin and I decided to pose a few more questions.

"What is your favorite dinner?"

"Lamb chops by Aunt Coretta."

"What is your favorite candy bar?"

"Baby Ruth and that's the truth."

"Who is your favorite all-time boxer?"

"Jack Johnson."

"Favorite baseball player?"

"Jackie Robinson."

"Who is your favorite basketball player?"

"Kareem. You can't defend the skyhook." (Muhammad loved this shot—it was the only one he would take when we played horse on the Deer Lake basketball court.)

"Who is the prettiest girl in the world?"

"Veronica." (I knew that would be his answer.)

"Do you have any regrets in life?"

The other questions he had responded to instantly. This one he thought about, then answered in a very heartfelt manner.

"Only one regret. That I turned my back on Malcolm X when he needed me the most. I was a young Muslim, not so sure of myself when it came to my faith, and when Elijah Muhammad told me to break ties with Malcolm, I did. I wish that I could have told Malcolm that I was sorry for turning my back on him at a time when he needed me the most, but Malcolm was killed before I had the chance."

The next morning we had just finished a run and Muhammad was heading toward the massage room when we heard the sound of a straining engine. We saw that an enormous bus was trying to make its way up the "monster" to the camp. The bus chugged its way up the steep hill and when it finally stopped at the top, the door opened and out jumped the singer Tom Jones.

"Hello, Champ! I told you I would make it up here someday."

Muhammad cupped his hands to his mouth and shouted his standard celebrity greeting. "Tom Jones has come to see Muhammad Ali! Look, everybody—come say hello to Tom Jones."

Tom was there about three hours—long enough for me to get the impression that he was a sincere and highly intelligent guy who, despite his superstar status, was very friendly and unassuming. Muhammad responded to that—he liked superstars who stayed true to their character in public and private. Tom and Muhammad were in Muhammad's cabin for about an hour, then they went to the kitchen, where Lana Shabazz cooked them a late breakfast. Jimmy Ellis and I sat on a bench, listening to the two superstars' conversation. At one point, Tom said, "You probably don't know this, Muhammad, but I used to box a bit."

"What did you box?" asked Muhammad. "Apples or oranges?"

We all laughed, and Tom had a "you got me" grin on his face. Before he left, Tom actually did get in the ring with Muhammad for some friendly sparring, and the singer definitely showed some athletic moves and boxing skills. Muhammad's taunts didn't stop the two of them from having a great afternoon together.

• • •

THE HOLMES FIGHT WAS SET for October 2 at Caesars Palace in Las Vegas. I flew in a few days ahead of time with John Travolta, Marilu Henner, and John's best friend from high school, Jerry Wurms. We checked into Kirk Kerkorian's suite at the MGM across from Caesars Palace, where Muhammad was staying with Veronica, Aminah Boyd (the mother of his second wife), and his oldest daughter, eleven-year-old Maryum. Veronica and I had both seen Muhammad looking sharp at camp, which calmed some of our worries, so we joined in the festive atmosphere around the fight and had a great time attending shows by Paul Anka and then Diana Ross.

Lola Falana was in town—at the time she was the highest-paid female performer in Las Vegas, earning $2 million for twenty weeks of shows at the Aladdin. I had the chance to show off the Kerkorian suite to her when she came by to say hello to Travolta. It was the first time I really had a chance to talk to her one-on-one, and I found her to be every bit as sweet as she was beautiful. I suggested that she record three oldies that I thought would be good fits for her sensuous look and warm personality, "My Guy" and "Two Lovers," both sung by Mary Wells, and "Drift Away" by Dobie Gray. I guess those suggestions gave Lola the impression that I knew what I was talking about, because Lola asked me if I would be interested in producing an album of oldies for her. That project never happened, but Lola did start singing "Drift Away" in her live act, and that time in the Kerkorian suite marked the beginning of a wonderful friendship.

Two days before the fight I was in the strange but enviable position of accompanying Lola and Veronica on a joint shopping trip. These two gorgeous women were trying on glamorous outfits and asking, "What do you think, Tim?" I think I just sounded like a tape loop: "You look fantastic. That's you. You look fantastic. What a color. You look fantastic."

Those were fun moments, but the reality check came when I watched Muhammad work out before the fight. When he had shadowboxed and hit the heavy bag at camp, his jabs were back to being lightning fast. Now, even though he had continued to lose weight, he seemed to be slow and lacking energy. With a lot of his punches and footwork, he seemed to be just barely going through the motions. I was worried again.

Muhammad wanted me to stay with him the day before the fight, so I went over to his suite the morning of the weigh-in. Even though he had slept late that morning—a rarity for him—he still seemed very tired. He didn't talk much, and everything he did, he did slowly. Watching him move around the suite, it hit me: he looked old. He didn't seem to have any of the spark he usually had before his fights, and he didn't seem to be the energetic, vivacious guy he had been just a month before in Deer Lake. I couldn't understand how he had lost so much energy so quickly. Was he sick? Had he overtrained? I was very worried.

The fight was terrible. It was everything that those who loved Muhammad had been afraid of. I sat with Travolta and Robert Shannon, and the three of us barely said a word to one another. My impulse was to get up and leave, but I knew I couldn't do that. It was terrible to see Muhammad looking so ineffective in a boxing ring—the space he had once dominated—and it was terrible to see Larry Holmes, a great fighter who idolized Muhammad, being put in the awful position of having no choice but to pummel his hero. After seven or eight rounds, it was obvious that there was no way Muhammad could win on points, and there seemed to be zero chance of him scoring a knockout. I saw that Angelo kept looking to Herbert Muhammad in the front row of the crowd, hoping to get a signal to end the fight. The signal didn't come. There were times during some rounds when it looked like Holmes himself wanted the referee to stop the fight. Finally, after Ali really got badly roughed up in rounds nine and ten, Angelo stood up to others in Ali's corner, asserted his official position, and angrily shouted to the referee, "I am the first 'second' here and I say the fight's over."

As the usual postfight crowd swarmed into the ring, Muhammad stayed slumped down on the stool in his corner. Larry Holmes, obviously feeling very conflicted about what had just happened, accepted his win at center ring with tears streaming down his face.

• • •

MUHAMMAD'S SUITE WAS USUALLY PACKED with people after a fight, but after this loss, people weren't sure what to say or do, and no one stuck around very long. Muhammad had agreed to do an interview with David Hartman of *Good Morning America* at 4:30 a.m. so that it would be broadcast live on the East Coast. As people began to leave his suite, he said to me, "Stay here."

"I'm not going anywhere," I answered.

By 1:30, the suite was nearly empty. Grandma Aminah and Maryum were asleep in one room and Abdul "Captain Sam" Rahaman—a Nation of Islam mentor to Muhammad—was around to take care of Muhammad's requests. Sam was the man who had first introduced Muhammad to the Muslim faith in the early '60s. He had been a loyal friend to Muhammad through the years, and I trusted him more than any of the other Muslims who hung around Muhammad.

Muhammad and I sat alone in the front room of his suite with the TV tuned to CNN. The twenty-four-hour news channel was just a year old at the time and Muhammad loved being able to see headlines from around the world at any time of day. He still looked down and not ready to talk. I could guess what was running through his mind: What had gone wrong? He lost the first Spinks fight because he didn't train hard enough. But he had trained very hard this time, had gotten his weight down, and went into the ring feeling like he had no energy for the fight.

"I don't know what happened," he said.

I hadn't wanted him to take on this fight in the first place, but in this moment I only wanted to offer him support. I told him that no matter what had happened in the ring, people all over the world still loved and respected him. I asked him if he wanted to lie down and rest a little before the interview. He shook off that suggestion.

"I felt slow, like an old man, with no energy. I wanted to throw punches, but I couldn't. I never felt like that in the ring before. I have always been able to throw punches in the late rounds. I couldn't do it this time." He paused a moment. "Do you think I was drugged?"

"You think somebody put something in your water?"

"I don't know."

"Well, you know Angelo would never allow something like that."

He started talking about other people in his corner and on his team, thinking about what motives any of them might have had for making him lose the fight.

"Muhammad—you know how I feel about those guys, but nobody wanted to see you get hurt. I just can't believe that anyone in your corner could have done such a thing."

He dropped that subject but we kept talking until it was time to get ready for the interview.

"How do I look?" he asked.

"You look like you've been in a fight, You've got a red, swollen eye. Do you want to wear my sunglasses? I think it will look better."

He tried them on, but decided against wearing them. At four a.m., Muhammad, Captain Sam, and I walked back down to the ring outside Caesars. Muhammad was going to be back in the ring for the interview, and we took seats in the now-deserted front row as a camera crew got their lights and equipment set up.

"How do I look?" Muhammad asked again.

"Ugly," I said.

Captain Sam was generally a very easygoing guy. Suddenly, though, he was very angry with me.

"Man, what are you saying?" he asked me. "Don't tell the Champ he looks ugly—not now!"

"No, man, he's right," said Muhammad. He asked for my sunglasses and wore them through the interview.

Just before dawn we were back up in the suite. Muhammad felt a little better, having said in the interview some of the same things he had said to me—that he didn't know why his energy was so low and that he had wanted to throw more punches but they just wouldn't come. Now Muhammad looked like he might be able to sleep, but he didn't go to the bedroom. Instead, he sat down on a couch.

"Where's Travolta?" he asked.

"He's at the MGM. I know he wanted to wish you the best after the fight, but he thought you might want to be alone."

"Bring him over when he gets up."

"I'll bring him over. But you've got to get some rest, Muhammad. Don't you feel like you could sleep now?"

"No."

He lay on the couch, turned his attention back to CNN, and almost immediately fell into a deep slumber.

NOT LONG AFTER THE FIGHT, I learned that Muhammad actually *had* been drugged—but, in a sense, he had done it to himself. As he began training, he was worried about how difficult it was for him to lose weight, and he consulted with a doctor who suspected that Muhammad might have a hypothyroid disorder, and suggested that he take a specific medication for his thyroid. Muhammad started taking the drug and lost weight like crazy. By fight time, he was down to 218, just a pound and a half heavier than he had been against George Foreman six years earlier. His sparring partners said he was as fast as ever and looking good in his sparring sessions.

Muhammad looked fantastic stepping into the ring to face Holmes, but he had been taking a powerful drug designed for people with thyroid disease. The drug had a long list of side effects and contra-indications. Feelings of weakness was one and sensitivity to heat was another. The Holmes fight took place outside on an unusually warm desert night. There was no doubt in my mind that Muhammad's use of a powerful medication could easily explain his slow reflexes and lack of energy throughout the fight.

AFTER THE LOSS TO HOLMES, Muhammad did not bounce right back to his usual fun-loving personality. More frequently, he seemed down or distracted. Muhammad, Veronica, Helga, and I continued to do things as couples, and we had some fun nights out going to concerts by Harry Belafonte, Donna Summer, the Spinners (who had been part of the entertainment back during the Rumble in the Jungle), and Bill Cosby (who cold-shouldered me once again). But things just didn't feel as loose and easy as they had in the past. Muhammad had always been the central figure in our foursome, and if he wasn't feeling well, the rest of us felt it, too.

Now that Laila was walking and talking, Helga and I were spending more time with Veronica and the kids. We were lucky enough to be able to take the two little girls on their first trip to the zoo and their first trip to the beach. I even got to take them on their first adventure trick-or-treating along a couple of blocks of Fremont Place (Hana was dressed as a little Wicked Witch of the West, and Laila was dressed as a tiny Wonder Woman).

Around this time I received some insight into my relationship with Muhammad from an unusual source—a Beverly Hills "psychic to the stars" named Alvaro. Alvaro wanted to do a reading for John Travolta in order to give him some career advice, but Travolta wanted Joan Edwards and me to meet with Alvaro first to judge his abilities. So, I found myself sitting with Alvaro in Joan's back bedroom with a deck of Tarot cards spread between us. Alvaro would touch the cards with his fingertips, visualize letters of the alphabet, and then ask me questions. I approached this kind of thing skeptically, but he definitely seemed to be able to tap into some other realm. He "saw" letters relating to first names of members of my family that I hadn't spoken to anyone about, and then described their homes and their lives in perfect detail. A "J" led Alvaro to tell me about how Travolta and I first met, and he accurately described the dynamics of our friendship. He saw an "R" for "Ronnie," then corrected that to "Veronica."

"She is a true friend to you and you are a true friend to her," said Alvaro. "Her husband is not jealous, nor is your wife. You all are trusting friends."

Then Alvaro saw an "A," and said he was sensing a person, "bigger than the president, bigger than the pope." He concentrated harder, then spoke.

"Ahh, now I see who it is. Have you wondered why Muhammad Ali has befriended you?" Alvaro asked.

The question hit me hard. It was a question that had been in the back of my mind ever since I met Muhammad, but it was a question I was almost afraid to ask.

"Yes, I have wondered about that," I said to the psychic.

"You and Muhammad Ali are friends because you both communicate on a higher spiritual level. Muhammad has befriended you because he sees in you what he sees in himself: a pure heart."

I still have no idea where or how Alvaro was getting his information, but I loved that answer.

TELEPHONE CALLS FROM MUHAMMAD WERE still rare, and this time he sounded especially serious.

"Tim, meet me at the house in two hours," he said. "The FBI wants to talk with us."

I half hoped he was playing some kind of joke on me, but when I got over to the house Muhammad was in fact sitting at his desk across from two FBI agents (he introduced me as his "administrative assistant"). What the agents had to say was shocking: they were about to arrest a man named Harold Smith for stealing $21 million from Wells Fargo while running an organization called Muhammad Ali Professional Sports, Inc.

Smith, aka Ross Fields, had first stepped into Muhammad's life back in Chicago. Smith said he wanted to create a Muhammad Ali Amateur Sports Club that would recruit exceptional track and field athletes from low-income areas around the United States and train them for the Olympics. Smith said he already had a team of investors in place, and he wanted to present Muhammad with a "good faith" gift of $40,000 in cash in return for Muhammad's signature on a one-page letter of intent that would allow Smith to use Muhammad's name in establishing the club. This was before Mike Phenner and Robert Abboud were involved in Muhammad's finances, and even though I counseled Muhammad not to sign anything, he signed. At first, Smith did make things happen—he promoted his own boxing events and organized the star-studded Muhammad Ali Invitational track meets in Long Beach. But he always seemed to be spending much more money than he was bringing in. Now it looked like a lot of the money that Smith had spent through the Ali amateur and pro clubs had actually been embezzled out of Wells Fargo accounts with the help of some bank managers.

The FBI wasn't sure how many people were involved in the fraud, which was why they were talking to us. Of course I knew Muhammad didn't have anything to do with it. I actually knew a lot more about Smith's business dealings than he did, since I had helped Smith get some big names to attend his events. But in the past, Muhammad himself had been the only victim of such rip-offs. This was a much bigger scandal that affected a lot more people. It was also a very public story that would tarnish Muhammad's reputation.

Muhammad was quickly cleared of having any knowledge of or involvement in the crime, but not before we spent another afternoon with FBI agents. They had seized Harold Smith's MAP office in Santa Monica, and were using a chalkboard there to sketch out the connections of people who might be involved in the scam. Muhammad's name was at the top of the board and various people were listed below. My name was up there under Harold's, and I was listed as "friend who introduced Smith to Ali." (This wasn't quite true—I initially brought Smith to Ali's house in Chicago only because Muhammad asked me to pick him up at the airport.) It was a little scary to be that close to a crime so big. But, as it turned out, the fraud was pulled off primarily by Smith with some inside help from a bank manager and a district manager (Smith eventually served a five-year term in federal prison).

• • • • •

EVEN AFTER A HUMILIATING LOSS in the ring and with a major financial scandal swirling around him, Muhammad could still occasionally look like a real-life superhero. In January of 1981, we were driving down Wilshire Boulevard in his Rolls one afternoon when we came upon a police road block. A distraught Vietnam vet was on a ledge of the ninth floor of an office building and was threatening to jump. Police negotiators, psychologists, and a minister had already failed to talk the man off the ledge. Without a word to me, Muhammad sprang out of his Rolls and approached the police officers who seemed to be in charge. They spoke briefly and then walked together into the building. A few moments later, I saw Muhammad's head poke out of a window close to where the vet was standing. I will admit that my initial reaction was not a hopeful one—it looked to me like this situation was going to have an awful end no matter who tried to talk to the guy. But Muhammad could still work wonders. From down at ground level we could see Muhammad talking to the guy for a very tense ten or fifteen minutes. Then Muhammad's head disappeared from the window he was at and, a moment later, appeared at the window the vet had stepped out of. Muhammad put his arms around the man, and slowly and gently pulled him back inside. Muhammad wanted to bring the guy home to Fremont Place with us—he felt bad for him and wanted to help him even more. The police, though they were amazed and appreciative at what Ali had just done, insisted that the vet be taken to a hospital for a psychiatric evaluation.

MUHAMMAD HAD ALL BUT GIVEN up any thoughts of an acting career, but in the spring of 1981 the Fremont Place house had a chance at its own starring role. For a couple of weeks, Sly Stallone and his film crew moved in, and Muhammad's home became Rocky's mansion in *Rocky III*. The place looked impressive on film, but for the couple that really lived there, life was getting a little harder.

One night I went over to Muhammad's place and found him alone and apparently not in a very good mood. We sat together in the office. He wasn't going to start the conversation.

"How are you doing, Muhammad?" I asked.

No answer.

"You seem to be a bit down. Is something bothering you?"

He said, "You don't have to worry about me. Worry about yourself."

"I'm a little down now, too," I said. "Maybe we can listen to some music to cheer ourselves up."

No answer. He wasn't interested in listening to music, or going for a drive, or going out to get ice cream. We just sat together in silence watching CNN. It always felt wrong to be anything but truthful with Muhammad—so, after a while, I asked what was on my mind.

"Muhammad, is everything OK between you and Veronica?"

"That's none of your business."

"OK—I know it isn't. I'm just asking because I'm concerned."

"Why? Is she talking to you? She should be talking to me. It's none of your business, so stay out of it."

I could see that he was working himself up and getting angry, and I knew that staying around him while he was in this state of mind would not be a good thing. I got up and headed for the door.

"I don't want you coming around here and I don't want you talking to Veronica anymore," he said as I walked out the door.

This felt more serious, and I wondered if by trying to ease any tension between Veronica and Muhammad I had actually ended my friendship with him. I drove home feeling sad and guilty, wishing that I had waited for a better time to have this kind of conversation. I couldn't sleep that night, and didn't sleep well the following nights, either. A few days later, though, I received this note on Muhammad's personal stationery:

Tim, you and Helga have been our good friends for the last few years, since I met Veronica. Friends come and go when you are famous, you and Helga

*have been true to us. You didn't hesitate to move with us from Chicago to Los
Angeles to start our WORLD foundation . . . You are a true friend.*

Love Always, Muhammad

A very rare shot of Muhammad with all eight of the children
he fathered. The group is starting out on a run around the
block on Fremont Place; the house is in the background.

THE LESS SAID ABOUT THE last fight of Muhammad's career, the better. He
knew how bad he had looked against Holmes and he got it into his
head that he wanted his final fight to be one in which at least he threw
some punches. Once the money people knew Ali was willing to fight
again, it was all but certain a fight would happen. He was matched
up against a young heavyweight contender named Trevor Berbick.
But because Muhammad could not get a medical clearance from any
state boxing commission, no U.S. venue was willing to sanction the
fight and no TV network was willing to sponsor it. So, the fight took
place in a makeshift ring on a baseball field in the Bahamas. As with
the Holmes fight, Muhammad dismissed all the concerns raised by

friends and family begging him not to get back in the ring. This time, though, I didn't want to be part of the debacle in any way. I didn't go to Deer Lake for training, and didn't go to Nassau for the fight. On December 11, 1981, Ali faced Berbick and lost a unanimous decision. Thankfully, in interviews after the fight, Muhammad finally admitted that his boxing days were over: "Father time has caught up with me," he said.

THE NEXT COUPLE OF YEARS were tough ones for Muhammad. I still enjoyed spending time with him, and we could always find some way to have a laugh, but his symptoms of physical decline and his mood swings were impossible to ignore. He and Veronica seemed to get along fine when they were together with Helga and me, and we still had some fun times together. But Veronica, Helga, and I shared so many close moments with Muhammad, we were each aware of the changes in him.

Veronica called me one night, and told me that she wanted to get another man's point of view about something she and Muhammad had been discussing. I don't remember what we started talking about, but we talked for a while. Then, suddenly, there was another voice on the line.

"Veronica," Muhammad growled.

Veronica and I both froze. Veronica and I knew that Muhammad would occasionally pick up a phone in the house to listen in on conversations. We were so engrossed with our conversation we didn't know how long he had been listening to us, but he was angry.

"You're telling Tim things that are more intimate than what you tell me," said Muhammad.

"Muhammad . . ." I started.

"Tim—I don't want to see you again. You're not my friend. Get out."

I was already sitting at home, so I assumed he meant for me to get out of his life—again. Even though I had been through this before, it hit me hard this time. I hated being in the middle of this. I hated the thought of losing Muhammad's trust, but I was worried for Veronica, too. I realized that whatever I tried to do to help might only make things worse. Perhaps the only way I could be a friend to these two people I loved would be to step out of their lives and let them work out their problems for themselves.

A few days later, Muhammad called. Veronica had talked to him and made him understand that she and I had simply been speaking as friends. He understood. He was over it. And he wanted to know if Helga and I wanted to go to the movies with him and Veronica.

We did.

BEGINNING WITH MUHAMMAD'S DECISION TO fight Larry Holmes, the WORLD foundation predictably fell apart. We spent two years doing everything we needed to do to get the foundation established as a nonprofit organization, but once Muhammad came out of retirement, WORLD was no longer much of a priority for him. Lonnie Rex told Muhammad that if he went back to boxing, the organization would have to be dissolved. Muhammad said he understood, and, for all the work we put into it, it took only a few hours to formally dissolve the WORLD foundation. Similarly, despite the hard work and good intentions of Robert Abboud, Mike Phenner, Bill Sutter, and Barry Franks, the attempt to straighten out Muhammad's finances was starting to look like a losing battle. They were such a great team and had worked incredibly hard for Muhammad, but their carefully thought-out plans for his business portfolio never had a chance because Muhammad's trusting, generous-to-a-fault nature wouldn't allow these experts to do what they could for him. I had been so optimistic about what these smart, dedicated financial minds might accomplish for Muhammad. It was heartbreaking that all their work could not set things right for him.

Life changed for Helga and me in 1983 when I was offered a prominent managerial position with Coast Medical, a major distributor of high-tech medical equipment. The catch was that the job required me to relocate to the San Diego area. I would have never initiated a move

Helga teaching Hana to braid hair.

away from Muhammad on my own, but when this opportunity arose, Helga and I realized that after so many years of having our lives intertwined with Muhammad's, it was probably for the best to put some geographical distance between us and Muhammad and Veronica. It had become very awkward for me to try to be close to both of them, and I didn't want either of them to think that I was meddling in their private lives. Helga and I believed the move would be good for our friendships.

I accepted the job, and Helga and I found a fantastic condo at the Solana Beach and Tennis Club, overlooking the beautiful Pacific Ocean. Helga had requested one balcony when she first moved to Chicago—this place had four, all with ocean views. She and I began a wonderful new part of our lives. And I hoped that from a little distance down the coast, Muhammad and I would have a better chance of staying close.

TWELVE

LONG-DISTANCE RUNS

"I'M STARTING TO WALK LIKE an old man," said Muhammad.

I was with him at UCLA Medical Center in 1983 as he went through a complete and rigorous physical with Dr. Dennis Cope, who had become Muhammad's go-to physician in Los Angeles. I was glad to see that Muhammad was being open and honest with the doctor. He had been out of boxing for a couple of years now, and his symptoms, instead of dissipating, had only gotten worse. Muhammad was well aware of this, and he wanted to know what was happening to his forty-one-year-old body.

Los Angeles was part of the sales territory for my new job and, despite some of the tough incidents we had been through before my move out of town, I called Muhammad every couple of weeks and tried to see him whenever I came back up the coast. I worked out my schedule so I would be in town to accompany him to his doctor's appointment at UCLA. For so many years, Muhammad had supported so many of the people around him, and he had been so generous about making me and Helga a part of his life. Now he was feeling down over his problems with Veronica and he was confused about what was happening to him physically. I was glad that I could be there for him. Muhammad and

Dr. Cope talked for quite a while before a series of physical and neurological tests was run, and Muhammad explained all the symptoms he was worried about.

"I stumble. I move slow. I sleep in late and I'm still tired. I feel a little trembling in my left hand, and I slur my words. People can't understand what I'm saying."

The tests Dr. Cope put Muhammad through that day were meant to look for signs of brain damage—the "dementia pugilistica" that so many boxers suffered after all those years of blows to the head. But Muhammad's symptoms didn't quite match up with that diagnosis. His mind was still as sharp as ever, and his scans revealed no obvious signs of brain trauma (frankly, considering the beatings he had absorbed in the ring over the years, I was surprised by this). It wasn't until a follow-up examination a few months later that a clear diagnosis was finally made: Muhammad Ali was suffering from parkinsonism. "Parkinsonism" could apply both to the Parkinson's syndrome that Muhammad had, as well as the more specific Parkinson's disease, but the bottom line was that Muhammad and all of us who loved him now had an explanation for what was wrong with him.

For me, the diagnosis explained everything I had been seeing in Muhammad for years. There was one particular detail of Parkinson's syndrome that stood out, though. While most of the symptoms were physical, because it was a nervous disorder, parkinsonism also affected emotions and moods. That didn't automatically excuse all of Muhammad's outbursts over the last few years, but it certainly made them more understandable. His out-of-character mood swings may have been a result of his worsening illness, or they may have been a result of increasing anxiety as he sensed that something was wrong with him.

Muhammad always trusted his doctors, and he put up no argument against the diagnosis now. He began to take several medications that his doctors hoped would ease his symptoms and slow the advance of the syndrome.

• • • •

THE MOVE TO THE SAN Diego area had the effect Helga and I hoped for on our relationships with Muhammad and Veronica—it was much easier to love them both from a distance. Veronica came down and stayed with us for a week so that she could take some dressage lessons at a nearby equestrian center. I went up to L.A. and stayed with Muhammad a couple of times during the city's hosting of the 1984 Olympics. I was there to watch him carry the Olympic torch for a mile on its journey to the L.A. Coliseum, and I went with him to a couple of the boxing events at the L.A. Sports Arena. As always, his presence at such an event got a reaction. As soon as he was spotted entering the arena, the crowd rose to its feet and began to chant "Ali, Ali . . ." I always expected that response from a crowd, but it still sent chills up my spine to be the guy standing next to "the Greatest."

At the boxing events we had the chance to watch Robert Shannon finally make his Olympic debut after having missed out on the 1980 Olympics. He was only twenty years old, and Muhammad loved watching the skill and passion this "kid" brought to the boxing ring. Robert won his first-round fight, but in the second round he came up against a crafty South Korean fighter named Sung-Kil Moon. The fight was more of a "slugfest" than anyone ever expected to see between a couple of bantamweights. Shannon fought with skill and determination and scored a standing-eight count against Moon. After two rounds he was ahead on four out of five judges' cards. Then in the third round, with Moon clearly hurt, Robert, at the urging of his corner, decided to go for a knockout. Instead of fighting defensively and staying away from his opponent, he came out swinging hard and left himself open enough that Moon was able to tag him hard and score a technical knockout. Robert ended up being the only member of that 1984 U.S. boxing team not to win a medal.

Muhammad wanted to see Robert after the fight, so I brought Robert over to Fremont Place. Muhammad was on the phone in his office when we walked in, but as soon as he saw Robert he got off the line quickly and hushed the other people in the room. He asked Robert to sit and then just looked at him for a moment.

Finally, he said, "You fought a good fight. You didn't do anything wrong, but your corner let you down. You should have gotten better advice about how to finish the fight. Whenever you lose, you have to learn from the loss. Remember this fight as a lesson. You're going to turn pro and you'll be a good pro fighter because I'm going to ask Angelo to train you. He trained Sugar Ray Leonard when I asked him—now I'll ask him to train you."

You could see how much Muhammad's words meant to Robert. Muhammad made good on his promise, too. Angelo did train Robert, who went undefeated in his first fifteen pro fights and went on to have a very respectable boxing career.

WHENEVER I CAME UP TO L.A., Muhammad and I would go for long drives up and down the Pacific Coast Highway. Once we stopped at the Self Realization Center in Malibu. Elvis had thought that it was one of the most peaceful places in Los Angeles, and we thought so, too. Muhammad wasn't interested in doing any exercise except for walking, so sometimes we would take long walks together, and as always he was happy to stop and talk to people we encountered along the way. A couple of times I was with him at his home office, and he just got up and headed for the front door. I followed, and we ended up walking around the Fremont Place neighborhood. Sometimes we would get out of the car and just walk for blocks and talk to people along the way. He was generally in good spirits and a couple of times during my visits he felt good enough to revive his old habit of calling up strangers out of the blue. I remember him calling a very surprised John F. Kennedy Jr., to wish him well after the young man had graduated from Brown University.

There were a few times when we were even able to get the four of us together just like old times. The first couple of Januarys that Helga and I were in Solana Beach, we made a point of coming back up to L.A. to celebrate Muhammad's birthday with him and Veronica (of course,

Helga baked Muhammad a special cake on those occasions). The feel of those nights was always easy and comfortable, and it seemed to us that both Muhammad and Veronica were able to relax with each other when Helga and I were there. He would still treat Veronica like a queen and they still seemed great together, even though we all knew a couple of good dinners probably wasn't going to solve all their problems. Those nights always reminded me that without Helga and Veronica in the picture, I would have never gotten as close to Muhammad as I was. I might have been as close as some of the other guys around him, but the fact that we could be together as part of two couples made the relationship much more intimate.

Those "problems" between Veronica and Muhammad were not just the result of his parkinsonism and his mood swings, though. One of the biggest problems was another woman: Lonnie Williams. Lonnie was a young neighbor of the Clay family in Louisville (she was eight years old when Muhammad first won the heavyweight championship in 1964). The families knew each other—Lonnie's mother was a close acquaintance of Muhammad's mother. In the early '80s, he helped pay for Lonnie to attend business school at UCLA and he paid for the condo she lived in. Veronica told me she knew about all this and, needless to say, she didn't like it. I'm sure Muhammad believed that his love for Veronica was true and complete, but his ongoing connections to other women showed a disrespect toward Veronica. It was that disrespect, not the parkinsonism, that was the real source of friction in their marriage.

MUHAMMAD HAD ONCE WARNED ME. "Nobody knows what I'm thinking," and he proved that point again during the 1984 presidential campaign when he endorsed Ronald Reagan. The move angered and confused some of the political figures that Muhammad had associations with: Jesse Jackson, Julian Bond, and Andrew Young (I believe Young even flew in from Atlanta to try to talk Muhammad out of the endorsement). Muhammad got a lot of grief for backing Reagan, especially after he appeared in billboard ads that had him, Joe Frazier, and Floyd Patterson standing with Reagan and declaring, "We're voting for the man."

I knew that the endorsement didn't actually reflect any great shift in Muhammad's allegiances. Despite the strong political stands he had taken in the '60s and all that he had been through, he never really cared about politics much at all. He had an innocent approach to people in general, and he assumed that most politicians acted out of good intentions. If anyone rose to a position of power, he respected that position. He respected the status of any president, king, or head of state, no matter what their actual policies might be. ("There are so many decisions that these people have to make, they are just doing what they think is right," he told me once.)

Muhammad had been to the White House to meet President Gerald Ford, and he went back just as happy to meet President Jimmy Carter. Still, it took Muhammad a while to warm up to Ronald Reagan. In 1979, when I was serving as secretary of the WORLD foundation, I received a call from Henry Salvatori, a wealthy entrepreneur who was part of Reagan's "Kitchen Cabinet" team of advisers. Salvatori wanted to set up a meeting with Muhammad, but Muhammad was out of town. I suggested that as Muhammad's "administrative assistant" I could take the meeting for him, and Salvatori agreed to that. The next day I headed over to Salvatori's Westwood office, where I found myself in a room with other Kitchen Cabinet members—Justin Dart, Armand Hammer, and, conferenced in by phone, Walter Annenberg. I felt as if I was meeting with some very wealthy, very powerful grandfathers, but they didn't seem all that different from some of the top doctors I was used to meeting with.

Salvatori got to the point fairly quickly: "We are here to tell you that Ronald Reagan will be the next president of the United States. He's going to be a winner just like Muhammad Ali is a winner, and we'd love to have Ali on board supporting him."

The group asked me how I thought Muhammad would respond to the request for an endorsement. I wasn't sure. Then they began to discuss some "incentives" they could offer—business opportunities that Muhammad might be a part of. I scribbled everything down in my notebook and took it back to Muhammad.

"Naahh, man," he said. "Reagan doesn't really like me. He called me a draft dodger."

Back in 1968, when Muhammad was trying to restart his boxing career, the California Boxing Commission was ready to grant him a license, but then–Governor Reagan announced, "That draft dodger will never fight in my state, period." So Muhammad didn't endorse Reagan in 1980—he stuck with Jimmy Carter. But by 1984, things had shifted— not so much for Muhammad, but for Reagan. I wasn't involved when Muhammad was approached a second time by Reagan's team (which included Senator Orrin Hatch of Utah, a major boxing fan), but at that point Muhammad felt he was being asked to support the president of the United States rather than to endorse a candidate, and, without regard for the criticism he might face, he went ahead and gave his support to the man in office.

DESPITE THEIR LOVE FOR EACH other, Muhammad and Veronica could not work their way past the problems in their marriage. By the end of 1985, they were in divorce proceedings. Just before the divorce was finalized, I was up in L.A. on business and went over to Fremont Place one night. Muhammad was reading through fan mail. For a while, he asked me what life was like down in San Diego, but that wasn't what was really on his mind.

"Veronica is going to take my kids away," he said quietly. "I won't be able to take Hana and Laila to school. I won't be able to buy them ice cream, or take them to the movies, or sing them songs in bed to put them to sleep. I tried my best to be a good father and a good husband. I tried to be there when I could. Now I'm rich and famous, but that means nothing without Veronica and my children."

I had tears in my eyes. I turned my head away, trying to hide them from him. But when I looked his way, I saw that his eyes were wet, also.

"How can I help you, Muhammad?" I asked. "What do you want me to do?"

He didn't answer. We sat there in silence for quite a while.

By 1986 the divorce was finalized. Muhammad, in exactly the kind of move that always drove his business advisers crazy, essentially tore up the prenuptial agreement he had signed with Veronica and worked out a very generous settlement with her on his own.

NOT LONG AFTER THAT, WE all got a lesson that there were worse things than divorce that could happen to a person. Muhammad's great adversary Ken Norton was driving home from a benefit at the Biltmore Hotel when he lost control of his 1980 Clénet on the Vermont on-ramp of the Santa Monica Freeway. By the time Norton was discovered and taken to a hospital, he was in critical condition and was rushed right into surgery. As soon as Muhammad heard about Kenny's accident, he wanted to be there, and he and Howard Bingham were among Kenny's first visitors.

Kenny had a fractured skull, dangerous swelling of the brain, a broken jaw that was wired shut, and partial paralysis. At that point, the doctors were not sure if he would ever walk again and were giving him a fifty-fifty chance of recovering without serious brain damage. (Norton's chances would not have been even that good, except that, at forty-two, he was still in good physical shape.) As soon as he could be transferred, Norton was moved to St. John's Hospital in Santa Monica, to be cared for by brain trauma specialists. Muhammad spent a lot of time there over the following weeks. I was training the hospital's nursing staff to use a new defibrillator and was able to sit with Kenny between my duties. Kenny couldn't speak, so when Muhammad visited, he would entertain the patient by performing some of his magic tricks or telling him jokes. ("What did Lincoln say after waking up from a two-day drunk? I freed the who?") Norton would later say that one of the great motivators for getting out of the hospital was that he didn't want to watch Muhammad make another handkerchief disappear or hear any more of his punch lines. But as Norton began his long, hard recovery, he never forgot that Muhammad had been there for him, and, when he could, he let Muhammad know how much that meant to him. (Kenny recovered enough that he could eventually make light of the experience. Years later, I heard him talking about his original prognosis and then saying, "Well, Muhammad, here I am walking on my own and chewing gum at the same time.")

BY THE END OF 1986, Lonnie Williams had become the fourth Mrs. Muhammad Ali.

Lonnie didn't seem very eager to foster connections with anyone who had gotten close to Muhammad before her marriage to him. Unfortunately, that meant that for "old" friends such as Helga and me, it suddenly became very difficult to stay in touch with Muhammad. And it became even harder to stay connected when, in 1988, he sold the Fremont Place house and moved with Lonnie to his farm in Berrien Springs, Michigan. After that move, I tried to stay informed of Muhammad's travel plans through Howard Bingham, who, as a friend not so closely associated with a former wife, had better access to Muhammad. Over the next several years, I asked Bingham to do me the favor of tipping me off when I, or Helga and I, might be able to see Muhammad alone, or with Bingham. Then I would rearrange my work schedule so that Muhammad and I could cross paths and spend some time together, usually in Chicago, Las Vegas, or Los Angeles.

Not long after the move, Muhammad came back to Los Angeles as part of a promotional campaign launching a Muhammad Ali cologne. Coincidentally, he checked into the Westwood Marquis for the weekend—a hotel I was already planning to stay at in order to meet with some cardiologists at UCLA. We didn't make a big deal out of our "reunion," but it was very nice to be able to spend time alone with him. You were never alone with Muhammad for long, though, and one of the highlights of that trip happened when baseball superstar Reggie Jackson came by to see Muhammad. They talked about a lot of things, but Reggie had one serious message for Muhammad that he wanted to share face-to-face. He said that because of Muhammad, millions of young black men started looking at themselves a whole different way. Reggie said that, before Ali, he was often embarrassed by his appearance as a black man, especially among white friends. But after hearing Ali proudly call himself "pretty" and telling the world, "I'm not gonna be who you want me to be—I'm free to be who I wanna be," Reggie felt a new sense of pride in who he was. Reggie said that Muhammad Ali completely changed Reggie's own self-perception, and he would always be grateful for that. I could tell from Muhammad's reaction that this meant a lot to him, and that he understood a little more now that he had truly made a difference in people's lives.

I had a great evening with Muhammad at the Marquis, and the next morning went down to have breakfast before I went to my meetings. As I took my first sip of coffee, I realized I was looking straight into the eyes of Clint Eastwood, who had taken a seat in the curved booth next to mine. He was joined a few minutes later by a reporter from the French magazine *Paris Match*, and I lingered over my breakfast long enough to eavesdrop on quite a bit of Clint's interview. I made a couple of calls in the lobby, then found myself approaching the valet station just as Clint did the same. I introduced myself, explained my connection to Muhammad, and said that Muhammad would love it if his "favorite actor" came upstairs and knocked on his door. Clint was tempted, but he was already late to pick up his daughter for a birthday lunch. When he asked what Muhammad was doing back in town, I told him about the new Muhammad Ali cologne.

"Ali cologne?" he said. "What does it smell like—sweat?"

"No, much sweeter," I said, which got a laugh out of Clint.

Through the years, Muhammad loved relating a story about the first time he had met Eastwood, in the greenroom of *The David Frost Show*. I asked Clint if he remembered that meeting, and he said he remembered it well. He said that Muhammad took him out in a hallway, made them stand twenty feet apart, and then instructed Clint to squint as only Clint could and say, "This town ain't big enough for the two of us. I'm giving you until noon tomorrow to clear out, or else." Ali whooped with delight and said, "You are one baaaad man."

Clint noticed a helicopter pin in the lapel of my suit jacket and asked if I was a pilot. I told him that I wasn't—the pope had given me that pin. Clint laughed, but I was serious. The year before, Pope John Paul II had visited Los Angeles for two days. He was going to travel around the Southland by helicopter, but he had a heart condition and so plans were made for him to be shadowed by a private medical helicopter outfitted with the latest medical equipment. Part of that equipment was a brand-new defibrillator/pacemaker/heart monitor made by my company, Zoll Medical—so new that it wasn't on the market yet on the West Coast. Dr. David Eisenhower of Good Samaritan Hospital was in charge of the pope's medical team, and he asked if I would train him and his nurses on the new machine. I did, and one morning, before the pope headed off for a Mass at Dodger Stadium, a group of doctors and nurses plus myself were lined up at the heliport atop Good Samaritan so that John Paul could present each of us with a special lapel pin, a replica of the new "LifeFlight" emergency helicopter, giving each pin a blessing. A great day for a Catholic boy from Milwaukee.

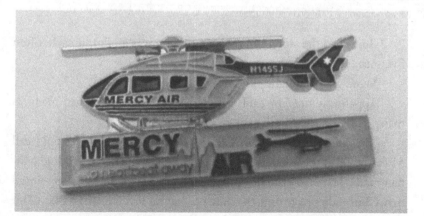

The "blessed" pin I received for being part of Pope John Paul II's
medical team during his visit to Los Angeles in 1987.
The pope blessed ten of these pins for the team.

Receiving a sales manager of the year award from Dr. Paul
Zoll, a brilliant man, the father of heart pacing, the salt of
the earth, and a wonderful professional mentor.

Clint liked the story, and told me that he was a pilot himself, often
flying the helicopters he used in his films.

"Wow, and I thought I knew everything about you!"

"Apparently not," he said, with the same squint that had made so
many bad guys weak in the knees.

The valet pulled up with Clint's Jeep, and he said he would call
Muhammad at the hotel later. I went back up to the room and told Muhammad who I had just been talking to. Muhammad was disappointed
that Clint didn't have time to come up, but he loved hearing that Clint
remembered their first meeting as well as he did.

•   •   •   •

ONE OF THE DISTRIBUTORS I worked with was in Louisville, so during some trips there in the late '80s and early '90s, I made a point of visiting with Muhammad's family: Mama Bird, Cash Sr., Aunt Coretta, Aunt Eva, and Muhammad's cousin Charlotte (also known as Duchess). Mama Bird was always warm and welcoming, and never tired of talking about what Muhammad had been like as a child. "Even when he was little," she told me, "Cassius wanted to take care of people. Once I was giving Rudy a spanking and Cassius came over and took Rudy by the arm and led him into the bedroom, telling me, 'Don't you hit my baby—you leave him alone.'"

Odessa also told me about some of young Muhammad's favorite pranks—he loved trying to scare his parents and his extended family, either by jumping out of a closet with a sheet over his head and yelling "Boo!" or by tying a long string to the curtains in his parents' bedroom so that he could move them from outside the room and make Cash and Odessa think their house was haunted.

Cash Sr. was even funnier than Muhammad, but he didn't know it. He was never trying to be funny, but when Cash got worked up on a subject, he could say things that sounded to me like brilliant comedy (though I was always smart enough not to laugh out loud). One day he and I were talking about the success of Kentucky Fried Chicken, and how well a small investment in that company would have paid off.

"Don't talk to me about investments, ummmm." He scowled. "I know everything there is to know about investments, ummmm." (He had a habit of adding those "umm"s at the end of sentences, as though he were weighing what he had just said.)

"You do?"

"I know investments better than anything. I know what to invest in, when to invest, and how much to invest, ummm."

"Well, then, Cash—why aren't you investing?"

"You need money to invest and I don't have any," he huffed. Perfect logic.

• • •

HELGA AND I DID NOT get to see Muhammad often, but we were always happy when we could spend time with him. In 1989 we visited Berrien to celebrate Muhammad's forty-seventh birthday (as usual, Helga baked an excellent cake for him). In the early '90s, Muhammad was making paid appearances at some of the casinos in Las Vegas—Caesars, the Mirage, the Paris. Vegas was part of my sales territory, so when I could, I would meet him there. I remember one great night at the Paris when Muhammad and LeRoy Neiman were the guests of honor at a dinner for "whales"—the casino's richest high rollers. Those Vegas times were fun because Muhammad would come to the city with Bingham, and he always seemed to be equally happy with a few of us in his suite or out among the public. He still had the amazing ability to be a humble soul and the center of attention at the same time. He was always aware of the commotion that his presence still created, and he loved it—though he would sometimes decline to appear at friends' special occasions for fear that he would take attention away from the person being honored.

In 1991, Muhammad, accompanied by Jimmy Ellis, came out to

Muhammad and Lonnie visit us at our home in
Rancho Santa Fe, California, 1992.

San Diego to be the keynote speaker at a big benefit dinner that the former boxing champ Archie Moore organized to support his boys' club. Moore had been a fierce light heavyweight who had dominated the weight class throughout the 1950s. Muhammad had briefly trained at Moore's San Diego camp as a young boxer; it was there that Muhammad got the idea for painting the names of boxing legends on large boulders at Deer Lake. Muhammad even faced Moore in the ring in 1962 in one of Moore's last professional fights (Muhammad predicted "Moore in four" and indeed won by a knockout in the fourth round). The night of the benefit sticks out in my mind because it was the last time I saw Muhammad in peak form at a public appearance.

When Helga and I met him up in his hotel room, he was still getting dressed in his custom-fit black tuxedo, and I helped him get his cuff links on. He was looking sharp, and he accessorized the look with his favorite African walking stick, a memento of his fight in Zaire with George Foreman. At the dinner, we all sat at a table in the front, and when Archie called Muhammad to the stage, he got up and climbed the stairs with no problem. Then he dominated the room, telling stories and making jokes that had the crowd roaring. His energy was great and his voice was strong and clear. I remember him making a big deal out of the fact that he and Archie had not been a very good match as trainer and boxer.

"I went to Archie Moore's training camp—the 'Bucket of Blood,' he called it," Muhammad explained. "Archie Moore wanted me to sweep the floors and peel the potatoes. I had to tell Archie Moore that I wasn't in training to be a housekeeper. I was there to box. So he started to teach me what he knew about boxing and he started trying to teach me some moves. But he was teaching me to move like *Archie Moore*. I don't move like Archie Moore and I don't box like Archie Moore. I box like Muhammad Ali and I'm not going to change my style for anyone!"

Archie himself was laughing and nodding along to everything Muhammad said. When Muhammad was done, he got a tremendous standing ovation. I think everybody in the room knew they had just seen something that was becoming rare: the Greatest at his best.

That same year, Muhammad and Lonnie came out west to attend the opening of a Muslim bookstore in downtown San Diego and visited Helga and me at our home. Muhammad liked our place, but he was more impressed by what we had in the garage—the Alfa Romeo Spider he had given us in Chicago back in 1976, which, thanks to Helga's loving care, still looked brand-new.

"This car looks better than you do," he said to me. I opened the hood to show him the clean engine, and he said, "I wish my engine looked that good."

Then I had a thought. While the hood was open, I asked Muhammad if he would sign a spot on the engine. He took a silver marker and wrote on the engine block, "This is my car, Muhammad Ali."

"If you ever sell this car, you better make sure that whoever buys it really appreciates it," he said.

The Spider is still in our garage. Nobody could appreciate it more than we do.

Compared to the warm, wonderful friendship we had all shared when Muhammad was with Veronica, it felt different with Lonnie. She did not seem all that interested in becoming friends, but Helga made a concerted effort to connect with her. Helga had always been open, honest, and welcoming to everyone she met, and I think even Lonnie could see how much Muhammad loved Helga as a friend. Helga's efforts were rewarded when we were invited to travel with Muhammad and Lonnie on a special trip to China in early 1993 (though the invitation did have to come through Howard Bingham).

Oddly enough, the trip was organized by none other than Harold Smith, who had finished his time in prison and was back to promoting boxing events, mostly overseas. It didn't really surprise me that Muhammad would get involved with Harold again. When asked about Smith's crimes, Muhammad would say, "He didn't hurt me. I didn't lose anything—he was just using my name." That sort of explanation used to drive me crazy, and I would often insist to him that his name was the most valuable thing he had. But he never wanted to hold a grudge against any individual who had tried to hurt him. He would say that the

Quran taught him to forgive. He said that whenever he felt angry, hateful, or vindictive toward someone he would ask himself, Would God accept this?

With Muhammad in the Presidential Suite of the Beijing
Grand Hotel. We're about to take our chauffeured Mercedes
to the Great Wall of China for a guided tour.

So Harold Smith was back in the picture. He had set up the first professional boxing exhibitions in China, and he knew that Chinese authorities were trying to put Beijing in consideration to be the host city for a future summer Olympics. He suggested that if the Chinese honored Muhammad Ali as the "Athlete of the Century," they could impress the Olympics selection committee with their ability to welcome westerners for a well-orchestrated event. With the prize of an Olympics on their mind, the Chinese officials agreed to everything that Harold Smith asked for. Muhammad Ali and his small group of traveling companions, which included the boxing promoter Bob Arum, were treated to a first-class stay in suites at the Grand Hotel in Beijing. Each of us had access to a chauffeured Mercedes 460, a bodyguard, a tour guide, and an interpreter.

Helga and I had traveled internationally before on Muhammad's behalf. In the '80s, we took a trip to Peru with Jimmy Ellis, and then a visit to the Marshall Islands to represent Muhammad when he was made an honorary citizen there. But traveling with Muhammad made this the most amazing trip we'd ever been on. Everywhere we went— grade schools, universities, hospitals, boxing clubs—the Chinese people poured out their love for Muhammad.

In being that close to him for ten days, though, I got a close look at what he was going through physically. In 1991, he had been in surprisingly good shape. Just two years later, he was not. His speech was now even harder to understand, and for the first time his symptoms started showing up in his facial affect: he was bloated because of the medications and he often had a dull, blank stare. Often, it didn't look like he was responding to anything around him. It was easy for people who just looked at him to assume that he was disengaged and out of it, but when I spoke to him one-on-one, it was clear to me that he was aware of everything going on around him. It had just become very hard for him to make all the fine-muscle facial expressions that go into normal responses of human emotion. Like the punches he wanted to throw in the Holmes fight, Muhammad felt those emotions, but couldn't express them.

He could still get amazed responses out of others, though. One of my enduring memories of that trip is of the awestruck faces of the Chinese flight attendants on our plane when Muhammad stood up in the aisle, told the first-class passengers to watch his feet, and "levitated" right in front of them.

ONE OF MY FRIENDSHIPS CAME to a sad end in 1999. Walter Payton was suffering from a rare liver disease. He was put on a waiting list at the Mayo Clinic for a liver transplant, but during his wait a cancer of the bile duct spread to the point that a transplant was no longer an option. I called

Walter when I knew I was going to be in Chicago, and he invited me to come visit him.

We sat by a man-made lake in front of his home. Walter was never a guy who showed much emotion, and I wanted to stay strong and positive for his sake, so we mostly talked about some of the funny memories we shared. I reminded him of the time he came knocking on my front door at six a.m., wanting me to go to the airport with him to pick up his brother Eddie. Helga answered the door and scolded Walter for waking us up so early.

"That's the last time I ever went to your house without you," he told me.

Toward the end of our visit, I shared with him a message that Muhammad wanted me to pass along—that as long as Walter loved God, he would be OK. Back in the kitchen with his wife, Connie, and their fourteen-year-old daughter, Brittney. Walter started talking about the magic tricks he had seen Muhammad do, and he asked me if Muhammad still levitated. I said that he did, and that he'd taught me to, as well. Walter wanted to see me do it, so I proceeded to "levitate" in Walter's kitchen. When it was time for me to leave, it was impossible not to acknowledge the sadness of the moment—that this was the last time we would ever see each other. I gave him a hug and said, "I love you, man." He couldn't respond with words, but he didn't have to. As I walked to my car, Walter was at the front door waving goodbye. When he went back into the house, I put my head on the steering wheel and bawled. Walter died two months later at the age of forty-five. Rest in peace, my friend.

AS THE YEAR 2000 APPROACHED, Helga and I were celebrating twenty-five happy years of marriage and twenty-two years of happy life in Southern California. Only occasionally, when we looked at old photos or shared old stories, did we think about how much we missed being as steady a part of Muhammad's life as we once had been. We knew we were incredibly blessed to have been as close to him as we were during those years in

Chicago and L.A.—maybe to hope for more now was just greedy. I would still call Muhammad in Berrien Springs, and could sometimes take time out of a Chicago business trip to see him there. We weren't truly ever out of his life—we just didn't see him as much as we wanted to, and we figured that wasn't going to change.

But it did change, thanks to our dear, sweet Hana Ali.

Hana was now a smart, beautiful twenty-three-year-old woman, living in Los Angeles. She was thinking about putting together a book—a daughter's perspective on Muhammad's life—and she reached out to Helga and me to help with stories from the '70s and '80s when she was quite young. We had never lost touch with her, but now that there was a reason to be more in touch we started talking a lot. I became "Uncle Tim" all over again, except that now, instead of taking Hana to the zoo or the ice cream shop, she and I were relating to each other as adults, and I think we both quickly realized just how much we treasured our bond of affection. Through Hana, Helga and I also rekindled our relationships with Veronica and Laila, and that in turn brought us closer to Muhammad than we had been for a while.

The night before Muhammad's birthday in 1999, Hana, Maryum, Rasheda, Jamillah, and I were sitting in his Beverly Hilton suite when Hana suggested going to a comedy movie in Century City. Muhammad and his daughters jumped into his Lexus SUV, and I followed them in my car. On Santa Monica Boulevard we had to turn left onto Century Boulevard, and I knew this was a very long stoplight. When it changed to red, I jumped out of my car and snuck up beside the passenger side where Muhammad was sitting. I knocked on the window and gave him my version of his signature "mean face" look and clenched fist. Though startled, he had a grin and gave me his mean face back with a fist. The girls screamed in the backseat when I knocked on the window.

When we were walking into the theater I asked Maryum what Muhammad had said in the car when I surprised him? He just said, "He's a brotha!"

THIRTEEN

IN HIS CORNER

IN 2002, HANA MOVED TO Berrien Springs to live with Muhammad. She loved her father dearly and had always had a special connection with him, and he with her, but now she felt compelled to be close enough to make sure that he got all the support and care he needed. The fact that Hana became such a part of Muhammad's day-to-day life meant that it was easier for me to connect with him, as well. Hana knew exactly what her father's friendship meant to Helga and me, and she always welcomed us into his home as a part of the family.

I made a visit to Berrien Springs not long after Hana moved in, and I got to see some of the new routines of Muhammad's life. Some people in Muhammad's physical condition might want to withdraw from the public eye, but for Muhammad it was always the opposite. He was energized being around people, receiving the love that came his way and giving it back the best he could. One afternoon Hana and I drove him over to Andrews University, one of the top colleges in the international Seventh Day Adventist school system, which was just a short distance from Muhammad's property. Muhammad brought a briefcase with him that contained about two hundred pamphlets with passages from the Quran. He had painstakingly signed every one of them, and then wrote

The entrance to "The Farm," Muhammad's home in Berrien Springs, Michigan.

"To:" with a space left blank for the recipient's name. Muhammad sat at a table in the student union with a pile of the pamphlets in front of him, and before long students were gathered around him, enthusiastically asking him all kinds of questions. He made a point of asking the name of every student he spoke with, and then gave them a signed pamphlet. He seemed very happy to be interacting with the students, and Hana told me it wasn't unusual for him to do that kind of thing two or three times a week.

In other outings around Berrien Springs, Muhammad seemed legitimately surprised that younger kids knew who he was. I can still picture one little girl who approached him and said hello.

"How old are you?" asked Muhammad.

"Ten," said the girl.

"And you know me? You weren't even born when I retired. How do you know me?"

"My daddy told me about you when we saw you on TV," she said.

Muhammad gave her a hug and a kiss on the cheek. As she walked away, he said to Hana and me, with a tone of amazement, "She's ten years old and she knows who I am?" (He was much more surprised about this than I was—I figured it was a safe bet that he was going to be known for generations to come.)

After buying the Berrien Springs farm back in 1976, Muhammad had always kept the huge wrought-iron gate to the property unlocked and open. But Lonnie was not so happy about putting up with strangers walking across the property or showing up at the kitchen door, so the gate was now locked and key-coded. That cut down on trespassers, but a new generation of young fans had heard that Muhammad hardly ever turned away a visitor, so the bell at the gate was being rung constantly. I was with him in his office—a small building closer to the entrance than the main house—when we heard it ring.

"Answer the gate," said Muhammad.

I went out and found three teenage boys on bicycles.

"Can we see the Champ?" one of them asked.

I told them he was busy in his office, but that they could come in for a quick hello. As soon as Muhammad saw the boys, he acted as if these were exactly the visitors he had been waiting for. He asked the boys what grade they were in and how they were doing in school. He asked what nationalities each of them had in their background (one had an interesting biracial look that I know Muhammad was curious about). Then he asked them what religion they were, and how much they knew about the Muslim religion. The boys didn't get to ask many questions of their own, but each one did get a signed pamphlet and also the thing that Muhammad felt was most important—a great memory of meeting the Champ.

Since childhood, Muhammad had enjoyed sketching pictures, and as his parkinsonism began to slow him down, sketching became a favorite pastime (along with reading and writing passages from the Quran, and watching hours of CNN or ESPN). I loved the style of his drawings and through the years had made several special requests for sketches of scenes from his career. One afternoon he was working on a sketch of himself and Frazier in the ring during their first fight when his personal secretary stepped into the room and reminded him that a call was coming through from London for a BBC radio interview. The call came in on speakerphone and I stayed in the room as Muhammad fielded the questions that were put to him. As the interview was winding down the moderator asked, "Muhammad, of all the celebrity friends that you've known all these years, who do you admire the most?"

"Elvis," Muhammad said without hesitation.

"Well, sadly Elvis is no longer with us," said the voice on the phone. "Of all your celebrity friends who are still alive today, who do you admire the most?"

"Clint Eastwood," Muhammad said, just as quickly.

"Why Clint Eastwood?"

"He's a great actor, he directs, he plays the piano, he composes music, he flies his own helicopters, he is humble like me, and he is older than me and still going strong so he must be the greatest."

"Muhammad, of all the fighters you have fought, who are you closest to?"

He again answered without hesitation: "George Foreman."

"Why is that?"

"Because George loves God, like me."

I got to pass this line on to George Foreman directly because, through Hana, I had had the chance to become close with George. Hana is a good friend of George's daughter Georgetta. (Hana is also best friends and was for years roommates with Ken Norton's daughter Kenisha.) I had met George briefly at the Fremont Place house and at some group events through the years, but had never really talked much with him because he didn't seem that approachable. Once Hana told George that I was one of her father's closest friends, though, that was all that George needed to hear. We really connected, and I could see right away what Muhammad loved about him—George was an absolutely lovable guy (pretty much the opposite of his intimidating image during the "Rumble in the Jungle" era). George and I hit it off well enough that he gave me his personal contact information, and we began staying in touch by phone and e-mail. What really meant a lot to me was that every time George's contact info changed, he got in touch with me to make sure I knew how to reach him.

It was amazing to me that George Foreman and Muhammad Ali— these two fierce competitors in the ring—could become such great friends after retirement. George would say, "Nobody loves Muhammad Ali more than George Foreman except for Jesus Christ." Early in their friendship, whenever George called he would give a shot at converting Muhammad to Christianity. I think both of them enjoyed the deep theological discussions they got into, but George figured out pretty quickly that he wasn't going to change Muhammad's mind (nobody ever does). He wasn't ever going to be Muhammad's pastor, but he was very happy to be one of Muhammad's closest friends.

George and I grew closer, too, and after we'd been in touch for a couple of years, he said something that astounded me.

"Tim, I'll do anything for you," he said. "I consider Muhammad to be my dearest friend, and you are one of my dearest friends, also."

"Wow, George. How do I possibly deserve that honor?"

"Because you took care of my dear friend through all these years when he needed somebody, and I didn't. You know that everybody took advantage of Muhammad Ali—even me. You were there when Muhammad needed someone."

It's still hard to express how much those words meant to me, but I can say that I love George Foreman and consider him to be one of Helga's and my dearest friends now. And these days George says, "No one loves Muhammad Ali more than George Foreman except for Jesus Christ—and Tim and Helga."

OVER THE YEARS, MUHAMMAD BECAME a more difficult patient. He had listened to his doctors at first, but there was no miracle pill for him to take; the drugs that helped him had side effects; and he started to grow tired with the shifting protocols, which had him taking medication throughout the day. At some point during his time in Berrien Springs he decided that he might be able to conquer his disease through his faith alone. He told me more than once that as a faithful Muslim believer, he would be taken care of by Allah. His sickness was merely a test of faith, a test he would endeavor to pass each day with inner strength and spiritual calm. With all that in mind, he began to skip his medications, not by refusing to take them outright but by putting his sleight-of-hand skills to use in a new way—palming his pills and simply drinking water (he got away with this once in a while, but Hana and Lonnie and Bingham were aware of his tricks).

Faith alone didn't cure him, though, and by 2004 Muhammad was aware that he needed more help with his condition. He and Lonnie began renting a home in Scottsdale, Arizona, in hopes that the warmer climate would be good for him as an alternative to the Michigan winters. Lonnie's sister Marilyn moved in, as well, continuing to serve Muhammad as a full-time caregiver. The move also put Muhammad closer to the Parkinson's experts at the Barrow Neurological Institute in Phoenix (which became home to the Muhammad Ali Parkinson Center). Muhammad and Lonnie bought a home in the Paradise Valley neighborhood of Scottsdale and began to live there. (Muhammad wasn't the first celebrity to live in Paradise Valley—his neighbors included Stevie Nicks, Alice Cooper, and the basketball stars Charles Barkley and Steve Nash.) Muhammad started on a new regimen of physical therapy and a new sequence of drug therapy. He responded well, and was able to stay active.

The move to Arizona made it easier for me to see Muhammad, as the state was part of my territory as a regional sales manager and I could always justify a trip to Phoenix or Tucson. On those trips, for the first time ever, I sometimes let some of my sales colleagues know that I was friends with Muhammad Ali. There was personal benefit in mentioning my connection—it actually helped close a deal at Scottsdale Memorial Hospital—but I also felt that I now wanted to remind people that Muhammad was very much still "here" and still "the Greatest."

When I visited Muhammad, I tried to be very mindful of his daily routines. In the mornings there was breakfast at 8:30, then time with the Quran, time for sketching, then some time for a favorite DVD (maybe Elvis's "Aloha" concert or a Clint Eastwood western). In the afternoon, Muhammad was driven to a physical therapy clinic a few miles from his home. Between 2005 and 2012, this therapy was intensive and included a tough regimen of treadmill runs, weight machine workouts, and agility exercises. When Hana brought Helga and me along on one of these workout days, it filled us with joy to see that Muhammad's fighting spirit was as strong as it had ever been. He really worked up a sweat as he used to do in the old days, and he would fight through the end of a workout on the weight machine the way he used to fight through the fifty-yard sprints at the end of our morning runs. Muhammad got so into his exercise one day that he told Hana and me to contact George Foreman. "Let him know I'm getting ready for him. Tell him to start getting in shape and to lose a few pounds. I'm going to have the press conference soon. We're going to shock the world again with Ali-Foreman II."

Hearing him clown that way always gave me goose bumps. I loved knowing that even with all he was going through, Muhammad's fun-loving character was undefeated.

In the late afternoon, Muhammad liked to spend time with his mail. Once he inscribed something on an Ali-Foreman fight photo for George, and then on a photo for Clint Eastwood, "Remember me and I will remember you." That struck me as a little strange. "Muhammad— do you really think that George Foreman or Clint Eastwood could forget you?"

"I'm starting to forget them," he said. "They might forget me, too."

MUHAMMAD MADE A SPECIAL TRIP to Los Angeles in the spring of 2007—Laila was a contestant on *Dancing with the Stars*. Muhammad came to the show with Lonnie, but of course the rest of Laila's family—Veronica, Hana, and Veronica's mother, Ethel Porche—were going to be there, too. Sweet Hana made sure that Helga and I were invited, and had us sit in the front row with her, her mother and father, Howard Bingham, and Laila's fiancé, Curtis Conway. At the taping, we all took our seats in the front row. On the other side of the stage, there were two beautiful women in the front row who began blowing kisses at Muhammad. Always the flirt, he pointed to them and smiled.

Veronica and Muhammad had not seen each other for a while, and now they were sitting close. The show was great and Laila was as beautiful as ever in an elegant red formal dress. She did a very special waltz just for her dad and at the end of the dance she went over to hand him a rose and to kiss him—an act of love that had the audience melting. The dance got high marks from the judges. During the other dancers' performances, Veronica was focused on what was happening up on the stage. But Muhammad was focused on Veronica. He just kept staring at her while she watched the show. Finally I reached over and tapped her on the shoulder and said, "Veronica, Muhammad wants you."

She turned toward him, and as their eyes met she had the biggest, warmest smile on her face.

"Hi, Muhammad. How are you feeling?"

He just nodded.

"It's good to see you again."

Muhammad nodded again, with the happiest smile on his face.

This tender moment between Muhammad and Veronica remains a jewel of a memory for Helga and me. Things had not worked out for their marriage, and each had gone on to build lives with other people, but I couldn't help thinking that Muhammad still saw Veronica as his one true love.

IN THE FALL OF 2007, I arranged a very special visit with Muhammad. Over the years, Helga and I had become close friends with Jerry and Cindy Schilling. Jerry was a member of Elvis Presley's "Memphis Mafia," and in many ways his friendship with Elvis paralleled the friendship I had with Muhammad. Knowing how highly Elvis thought of Muhammad,

Jerry decided that he wanted to give Muhammad a very special gift—a gold friendship ring with a black onyx stone that Elvis had given to him back in 1974. To get a sense of the value of this gift, I called Bonham's Auction House in Los Angeles and was informed that at auction such a ring with an Elvis-Muhammad pedigree could go for close to $500,000 if it were in Muhammad's possession when it was evaluated. I decided to relay that information to Jerry, and asked him if he was sure he wanted to give Muhammad this gift.

Receiving Elvis's friendship ring from Memphis Mafia man Jerry Schilling.

"Yes," said Jerry without a moment's hesitation. "I know that Elvis would want Muhammad to have this ring."

Helga and Cindy came up with the idea of setting the ring in a custom black velvet case with a gold inscription plate. I scheduled with Marilyn to find a day when Muhammad would be alone at home and available to receive a visitor. Jerry flew out from L.A., and I picked him up at the airport and we got to Muhammad's house around one p.m. As we stood at the door, I could see that Jerry—the man who had been at Elvis's side for so many historic moments—was feeling the weight of this moment.

"I'm actually nervous," he admitted.

Muhammad was in the den, sitting in his easy chair in front of a huge TV screen (his "throne"). I gave Muhammad my usual greeting, putting my arm around his shoulders, kissing him on the cheek, and saying, "I love you, man."

He answered, "Maaaaaan, maaaan!"

I explained that I had brought a special guest with a special gift. I introduced Jerry as "Elvis's best friend" (you can't have a better introduction than that). I explained a little bit about Jerry's career as a manager for Billy Joel, Jerry Lee Lewis, and the Beach Boys, but mostly I explained how close Jerry had been to Elvis.

Muhammad said, "Jerry is Elvis's Shanahan." That was beautiful to hear.

Jerry and I kneeled on either side of him, and Jerry presented him with the black case, opened it, showed Muhammad the ring, and read the inscription: "To Muhammad Ali, Elvis gave me this ring as a symbol of our friendship. I am giving you this ring as a symbol of your friendship with Elvis. Elvis would want you to have it. Sincerely, Jerry Schilling."

Muhammad took the ring out of the box and gently put it on his ring finger. He looked up at Jerry and whispered, "Thank you." Muhammad kept touching the ring and staring at it lovingly as he listened to Jerry tell him the story about how Elvis had given Jerry the ring. It was a wonderful moment for all of us. And it only got better. Jerry had also brought an amazing Elvis personal family photo album full of shots of Elvis through the years. Boy, did Muhammad get excited over that. Muhammad looked at each photo intently while Jerry told him the story behind each one. Then Muhammad started pointing at pictures and asking Jerry questions.

"That's Elvis?"

"When he was eight years old."

"Who's that?"

"That's Priscilla—Elvis's wife."

"Who's that?"

"George Klein. Another good friend."

Muhammad pointed at a picture of a young guy with a very full head of hair.

"Who's that?"

Jerry said, "That's me."

Muhammad looked at Jerry, looked back at the picture, and had a big smile on his face.

"Well—that was the hairstyle back then," explained Jerry.

The afternoon was everything I wanted it to be, and everything I know Jerry wanted it to be. Just before we left, I wondered if maybe we could cap off the meeting with a little magic.

"You know, Jerry—Muhammad can levitate."

"I knew he could do a lot of things, but I didn't know that."

"Muhammad, can you still do it?" I asked.

He quickly grabbed both arms of the chair and pulled himself out of his chair. I walked him over to a kitchen counter, where he put one hand down to get a little leverage. I told Jerry to watch Muhammad's feet. Muhammad positioned himself just right and, to my amazement, he had the strength and the balance to pull off the illusion just as he had so many times before.

AS THE YEARS PASSED, RUNNING into old friends could be a bittersweet experience. In 2008 I was in Chicago on a business trip, and Jimmy Ellis had come to town from his home in Louisville to sign autographs at a sports convention. I met him at his hotel and was saddened to see that he was beginning to suffer the memory loss associated with dementia pugilistica. Jimmy said he was surprised himself that he remembered me and

Helga. Jimmy could maintain a conversation, but it was like speaking with someone who is a little drunk. The important thing for me was that he recognized me and Helga, and was as happy to see us as we were to see him. His condition worsened through the years, and when he passed away in 2014, I was thankful for that last visit.

A happier reconnection occurred in 2008 when Helga and I went to see Kris Kristofferson in concert at the Escondido Performing Arts Center near us. I had stayed in touch with "KK" through the years, and made arrangements to see him after the show. I brought along a lot of photos I had taken of Kris and Muhammad through the years—most of which Kris had never seen. He told me he had not seen Muhammad in years, but would love to invite him to come to his home in Maui. Almost bashfully, he asked if I would give him Muhammad's phone number. Of course I would—but I advised him to make any travel arrangements through Marilyn Williams.

A few days later, I got a very excited call from Marilyn.

"I couldn't believe it. Kris Kristofferson called, and I got Muhammad on the phone with him and all I heard was Muhammad saying 'Yeah! Yeah! Yeah!'"

Marilyn worked out the details with Kris's wife, Lisa, and it wasn't long before Muhammad spent a week of Hawaiian vacation with Kris. Once Kris knew that Muhammad was coming, he invited Willie Nelson to join them. Muhammad told me he had a great time sportfishing with Kris and Willie, and he said that he and the other two veteran practical jokers spent a lot of time talking about favorite pranks.

MUHAMMAD AND I STAYED IN touch mostly through Hana and by phone (when we couldn't be with Muhammad on a birthday, Helga made sure to Fed Ex him one of his favorite cakes). Hana had told me the best time to call her father was between nine and eleven in the morning, when the drugs from the previous day had worn off and before his morning dosage had kicked in. On some of those mornings, I felt like I was talking to the Ali of thirty years earlier—he was alert, sharp, conversational, and as funny as ever. He loved hearing old stories (buying the Rolls in L.A. was a favorite) and, without fail, he would ask where Helga was and how she was doing ("Is she cooking?" "Is she still a fox?"). Whenever I had a great conversation with Muhammad, I would call Hana right away and tell her that it was a "good day" and that she should give her dad a call. Sometimes it would work the other way, with Hana calling me to let me know that it was an excellent morning to give Muhammad a call.

I never spoke about the specifics of treatment or medication with Muhammad, but I was kept up to date by Marilyn. As new medications became available, new regimens were developed for Muhammad, and Lonnie and Marilyn were always keeping up with any available advances in treatment. In some ways, the medications and his physical therapy helped him beat the odds—he was in good shape for someone who had been living with parkinsonism for as long as he had. ("Thirty years ago they gave me ten to fifteen years to live," he would say. "Now it's thirty years later and I'm still in the fight.") There were bad days too, though, when keeping up his side of the conversation seemed to take too much effort. On those days, I would talk to him as I always did, telling him old stories, keeping him up to date on his friends ("Chubby Checker sends his love"), and just trying to entertain him for twenty or thirty minutes.

Even though it became harder for him to get out, Muhammad still loved to be among people. He was at the inauguration of Barack Obama in 2009. He was in London for the opening ceremony of the Summer Olympics in 2012. He especially enjoyed making appearances at the annual Celebrity Fight Night held in Phoenix. That event was the vision of Jimmy Walker, who started it in 1994 as a way of raising money for a number of charities with a single fund-raiser. In the event's third year, Muhammad became the featured guest of the night, and from that night on, Fight Night really centered on him. Through the years, the night showcased the talents of Muhammad's friends, some of whom I first saw as names in his little black book, and some newer: Billy Crystal, Garth Brooks, Robin Williams, Diana Ross, Madonna, Cher, and especially Reba McEntire, who continues to do a fantastic job as the event's emcee.

I believe that the years Hana spent living with her father had a lot to do with keeping him healthy and active. She always wanted to do whatever she could for him, but at some point both of them agreed that she needed to make a life for herself. In 2009 she moved from Berrien Springs to Los Angeles to pursue a professional career as a teacher and author, calling her father daily and visiting him in Scottsdale whenever she could. In 2011, I was honored that Hana asked me to help represent the family when the stunning *reALIze* installation—the artist Michael Kalish's tribute to Muhammad—was dedicated outside the Staples Center in Los Angeles before a Lakers-Knicks game.

For Christmas of 2012, Helga and I received the greatest gift either of us could have hoped for—a chance to visit Muhammad together. It was wonderful to spend time with him. Muhammad still loved to be out people-watching, so one day we picked up some fried chicken for lunch and drove down Scottsdale Boulevard, cranking up one of his new favorite Andrea Bocelli CDs. We made stops in the Old Town neighborhood so that Muhammad could interact with fans, which reminded me of our days in Chicago, when we would cruise Lake Shore Drive and then, at Muhammad's insistence, stop at the Navy Pier to sign autographs.

Another of Muhammad's favorite things to do was go to a bookstore and look at photography books. One afternoon, after we took Muhammad out for a picnic in the park, Helga, Marilyn, and I brought him to a Barnes & Noble bookstore. Helga and Marilyn sat with him in a comfortable reading area, while I tracked down photo books with subjects I knew he would enjoy (the Beatles, Elvis, Marilyn Monroe, Sophia Loren). As I carried a stack of books to the sitting area, I heard Helga speaking to Muhammad, telling him about that beautiful night thirty-six years before when she prepared the first home-cooked dinner for him and Veronica at the South Woodlawn house; the night he and

I had made a deal to rock side by side in our rocking chairs when we got to be old men; the night he had written us the note that said, "The Chef that prepares a good dish makes a greater contribution to Human Happiness than the Astronomer who discovers a new star."

"Do you remember that night, Muhammad?" Helga asked.

Dr. Veronica Porche and I having dinner at the Beverly Wilshire Hotel, 2012, where she and Muhammad were married in 1977.

"No," said Muhammad. He bowed his head, shook it slowly side to side, and began to cry.

Helga held Muhammad's head to her chest. She spoke to him using the nickname she'd had for him almost since they'd first met. "Don't worry, MuMu. It will come back to you another time. The next time I tell you about that night, you will remember it like you always do. Don't cry, MuMu. We love you. It's all right. Please don't cry."

He stayed bent forward. She put her arms around him, then looked up at me. "Sing to him, Tim," she said.

I was crying now, also. My singing had always managed to get smiles and laughs out of Muhammad, so Helga was right—now was the time to sing again. What song, though? Before I even had a chance to think about what Muhammad might want to hear, my mouth was open and the words were coming out loud and strong—words I had sung to him years ago in Deer Lake as we watched his friend Elvis in *King Creole*.

"If you're looking for trouble, you came to the right place. If you're looking for trouble, just look right in my face. . . ."

Muhammad looked up at me. His eyes were still wet, but a smile began to spread across his face. I kept singing and began to throw in a few Elvis moves for dramatic effect. Other patrons started coming over to us to see what was going on—but nobody asked me to stop. In fact, when I got to the end of "Trouble," there was a polite smattering of applause. Muhammad clapped, too, so I launched right into two choruses of "Ball of Confusion" with some Temptations' dance moves, and then finished with my heartfelt take on the Shirelles' version of "Dedicated to the One I Love." There was more applause and Muhammad was still smiling. I gave him the mean face and he gave it right back. We helped him up, and Helga walked Muhammad out of the store and back to the car. The singing really did seem to cheer him up, but we worried that he might spend the rest of the night troubled about his memory lapse.

We didn't need to worry. By the time we were in the car, Muhammad was back to being Muhammad: he wanted to stop for ice cream. So, we did. Muhammad's life had been complicated at times, but this simple treat had always made him happy. I was not as big a fan of ice cream, but in the nearly forty years of being Muhammad's friend, simply being around him had always made me happy. He welcomed me into his amazing life, and in doing so he made my life richer in ways I could never have dreamed of. In these later years, which were a struggle for him, I felt closer to him than I ever had before. Whatever little thing I could do for him wouldn't come close to repaying him for everything he had given me through the gift of his friendship.

But those aren't the kinds of things you say out loud to the three-time heavyweight champion of the world when he's trying to enjoy a banana split. As Muhammad had often said, true friends could be comfortable in each other's presence saying nothing at all.

So, just as I had so many times through the years, I sat there quietly with my friend and had some ice cream. It tasted better than ever.

EPILOGUE

BLACK SUPERMAN

November 2013

THE SETTING WAS BEAUTIFUL AND the day seemed perfect for an outdoor wedding. There was a clear blue sky above us, and the warm afternoon sun lit up the foothills of the Santa Monica Mountains. The Mountain Gate Country Club was just a short drive off Los Angeles's traffic-clogged 405 freeway, but, nestled in those foothills, the club grounds felt far away from everything ordinary. Lights were strung in the trees, and large scented candles marked the rows of white chairs set up on a perfectly manicured lawn. A colorful trail of rose petals marked the aisle the bride would walk down.

This wedding, like any other, was a day for the bride and groom to take their first step toward a new future. I couldn't help thinking about a past that was full of so many wonderful memories, though. This particular bride, Hana Ali, had grown into a beautiful woman, and today she looked absolutely stunning in her elegant white dress with a flowing train. But it was still hard for me not to see the little girl I'd shared so many happy moments with. I thought about the times I had taken her and Laila to the beach, the zoo, trick-or-treating, out for ice cream. Frankly, Hana had been a very special person to me from the first time I had held her as an infant in my arms. With Hana, Muhammad had become the father to a sixth daughter (Laila would make it seven), and I remembered him back in Chicago, expressing some nervousness at welcoming another girl into the family.

"Another daughter, another daughter," he said, shaking his head. "I've got to worry about another daughter."

I couldn't resist teasing him about being an overly protective father. "Well, Muhammad, this will be just like the other girls—you'll have to sit on the porch with a shotgun, waiting for some boy to bring your daughter home from a date."

He looked at me with his mean face—then his expression softened and he just snorted a little laugh.

"Even more so. I'll be out on that porch when the boys come to pick her up. They'll get the message."

The only message being sent this day was one of love. Hana was marrying a good-looking guy named Kevin Casey, who, in Ali family tradition, was also a fighter—a mixed martial arts pro and karate instructor. The bride and groom were clearly devoted to each other, and all of us who loved Hana wanted this day to be a fitting celebration of the love between Hana and Kevin.

I believe Hana and I would have shared a special connection no matter what, but I know the connection was even deeper because of Helga, whose advice and guidance Hana always valued. It meant a great deal to Helga and me to be there for Hana's wedding, and it meant even more that Hana invited us to be seated at her father's table. Hana once told me that I was like a second father to her, and on this special day I felt as proud of her as a father could be.

When the service began Hana walked down the aisle arm in arm with Veronica. At the end of the aisle, she stepped over to Muhammad, who was sitting in the front row. She bent down to kiss him and share a moment with him, then walked over to take her place with her groom. The ceremony was perfect, and once the beautiful couple were officially pronounced husband and wife, the guests headed to the club's ballroom for the reception.

Muhammad always wanted to carry himself with dignity, and for years, even as his Parkinson's greatly restricted his mobility, he refused to use a wheelchair. As hard as it was for him to get around in arenas and airports and such, he would always decline any offers of a chair. If it took him a half hour longer to get somewhere, fine—he would put in the greater effort required to walk wherever he was going. Occasionally at a public outdoor event, when tougher distances had to be covered, he would allow himself to ride in a golf cart. But never a wheelchair. I knew that staying out of a wheelchair wasn't just a matter of pride. Muhammad had never forgotten the image of Joe Louis, broke and ailing, parked in a wheelchair in the front entrance to Caesars Palace back in 1978 before the first Spinks fight. That image symbolized everything Muhammad wanted to avoid in his later years.

At Hana's wedding, though, Muhammad was in a wheelchair. I knew he wasn't happy about this, though to me he looked just as dignified as ever. I decided that when I had the chance to talk to him at the reception, I would let him know that I understood how he felt. After he had been pushed to the main table in the reception room, I went over to him, put my arm around his shoulder, and gave him a kiss. "I know you hate that damn wheelchair," I continued, "but at least you're not broke. One out of two ain't bad."

"Unnh," he grunted. He didn't smile and didn't respond any more than that.

During the time I had to talk with Hana before the ceremony, she said that the only hitch in the wedding day so far had been her father's unresponsiveness. Usually, even on what were physically demanding days for him, he would perk up in the presence of Hana, Laila, his other children, and his grandchildren. He especially enjoyed being a loving grandfather, and his sly sense of humor would almost always come out when grandkids were around. And, though he and Veronica rarely had the chance to see each other, Muhammad always made an extra effort to be "on" when she was around. But on this big day, in a room full of people who loved him, he wasn't responding to anyone. Everyone in the family appreciated how hard it must be for him to get through a big occasion like this, so nobody pressed him to become more involved in what was going on around him. It just seemed very sad that he couldn't enjoy a day that would otherwise be such a special one for him.

At the main table, Muhammad had Lonnie on one side of him, and his daughter Rasheda on the other side, with Marilyn next to her. Hana had placed Helga and me across from her father so that he could see us more easily. As people got up after dinner to mingle and dance I kept my eyes on Muhammad, but he kept his head down, sometimes with his eyes closed. Rasheda and Helga were talking about how unusual the situation was, and I got the sense that there was growing concern that the whole celebration might slip by without Muhammad really being a part of it. I waited and waited and watched him across the table. Finally, he did look up. He zeroed in on me, and our eyes locked.

I did my own version of the mean face, held a fist up, and gave it a shake in his direction. He had told me so many times through the years that I was the only one who looked uglier than him making that face. I was hoping my face could still get a response—and it did. Muhammad smiled—a full, real smile—and then he made the face right back at me. And he stuck out his tongue, like I always did. I took my taunting fist and began throwing jabs in his direction. He began throwing jabs right back at me. Just what I had hoped for. His jabs were in slow motion, but at least he was throwing them.

I knew he was in there. I knew he was always there, even when he didn't show it. Now it was time to bring him all the way out. It was time to sing again.

I kept my eyes locked on his across the table as I stood up, emphatically planted my feet, and gave my shoulders a dramatic roll, making myself stand as big and tall as possible.

"I knew it, Muhammad," I called out. "I know what you're waiting for." With that, I began belting out the opening lines to "Black Superman," a novelty tune by a British songwriter named Johnny Wakelin that had come out in 1975 after Muhammad's epic "Rumble in the Jungle" with George Foreman. The song had a Jamaican feel to it, and the lyrics were delivered in a kind of rap patterned after the way Muhammad often spoke in rhyme to the press. The song wasn't a masterpiece (rhyming "Clay" with "Ali," for instance) and Muhammad hadn't been all that thrilled with it when it first came out. But through the years it had grown on him, and he always seemed to enjoy hearing me sing it.

Hana saw what was happening and started calling more people over to gather around our table. I sang on, and Muhammad was watching my every move, alternating between grins and his mean face, and he continued to throw those slow jabs in my direction. I got into the first chorus and did some butterfly dance moves and then added some bee stings with my hands. Muhammad stung back at me, smiling the whole time. I headed right into the second verse and suddenly I had a full chorus of backup singers: Hana, Kenisha Norton, Rasheda and her twin sister, Jamillah, Muhammad's oldest daughter, Maryum, Howard Bingham, and other friends and family members. They all sang the song's horn parts and added some choreography of their own, as people at the nearby tables stood up and clapped along. (Bingham whispered to me, "Shanahan, your bee sting needs some work!") All together, we gave the song a big ending: "Muhammad, the Black Superman, who calls to the other guy, 'I'm Ali—catch me if you can . . .'"

Muhammad applauded along with everyone else and really seemed to get a kick out of this impromptu tribute. Hana had a huge smile on her face, thrilled to see that her father was now fully part of her celebration. I had an idea for keeping the moment going. Hana had asked me for a list of songs Muhammad might want to hear, so now I had the DJ cue up Muhammad's own version of "Stand by Me" (recorded for his 1963 album of songs and poetry, *I Am the Greatest*). I started singing again *to* Muhammad while singing along *with* Muhammad, and he kept smiling, making the mean face, and throwing his jabs.

I wasn't quite done with him. I came around the table and stood by his side. When he looked up at me, I launched into my other big "hit"— "Trouble" from *King Creole*.

I ended with a mean face and I got one back from the Champ.

There was a little extra buzz to the party now. Hana gave her father a big hug and I sat down again across from him. I knew he had enjoyed the show and had appreciated the fuss made around him. But within just a few minutes his smiles faded away and he was back to being unresponsive. Before I left that night Helga and I gave him goodbye kisses. I made one more fist for him and told him I loved him. He tried to smile just a bit and nodded slowly.

A few days later, I got a note from Hana saying that she considered those few moments when her father was laughing and clapping to be the highlight of her wedding. She wrote. "Thank you. Thank you. Thank you. This will be a moment we will all be thankful for in the future." It meant everything to me that I had a role in giving Hana the gift of her father's smiles on her wedding day. Muhammad's life was still full of friends and family who loved him, along with millions of fans around the world who still loved him, but at Hana's wedding I was willing to "act a fool" in order to add a little joy to his day. After all the happiness he had given me, it felt great that I could still make him happy in that small way.

With my sweet, beautiful Hana, who visited us at our
home in Rancho Santa Fe, California, 2015.

• • •

I STILL CALL MUHAMMAD WHENEVER I can, usually when Hana is with him, though it has become very hard for him to speak on the phone. I talked to him on his seventy-third birthday, when Hana was there with him to help translate what he was trying to say. When he heard that it was me on the speakerphone, he mumbled something that I couldn't understand. He repeated it for Hana, and then she told me what he was asking for.

"He wants to hear the Rolls-Royce story."

I told him all about the time he drove a new Rolls off the floor of the showroom in Beverly Hills—a Rolls he "paid" for with a business card—and then I kept talking for twenty minutes or so, telling him a bunch of the other stories I knew he liked to hear.

When I was done, he spoke again—this time clearly enough to be understood.

"You've got a good memory," he said.

Even after decades of being a part of Muhammad Ali's world, it still feels like the most incredible honor to speak of him as a friend. I don't know exactly what he saw in me when we first met, but I will second what George Foreman once said: I am happy to have lived during the time of Muhammad Ali. It has been a privilege to be a part of Muhammad's life, and so much of the joy and happiness I have experienced in my own life has come directly from my friendship with him. That friendship is what makes my memories my greatest treasure. So I'll end here with some words that capture everything I've wanted to say in this book:

It has been a thrill and an honor running with you, Champ. Thank you for being my friend. I love you.

My favorite shot of the Champ:
The Greatest of All Times.

ACKNOWLEDGMENTS

TO MY SWEET HANA: the love shared between you and your father is an inspiration. You said, "Shanahan, you have so many great stories about my dad, you should write your own book." I would not have done this book without your encouragement.

To George Foreman: I asked your advice and you told me that the world needs to hear about my friendship with the Greatest. You really convinced me to write this book. Thank you.

To Jerry Schilling: You wrote your book about your friendship with the King and you told me to write my book about my friendship with the Greatest. I asked you to be my literary agent and you accepted. Thank you.

Thank you, Jerry, for teaming me up with Chuck Crisafulli, who told my story the way it needed to be told.

Thank you, Bob Bender, for having confidence in me and giving me the support and encouragement that I needed. You really did follow Richard Simon's goal concerning publishing books when in 1924 he said, "I only want to publish good books." And this you have done for over thirty-five years.

Thank you, Dick Enberg: As with George Foreman, when I asked for your advice, you told me that the world needs to hear about my friendship with the Champ.

Thank you, Dr. Veronica Porche, for your friendship with Helga and me for forty years. You know that we love you and we are so happy that you are in our lives.

Thank you, Kris Kristofferson, for being Muhammad's friend; so true, so loyal for forty-five years. You really love Muhammad.

Thank you, Howard Bingham, for being Muhammad's closest friend for fifty-four years. Ali fans and friends can't think of Ali without thinking of you. You have been such an important part of the Champ's life.

Rahaman Ali: You and your brother have been as close as any brothers could be, and he loves you as much as anyone in his life.

Captain Sam Saxon, the most devout Muslim whom I've ever met. You were truly Muhammad's mentor on the Islamic faith; you were sincere and honest, and you love Muhammad.

Angelo Dundee and Ferdie Pacheco, thank you for your love, advice, and service to the Greatest. You two men were as close as anyone to Muhammad.

Chubby Checker, another friend of the Champ's for fifty years; you are a good man and a good friend. Thank you.

To Connie Payton: Thank you for your friendship of forty years. Didn't we have fun? I miss Walter. You are doing great things with the Walter Payton Foundation.

My special thanks in memory of Jimmy Ellis, Odessa Grady Clay, Cassius Clay Sr., Aunt Coretta, Aunt Mary, Aunt Eva, Lana Shabazz, Kenny Norton, and Gene Dibble.

To Muhammad's favorite cousin, Charlotte "Duchess" Waddell—a talented artist and a pistol.

To beautiful Joan Edwards, still one of Helga and my closest friends. What a journey we have had together. Stay healthy, all our love.

To dear Lola Falana, our wonderful, beautiful friend and the daughter of Christ.

To Howie Frank, John Hirschboeck, Joe Graf, and Chuck Nagle, my closest Marquette University High School friends: Weren't we devils? We were the original *Animal House* in spite of six-foot-four, 230-pound Father Jerome T. Boyle trying to rein us in.

Thank you, Mrs. Pat Richter (Rene Sengstock), for paying attention to a lovesick twelve-year-old at McKinley Playground. A Junior Miss Wisconsin–West Allis, 1960, and my first love!

My mother, Mary; I don't know how you handled five sons and nine cousins in a small house. It must be a miracle. To my brothers, Pat, Michael, Terry, and Kevin—my first support team in my life.

Thank you, Auntie Ora, Auntie Lillian, Auntie Evelyn; without you wonderful women in our lives things would have been a lot harder for all of us as children.

Thank you, Father Tom Shanahan S.J. ("Unc"), for helping me get through Creighton University. Thank you, also, for being a father figure to all of those terrific Creighton University basketball players who needed your love and guidance all those years, including Kyle Korver and Doug McDermott.

To Hank Aaron, for being my idol and an excellent role model for an eleven-year-old boy. And thanks for the ride home.

Thank you, Glenn "Doc" Rivers and Dwayne Wade, for being the best representatives of Marquette University and for showing the world what a Jesuit education can do for a young man.

A special thanks to all these men who tried their best to give Muhammad financial security: Robert Abboud, Mike Phenner, Bill Sutter, Barry Frank, and Robert Richey. I know you all did it out of love for Muhammad.

To Jimmy Walker: You have dedicated yourself to putting on the annual Muhammad Ali Fight Night to benefit the Muhammad Ali Parkinson's Center in Phoenix. You have done an amazing job, and you have made a difference.

Thank you, Rick "Rico" Abrahamson, my army basketball buddy and Oregon Duck, for allowing me to share the experience of a lifetime with you and the U.S. handball team at the 1972 Munich Olympics.

To my good friend and four-year college roommate at Creighton University, Bob Portman. Bob was the all-time leading scorer in basketball at Creighton for twenty-five years, while playing only three years and with no three-point line. That is amazing.

A special thanks to Mike and Gloria Franks for your tireless work on Carl Reiner's Pro Celebrity Tennis Tournament for twenty years to benefit special education elementary schools in L.A. Thank you for letting me contribute. It was an honor.

To my good friend, my tennis partner Gebre Wallace, the "Teaching Tennis Pro to the Stars," especially Charlton Heston and Peter Morton (Hard Rock Café).

Thank you, Larry Elder, for giving me your good professional advice concerning writing a book. I am so glad that you are back on the radio airwaves where you are meant to be. TV is next.

To my beautiful, talented, wonderful wife of forty-two years, Helga: You have always been my best friend. Thank you for being Muhammad's good friend along with me.

To my friend Muhammad Ali: You told me your story about how you were crushed when Sugar Ray Robinson didn't give you his autograph, and you told me, "People will forget what you say. They will forget what you do. But they will never forget how you made them feel." I can't imagine how many millions of people in the world you have made feel special, but you can count me as one of those people. Thank you for being my friend, Muhammad. I love you. Maaaaaaan!

INDEX